Praise for *Vision and Division in Israel*

"A values-driven activist, Kreimer brought to the conflict arena her unique approach — a bridge of dialogues over an ocean of hostilities. Her dedication and initiatives made her the recipient of the 2002 Award of the Speaker of the Knesset for Contributing to the Quality of Life in Israel. *Vision and Division* should be read by all who refuse to lose hope."

—Avraham Burg
Former Speaker of the Israeli Knesset

"An amazing and critically important book that tells the immensely complex story of life in Israel over the last four decades through the eyes of a person immersed in working for important social, economic and political change. Sarah Kreimer raises the toughest issues of the future, weaves them in and out of a real life of economic development work, personal love and loss, motherhood, and the kind of reflection that most of us do too little of. This is a must-read for anyone still committed to building peace in the Middle East — and reminds us that change is never smooth."

—Ruth W. Messinger
Global Ambassador, American Jewish World Service

"In this beautifully written, emotionally compelling work, Kreimer models how a Jew can be a passionate critic of Israel while remaining a passionate lover of Israel. Sarah Kreimer and I will likely never vote for the same Israeli party, nor will we agree on how to solve the Palestinian-Israeli conflict or which side deserves the greater blame for the absence of peace. But what unites us is no less important than what divides us. We both want a just and decent Israel. Her story needs to be heard with respect by Jews who disagree with her — especially by Jews who disagree with her."

—Yossi Klein Halevi
Author and Senior Fellow, Shalom Hartman Institute

"A fascinating read, written by an expert who has lived many years on the seam-line between the peoples in Israel, and beyond that, in the Middle East. Engrossing and stirring, her book is a must for those who care about Jewish-Arab relations in Israel."

—Judge Muhamad Massarwa,
Former Consul General of Israel to the Southeast United States

"A book for all who love Israel's Declaration of Independence. Sarah Kreimer shines a harsh but accurate light on Israel's deepest internal problem: the Israeli Arab/Israeli Jewish divide. She remains true to her idealist self through very challenging times."

—Rabbi Brian Lurie,
Former Executive Vice President, United Jewish Appeal (UJA)

"A riveting view of Israel society over the past forty years from the perspective of an extraordinary leader in Israeli peace and justice efforts. Sarah Kreimer gives us an intimate view of her work for economic equity for Palestinian citizens of Israel and for advancing the possibility of Israeli-Palestinian shared citizenship. Her book is a page-turner."

—Rabbi Amy Eilberg
Author of *From Enemy to Friend:*
Jewish Wisdom and the Pursuit of Peace

"One of the profound challenges facing this Jewish generation is how we choose to engage in the rebuilding of our people's national home. Kreimer has put her life, heart and soul into the struggle for Israel's future, and her stories are vital for all engaged in the struggle."

—Jeremy Ben-Ami
Founder and President of J Street

"Sarah Kreimer steels herself to ask the hardest questions and commits to building relationships and organizations that may forge new, previously unimagined answers. Her life's work, including this memoir, aims to create new trajectories for all of Israel's children."

—Rabbi Deborah Waxman,
President, Reconstructionist Rabbinical College
and Jewish Reconstructionist Communities

Vision and Division in Israel

Forty Years of Activism
Along the Seam

To the memory of two people, who changed the trajectory of my life in Israel:

Rabbi Bruce Cohen, founder and director of Interns for Peace
Shuki Komarov, my late husband and father of Shai and Liad

Blue Thread Books and Music

Cover design by Lawrence Bush.

ISBN 978-0-9903524-9-5

Yehudah Ben Tema used to say:
A twenty-year-old begins pursuit [of livelihood];
A thirty-year-old attains full strength;
A forty-year-old attains understanding;
A fifty-year-old can offer counsel . . .
      —The Sayings of the Fathers (*Pirkei Avot*) 5:25

Table of Contents

Acknowledgments

So many people have been midwives for this book, which had a decade-long gestation period. My thanks go first of all to my sister-in-law, Nancy Fuchs-Kreimer, who encouraged me from the beginning, read the chapters, taught me to be a little less earnest and a little more conversational, and gave me the gift of an editor, Ellen Frankel, who helped provide form to the book when I was floundering. Thanks also to Nancy's father, Victor Fuchs, who believed in me and this enterprise and gave me insightful comments on every chapter.

Thanks to Lois Blum-Feinblatt, for providing support that enabled me to take some months off from work to get started with the writing. Speaking of taking time off from work, many thanks to Amos Gil, who provided a critical eye from the point of view of an activist and made sure that no one bothered me on my "writing day" each week when I was working for Ir Amim.

A huge thank-you to Judy Labensohn and the gifted women of our writing group in Israel — Shoshana London Sappir, Judith Laurence, Judith Sudilovsky, Judit Frigyesi, Diana Flescher, Sarita Perel — with whom I workshopped most of the chapters. Judy created a dynamic combination of respect, creativity and critique. So many scenes in the book came to life because of her instruction to "show, not tell!"

Much gratitude to Lawrence Bush, editor of *Jewish Currents* magazine, for his skilled editing. Our public correspondence in that magazine when I first came to Israel in 1980 launched my writing career, so there is poetic justice this book's being published, thirty-six years later, through the magazine's Blue Thread imprint.

Thank you to my sons, Shai and Liad, who put up with me holing up to type in my room, and trusted me to write about our lives. And thank you to my brother, Seth, and my partner, Yehudah Livneh, who supported me in getting through the hard times and bringing so many endeavors to fruition.

Prologue

September 27, 1998 dawned a beautiful, crisp fall morning in Israel. I drove an hour north from my home in Tel Aviv, leaving the coastal highway to enter Wadi Ara, a valley winding past broad kibbutz fields and along Israeli Arab villages. The hills between villages bristled with olive trees, their gnarled branches heavy with fruit.

At the entrance to Umm el Fahm, one of Israel's largest Arab cities, I drove up a steep road to the new Comprehensive High School, poised on the crest of the hill. Inside the school's carpeted, air-conditioned library, I took my place with urban planners from Arab towns throughout Israel to hear an official from the Israel Lands Authority explain the National Plan for Forestation. As co-director of the Center for Jewish-Arab Economic Development, I had come to congratulate the participants on their completion of the Center's course, "Environmentally Sustainable Development."

Nearly three years after the assassination of Prime Minister Yitzhak Rabin, the Center continued its quiet, uphill struggle to advance cooperation and equality of opportunity in economic development in Israel.

" . . . The Forestation Plan takes into consideration development needs, as well as environmental needs," said the official, pointing to a detailed topographical map on a stand next to him. "For example, right here in Wadi Ara, you can see in the midst of this planned forest a blank space: the site of a future town of Jewish, perhaps ultra-Orthodox, residents. The Ministry of Interior

1

marked this for development, even though today it is forested."

"What about the area we requested as an industrial zone for Umm el Fahm?" asked Mohammed, the city's environmental engineer.

"No, that area is zoned as forest land."

Appealing to reason, Mohammed continued: "Last year, Me Ammi, the small Jewish community up the road, received approval for an industrial area in an area designated as forest. Why shouldn't we?" On the last syllable, Mohammed's voice squeaked in frustration.

I felt the blood rising to my temples — at the banality of the bureaucracy, which is able to bend the rules to enable the development of Jewish towns, while being stymied by the needs of neighboring Arab areas.

"We have no industrial area for a city of over 30,000 people," Mohammed continued, walking to the map. He pointed to the built-up area of the city, surrounded by land shaded in green, for forest, with virtually no margin of land reserved for future development. "For years we've been applying for approval of an industrial area — either here or there." He poked at two green blotches on the map. "Every time, we are turned down, because of the need for 'green areas.' In the meantime, factories operate in residential neighborhoods, and send toxic wastes into their neighbors' yards. As an environmental engineer, I ask you — is this better for the environment?"

Before the lecturer could answer, rifle shots cracked outside. A minute later, two students burst into the library, eyes red, gasping for breath. One of the Arab urban planners jumped up to tend the students; others rushed from the room.

Mohammed had vanished. Besides the lecturer from the Israel Lands Authority, who was nowhere to be seen, I was the only Israeli Jew in a school of hundreds of Arab Israeli kids. I was practically the only woman, as well. Male teachers pushed through the door into the library to find out what had happened. They pressed to the windows to see, through the trees below, jeeps and armored personnel carriers of the Israel border police, amassed at the main entrance of the city, near the turn-off I had used less than an hour before.

Mobile phone to his ear, one teacher called out in Arabic,

"They destroyed the protest tent; Sheikh Raed was injured!"

I phoned a news reporter, to alert him to the events in Umm el Fahm. Over the past days, Sheikh Raed Salah, the city's mayor and national leader of the Islamic Movement in Israel, had been staging a sit-down strike on a plot of Arab-owned land, to protest army plans to seize it for a firing zone in the hills across from the city.

Two more students pushed through the doors, struggling to carry between them a moaning boy. They laid him heavily on the floor; he writhed and clutched his eye. Blood spattered the fresh blue carpet.

I lingered in the library near those students, afraid of what I would see outside the door. I thought of my two sons, Liad, age 6, and Shai, age 7, whom I had sent safely off to school this morning in Tel Aviv. I was now paralyzed with fear. If I went out that door, I might get shot. What would my kids do if anything happened to me? Yet, I could not stay in the school library forever, trapped by my cowardice.

Cautiously, I opened the door. The halls were empty, eerily quiet. I stepped out. An unfamiliar odor hung in the air, stinging my eyes, my nostrils — tear gas. Then the school bell rang, announcing the end of the period. In a rush of running students, I was pushed out into the schoolyard. There, two Arab planners from our course stood facing an Israeli soldier at the schoolyard gate, blocking his entrance to the school.

"Where do you think you are, Gaza?!" yelled Mohammed, the Umm el Fahm environmental engineer, in perfect Hebrew. "This is Israel; you're not allowed to enter a high school without permission from the principal!"

A boy running out of the building pushed past me, screaming in Arabic, "*Idbah il Yehud!* Death to the Jews!"

Shocked, I yelled back, instinctively, in Hebrew, "What? I am a Jew!" His eyes widened and he swerved away from me into the crowd. I realized he had aimed his words at the police, but they had hit me, as well. I definitely did not belong here.

I slipped outside the main gate of the school and halted only meters away from twenty border policemen. They stood shoulder to shoulder in full riot gear, some with tear gas guns, some with regular rifles. On a knoll above them, marksmen crouched behind boulders, guns trained into a crowd of yelling students pressed against the fence in the upper level of the school yard, to my left.

Students shouted taunts at the soldiers. Some threw stones. One marksman took aim. I heard a shot. Someone screamed.

I froze, terrified of the border police, of the students' hatred. I tried to imagine these same teenagers sauntering into school this morning, clapping a friend on the shoulder, chewing a lip in anxiety about a math test. Outside the main gate, I saw the principal and a number of teachers pacing between the soldiers and the students, out of range of the stones, and out of the line of the marksmen's fire. The teachers shouted alternately at the students to go back into the building and at the border police to leave the school.

The students, quarantined in the schoolyard with no intention of returning to the building, baited the police with cries of *"Allahu Akbar!* God is great" and "Soldiers, go home!" The police, presumably trying to keep the students from joining the protest tent, could not turn tail and run. Paralyzed and powerless, I wished I had left with the Israel Lands Authority official.

I had only one advantage: I was out of place. Neither students nor police could fit me, a tall Jewish woman in high heels and a flowered dress, amidst hundreds of Arab men and boys, into their standard mental images. Perhaps that incongruity could trigger a non-standard response. From past experience, I knew that Israeli security personnel exercise greater restraint in the presence of Israeli Jews. After another moment of hesitation, I stepped out to join the teachers walking back and forth between the two groups, trying to mediate an end to the stand-off.

As I approached the soldiers, I scanned the uniforms and taut faces, searching for the officer in charge. A young man barked into a walkie-talkie, "I told you, a Jewish woman! . . . Yeah, here!"

The soldiers eyed me suspiciously. One had his hand on his gun. I took a chance on the soldier with the walkie-talkie. "Who's in charge here?" I asked, trying to look stern and knowledgeable.

"I am."

"What are you trying to do? You have the kids locked into their schoolyard and you're shooting!"

"We're trying to keep the peace, ma'am."

"What peace? The only reason there isn't peace is because you're here. As soon as you leave, they won't have anyone to throw rocks at. The whole thing will end. Kids are being hurt!"

An ambulance screeched, siren wailing. Medics jumped out and ran toward the library. Teachers lifted injured students into the ambulance.

"Believe me," growled the officer, "I want to leave! You think my men aren't being injured? I came here on orders; I leave on orders!" He barked incomprehensible jargon into his walkie-talkie.

Another volley of stones; more shots.

The principal, teachers, and I caucused quickly. We agreed that they would try to keep the kids from throwing stones; I would try to get the border police to leave. Kids yelled curses. A few stones fell near the teachers. The principal strode to the fence of the upper schoolyard and barraged the students with stern threats.

I stood by the soldiers. Their faces were tense. "Look, if you let the principal take care of things," I said, "it will calm down."

The officer called out, "If there is quiet for five minutes, we will leave."

"If you leave, there will be quiet," screamed a teacher.

A car of parents pulled up, then another, and another. Fathers leapt out, yelling in Hebrew at the soldiers: "Get out of here . . . you have no right to be here . . . leave our children alone!"

The tension mounted. More stones, more shots, more screams. Someone shoved a bleeding kid into a father's car. Wheels spun on the gravel; the car careened down the road.

"When will you stop?" I urged the officer.

"Get five minutes quiet! Tell the kids to go straight home!"

The teachers paced by the upper yard, yelling, sweating, searching the crowd with their eyes. Suddenly, the officer gave the order to evacuate. Soldiers shot a parting volley of tear gas and more rubber bullets. Everyone started running. The border police jumped into their trucks and jeeps and sped off, in a cloud of tear gas, under a shower of stones.

The students poured out of the schoolyard and down the hill.

In minutes, the school stood silent, littered with rocks, rubber bullets and tear gas canisters. Impaled on the gate, a bloody school shirt flapped in the breeze. A handful of teachers stood, stunned, tears in their eyes, ostensibly from the tear gas still clinging to the air. No one spoke.

After a moment, one teacher with bloodshot eyes muttered,

almost to himself, "We were in the middle of teaching . . . This is the education we give our children . . . What do they think this is, Jabalya Refugee Camp?"

Mohammed and I stood on the steps of the school, overlooking Umm el Fahm, our eyes smarting, our throats tight. We had worked together in various projects for years. Whatever goodwill we had created in those years seemed to dissipate in the acrid breeze.

Far below, border police units patrolled the deserted main street. Bullhorn voices wafted up to us: "Clear the streets! Everyone in their homes!" As if watching a movie, we viewed distant figures of the border police running through a neighborhood on the opposite hill. From a house, stones pelted them. The sound of shots drifted up, as did the dissipating tear gas. Someone arrived with onions and damp scarves to ease the sting in our eyes.

I sank onto the stone steps, realizing that my back hurt and my legs felt weak. It was 3:00; I hadn't sat for hours, and I was tired, hungry, wanting to go home. Umm el Fahm was still under siege, but there was nothing left for me to do. The police had blocked the main entrance to town, so Mohammed led me in his car through back roads to the main Wadi Ara road. I said goodbye and drove down the deserted highway, which was officially closed under police orders.

The adrenaline that had kept me going over the past hours seeped away, leaving my body limp. Seeing the gas station/restaurant at Kfar Kara, I pulled over. As I rose weakly from the car, I met a group of police officers on their way out. Shaken by all I had seen, I blurted out, "What are you doing in Umm el Fahm? Why did you fire at students in their schoolyard?"

They looked with surprise at a haggard, dark-haired Jewish woman on the closed Wadi Ara road. For a moment I thought they might arrest me for violating the police closure.

A meaty police officer stepped close. "Did you know that from the mosques there was a call to go down to the road, to the tent?" he said. "Did you know that schools released their students with orders to go throw stones? Can you guarantee that next year there won't be an *intifada* here in Wadi Ara? Ma'am, you have a very limited view."

I looked at him in stunned silence as he folded himself into the patrol car and closed the door. I knew that for years, Umm el Fahm's mayor, Sheikh Raed Salah, had been warning of Israel's intentions to undermine and destroy the Al Aqsa Mosque in Jerusalem. I knew that he led a growing fundamentalist stream of the Islamic Movement in Israel. Perhaps this police officer was right, and there had been incitement in the mosques. Perhaps the soldiers and police had taken important action to prevent greater violence.

At the same time, I saw my country creating its future that day, a future in which an Arab student goes to school in the morning and comes home without an eye; a future in which my children and the children of Umm el Fahm are not seen as citizens of the same state.

Indeed, in this gnarled reality, I could not guarantee that next year there would not be an *intifada* in Wadi Ara. Or the year after.

Into my exhausted brain popped a picture of my mother, sitting at the kitchen table in Pittsburgh, asking, "What are you doing, living in Israel?"

Why *was* I living in Israel? I could easily reel off a list of good reasons: I was in Israel because I was Jewish; because I believed that the Jewish people need and deserve a homeland, here in the land in which Judaism was born. I was in Israel so that I would not be discriminated against, as was my father in America; or persecuted, as was my grandfather in the Ukraine. I was here to contribute my part to this country, not ten years older than I — where despite doomsday warnings of the clash of civilizations, my pediatrician was an Algerian Jew, my dermatologist an Israeli Muslim Arab, and my own physician a Christian Armenian; where all these and more met in the *shuk* (market) on Friday afternoons and bargained in a ridiculously loud Babel of languages; where people I didn't know came up to me on the street and told me that my child needed a hat.

If I looked deeper, there was more. After graduating from Yale, I could have gone to law school, as my older brother had done, as my father wanted me to do. Instead, I had traveled America with a backpack, worked as a cocktail waitress and a horse breeder, led Outward Bound programs for delinquent boys, and hiked the Appalachian Trail. Truth was, I liked pushing myself: the daugh-

7

ter who could take risks her mother never dared, the little sister who could be strong. I had trained myself in my young adulthood not to fear coming up to the edge. I had grown to like living there.

The edge I had pushed myself to this time was more rugged than any wilderness in which I had set up camp in America's West. Here I was a Jew with ideals of what Israel should be — but as a Jew, what fulfillment could I find when Jewish police shoot into a crowd of Arab students in their schoolyard? What refuge could I find when my fellow Arab citizens hate me as a symbol of all the Jews who have settled on their land? What home is this, where forests are cut down to accommodate the needs of Jewish citizens yet planted to limit the development of Arab citizens? And how much difference could I, one American Jewish woman, her Israeli citizenship not yet two decades old, really make? How to keep on keeping on?

This book is about Israel and the specific challenges it faces. Many of these challenges and contradictions — between maintaining a particular national character and upholding universal values of equality and democracy — are hardly unique to Israel. Indeed, they lie at the heart of many conflicts in the world today.

I wish I could say that I have answers, both to the questions tearing apart Israeli society and to the more universal question of how we keep on keeping on. I do not. What I do have is fears, and hopes, and a sense of direction.

I fear that clinging to the visions that have guided Israel in the past will destroy what has been built. I fear that I will grow weary of the fight, when so often my small triumphs have been overwhelmed by disastrous moves by others who are many times more powerful than I, creating a painful reality beyond my control.

I hope for my two sons, and for the children of Nazareth and Tel Aviv, that it is yet possible to build a shared future out of a disputed past and a bloody present. I believe that our chance to reach this future depends on the ability of Israelis, and those who love Israel from afar, to look honestly at the pain and the aspirations of those Israelis — Arab and Jewish — who live here now. It depends on letting go of the old dreams of what a Jewish state might be; on embracing the reality of our wounded country, still locked in a struggle between two peoples; on building a new vision.

This book is the story of how I, too, have struggled to build and rebuild vision out of the broken pieces of my dreams. I hope that these intertwined stories of triumphs and anguish, of torn dreams and new possibilities, will bring you, the reader, into a deeper understanding of the complexity of Arab and Jewish relations in Israel today. Perhaps it will also help you to see your own story, your ideals and the obstacles you have encountered, in a fresh light.

I. At Twenty: Beginning Pursuit
(1980-1984)

Chapter 1
"Things That You See from There, You Can't See from Here"

You took my hand, showed me the way to many things;
You brought a smile, lovely as a flower, and the strength to believe;
I still remember the song that you sang, the good part of all you said.
Hey, angel or devil, will you come back to stop time?
Things that you see from there — you can't see from here.

—"You Took My Hand in Yours"
music by Matti Caspi; words by Yankele Rothblitt

"**W**omen in Tamra have power, but no status," remarked Dina, as she showed us around our new home in this traditional Israeli Arab town of 18,000 Muslims — and now four American Jews, with Sue and I moving in for the next two years. "On the outside, it looks as if the men make the decisions. But when you see how things really work, the women are running the household. They manage the family budget, raise the kids, and guide their choices about education. But if a teacher asks to speak with a parent, it's the father who goes, not the mother."

I wondered what it would mean for me, an unmarried Jewish woman with no household to run, to live and work in an Arab town where women have no status. Despite my excitement at starting this journey, I felt a bit like the furniture in the apartment looked, sparse and scuffed.

Dina was moving on to the livingroom, where bare bulbs hung

from wires in the ceiling, and foam mattresses, covered with dull patterned material, lay on straw mats around the edges of the room. In the kitchen, two stove-top burners sat on the counter; there was no oven. The bathroom contained a showerhead that drizzled cold water when I turned it on.

Dina explained: "We have a solar water heater that's great in the summer. In the winter, we just heat water in a kettle on the burner, and pour it over ourselves to take a shower."

"Where's the phone?" I asked.

"We don't have a phone line," answered Michal, who had been here with Dina over the last two years, "We use the phone at the community center."

I walked into the one bedroom, which was furnished with a creaky brown closet and a desk. "Where are the beds?" I asked.

"Oh, we sleep on the *frash*," Michal told us. "That's what they call the mattresses on the floor over there. A lot of people in the village sleep on them. In the morning, we fold up our sheets and blankets, and the *frash* are ready to take guests. You know, that's how all the women entertain here — we all sit around on the *frash*, throw a sheet over our legs, drink tea, eat sunflower seeds and gossip. The women in Tamra are great!"

With that, the four of us set out to make our first house visit, to our landlady across the street. Our apartment, the first floor of an unfinished two-story home, was being built slowly, as money allowed, for the owner's oldest son, Musa, who would move in

Gathering on the *frash* (mattresses on the floor) in Tamra;
Sarah is third from right.

when he got married. Out of respect, we called our landlady and her husband "Im and Abu Musa," Mother and Father of Musa, who would someday inherit our home. Beyond the circle of close friends and family, people in the village addressed one another by their oldest son's name. Those unfortunate men who had only daughters were known jokingly as Abu Banat, father of girls.

Years later, after I had my first son, Shai, I suddenly understood this custom, not only as an expression of clan relationships, but as a universal description of parenthood. From the moment I emerged from the maternity hospital, I became Im Shai, Shai's mother. When Shai went to kindergarten, I was never really Sarah, but Im Shai. To the violin teacher, to National Insurance, and to the neighbors who were awoken by my baby's cries at 5:00 a.m., I was definitely Im Shai.

It was March 1981 and I was 25. My decision to come to Israel had been sparked in November 1977, in the midst of serving drinks in the cocktail lounge of the Conrad Hilton Hotel in Chicago, a job I'd taken as I traveled around America to "find myself" after graduating from Yale. Unexpectedly, I found myself riveted to the bar's TV as Egyptian President Anwar Sadat, peering through thick glasses, addressed the Israeli Knesset during his historic visit to Jerusalem. Tears stung my eyes when he spoke the simple and stirring words: "Today I tell you that we accept to live with you in permanent peace based on justice."

I never cried over the news in America. Why was I crying over Israel?

As I continued my trip around America, I found myself seeking out Jewish communities, meeting people who had run guns for Israel in 1948, and increasingly drawn to the history of the Jewish State. Israel was only eight years older than I. In three decades, the country, born of an idea, had undergone four wars and ongoing onslaughts of terrorism, and had attracted and absorbed millions of immigrants, providing them with education, housing and decent health care. The *kibbutzim*, started even before the State, represented a bold experiment in Jewish socialism, from the bottom up. Israelis' brash belief that, as Herzl said, "If you will it, it is not a dream," had led to an outpouring of innovation in agricultural as well as military technology.

Much was wrong with Israel, too. Many of the Jewish immigrants from Arab countries, the *Mizrahim*, were unemployed, second-class citizens in peripheral development towns. One out of every six Israeli citizens was Arab, but most of them lived in poor towns that lacked sewage systems and basic infrastructure. Still unrecognized as a nation by most of its neighbors, Israel had occupied and denied national recognition to over one million Palestinians in the West Bank and Gaza for a significant part of its lifespan.

Oddly, the more I had learned about Israel's difficulties, the more I wanted to be involved, to be part of it, to help it be the best society it could be. I wanted to give something to this fabulous Jewish collective effort of the 20th century, perhaps because I felt that, in some way, it represented me as a Jew.

At Yale, I had heard a young Reform rabbi with a captivating smile, Bruce Cohen, speak about the new program he was starting in Israel to address the deep divisions between Arab and Jewish Israelis that had been exposed when six young Arab Israelis had been killed by Israeli police during a civil-rights demonstration the year before. Rabbi Cohen's Interns for Peace (IFP) was based demanded a two-year commitment to live and work in Arab and Jewish communities in northern Israel, in order to create a network of joint community projects and build understanding by doing things together. I had done some community organizing with the Welfare Rights Organization in Pittsburgh; IFP sounded like a serious and exciting way to jump into life in Israel. In 1980, I did so, joining Interns for Peace to contribute two years to the bold effort of building a country out of an idea, to see how I was connected, and, yes, to have an adventure.

Sue Wish and I had just completed, along with our male col-leagues, four months of training to become IFP community workers. At Kibbutz Barkai, we had worked in the fields and children's houses in the mornings, and studied in the afternoons: community work, sociology of Israel, history of the Arab-Israeli conflict, and Arabic language and customs. We had each been "adopted" by a *kibbutz* family, as if we were going through immigrant absorption, although none of us was planning to make *aliyah* (which means, literally, to "ascend") and stay in Israel.

In our training, we learned that most Arab and Jewish citizens lived separately in Israel, either in Arab villages or Jewish towns. The two towns in our area, Tamra and Qiryat Ata — a working-class Jewish town, fifteen kilometers away — were no different. Our job, as the new staff of IFP in the Western Galilee, was to create joint community projects between the two, in order to begin a network of relationships that did not now exist.

Our Israeli Arab colleague, Ghaleb Haikel, who was to be the third member of our team, had driven us to Tamra in his old car, grinding up narrow streets from the village fields below (where two-thirds of Israel's cucumbers are grown), to arrive at the apartment rented for us by the municipality. Sue and I were to live there, replacing the current IFP staffers Dina and Michal, who had been in Tamra over the past two years. Ghaleb, who before joining IFP had worked in construction after graduating from college, would live in a separate apartment, across the yard. In the village, unmarried men and women could not share a home.

On our first night in Tamra, Sue and I lay on the *frash*, the mattresses, on the floor, together with Dina and Michal. We had turned out the lights, but none of us was ready to sleep.

"Have they ever really accepted you in Tamra?" I asked.

"Yes, and no," answered Dina. "We have a circle of friends who love us and accept us as daughters, sisters, friends. And we have a circle of work colleagues at the community center, in the municipality, in some of the schools, who know what we are trying to do here, and appreciate it. And then there are the people who see us around and think we're English teachers, or CIA agents, or foreigners looking for an Arab husband."

"For the first year," added Michal, "many people, particularly the more politically active, thought we were Shin Bet (the Israeli Security Services) or CIA agents. Given the pervasive presence of informers in the village, it may not have been as paranoid as it sounds. You know, no one here gets to be a teacher, and certainly not a principal, without the approval of the Shin Bet. In any case, it took us thousands of cups of coffee in people's homes, hundreds of hours of teaching English at the community center, before people began to accept that we are really here for our stated purpose — bringing together Jews and Arabs from the region."

Sue hesitated before she asked, "Were you ever scared living here?"

15

Silence. I could feel Dina looking at Michal through the dark, consulting wordlessly.

My mind flashed to Yaakov, a thin young man I had met while volunteering with Project Renewal in Safed just a few months before. In 1974, his 11th-grade class had gone on a field trip to the Golan Heights for Independence Day. They had bunked in a high school in Maalot. Yaakov awoke in the middle of the night; men in uniform were moving about the room. He first thought they were Israeli soldiers, but, somehow, in the shadow, realized they were terrorists. He leaped from the window and broke his leg, escaping the Maalot massacre by the Palestinian Democratic Front for the Liberation of Palestine, which murdered twenty-two of his classmates.

I shuddered, listening to the silence of the village night.

Finally, Michal answered. "Once the house was broken into, and we never found out by whom or why. But that was a long time ago. You know, you still can get into the house from the side window; sometimes we do that, if we forget our key."

Only later did I hear the full story: that a man had entered our Tamra home at night, while Michal was sleeping. She ran outside to the neighbors, escaping unharmed. The incident was not repeated, but it stayed as a shadow in the back of my mind.

As our words, fears and memories rolled into the stillness of the village night, the conversation on the *frash* curved to more familiar ground. "This feels like those first nights at summer camp," mused Michal, "when we all talked about our boyfriends." Giggles rippled through the room.

Quickly checking that the shutters on the window were closed to ensure that the neighbors couldn't hear, we began to tell of old boyfriends and romances. Tamra melted away, and we were all back in Pittsburgh, PA, Buffalo, NY, Cleveland, OH, seeing one another in the tender and embarrassing moments of young love. We were undoubtedly the only unmarried women in Tamra's history ever to laugh together over our rich and varied premarital romances. We giggled hysterically at the clash of the familiar and the forbidden.

Two weeks later, Michal and Dina left, and Sue and I were on our own, trying to become an accepted part of the life of the community. We soon learned that we could not just fit into the niche carved out by our predecessors, starting our work where they left off. We would have to build our own base of trust, relationship by relationship. This realization was disappointing for both of us, but especially for Sue, who was impatient to start on the work we had come to do, forging joint community ties between Arab Tamra and Jewish Qiryat Ata.

We began by teaching English and visiting families from the veteran Diab, Hijazi and Abu Rumi clans, as well as from the families of the "internal refugees," those who had come to Tamra from Galilee villages destroyed in the 1948 War of Independence. Without a car, in a town with few buses, we walked everywhere, climbing steep, narrow, winding, ill-repaired streets without sidewalks. Since there were no parks, we often passed kids playing soccer in the streets, or in rock-strewn lots. In the midst of residential neighborhoods, along the main roads, carpentry shops, cheese factories, and garages operated on the ground floor of homes. Smells of sour milk and grease wafted through the neighborhood as — in the absence of a sewage system linked to the national infrastructure — production waste flowed in the streets.

Two *azhnabiyat* (foreign women) walking unescorted down the street, hair uncovered, dressed in slacks (though never in sleeveless tops), attracted attention. Sue, slight, with flowing blond hair, turned more heads than me, tall with unkempt curly brown hair and glasses. We were hailed with constant invitations from women of the homes we passed: *"Tfadalo"* — Please, come in!

For days we barely managed to get anywhere, accepting every invitation, lest we offend our eager hosts.

When we told Ghaleb about our predicament, he laughed. "If an invitation is offered as you approach a house, it is intended. If it is called out after you have passed the doorway, they're just being polite. Call out *'Mar't e-jai, in shallah'* (Next time, God willing), and keep walking."

For many women in Tamra, marriages were arranged. Oddly, after talking to scores of women in the village, I came to the conclusion that the proportion of such marriages that worked well was probably not much different than the proportion of freely chosen marriages in Western society. However, the fate of women

A wedding procession in Tamra.

stuck in the ones that didn't work was very different.

Sue and I joked that our relationship fit right in. We had not chosen to live together, to run a household together, to present a public face together, to comfort one another, to deal with cultural translations together. Our styles were different. Sue's emotions were close to the surface. She would size things up quickly and go into action. I was more cerebral, and felt the need to probe and analyze, sometimes ad nauseum. Neither of us wanted to spend much time taking care of the house.

Yet here we were, our private lives bound together, as we tried to learn the ways of the community around us, and to be catalysts for greater ties with the community down the road (which we also strived to understand). I needed Sue desperately, and she needed me, as an island of familiarity in this alien sea. We worked to appreciate and support one another and create a common home, despite our different styles and outlooks.

As we began to fathom the cultural rules in Tamra, Sue and I developed some basic codes for our own conduct:

• No boyfriends or alcohol in our house; both are prohibited by Moslem law or custom. The few male friends we invited to visit spent a lot of time with Ghaleb, and, of course, slept at his house, not ours.

• Never visit a man in his home unless someone else, preferably a woman, is in the house. Corollary: don't allow men from the village to visit our home if one of us is alone in the house. If you have to lie and tell the would-be visitor that he can't come in because you are about to go out, so be it.

• Never allow anyone to plant jealousy between us. The women of the village, constantly on the alert for gossip, would test us. "Your Arabic is better than Sue's," someone would say to me (or the opposite to Sue). Whichever of us was being complimented would answer: "Oh, no, her Arabic is much better!" Even when Sue and I were in the midst of a domestic squabble, we rigorously defended one another in public.

• There is no such thing as privacy. Always assume someone can see you, and is watching — no matter where you are, or what time of day. We took for granted that our neighbors, Im and Abu Anan, knew things about us, or imagined that they knew things about us, that would soon be known by the entire village.

One spring day, Im and Abu Anan invited Sue and me to join them and their kids for a walk up the hill above Tamra to collect herbs and plants for cooking and home remedies. It was magnificent out, sunny with a cool breeze and rain-washed air. Winding our way up the hillside, we picked sage, *za'atar* (a cousin of oregano) and a variety of mints for tea from among the rocks along the way. When we reached an area of trees, just below the summit of the hill, we rested. Im Anan, like a rotund Mary Poppins, began unpacking dish after dish from a brown cloth bag — homemade *kubbeh* (meat-filled dumplings), tangerines, and cucumbers grown in Tamra. As the adults finished eating, the kids played tag. Then we all climbed the rest of the way to the top of the hill.

Looking out over the Western Galilee's rolling, rocky hills, which were brushed with low carob trees, we saw red roofs sprouting on the hilltops in the distance, signaling the construction of new Jewish communities. The crown of our own hilltop had been cleared and flattened, making space for a number of homes in various phases of construction. We stepped into the uncompleted, still-dirt yard of a neat, white house with red roof.

"They call this Mitzpe Aviv (Aviv Lookout), but some of the land around here belonged to my grandfather," said Abu Anan, peering around with proprietary interest. "Sometime in the 1950s, I think, they confiscated it. I never received compensation." He paused. "But I didn't want money, because then it would seem like

19

I agreed to give up my land. Now, they're building a Jewish settlement on it — to 'look-out' over Tamra. What are they looking for?"

"They" — the Israeli government — looked to halt unauthorized Arab expansion on the lands of the Galilee. In the United Nations Partition Plan of 1947, which proposed dividing the land of the British Mandate of Palestine into two states, Palestine and Israel, the Galilee had been slated to be part of Palestine, not Israel, because the overwhelming majority of the population was Arab. Although Israel took over the Galilee in the 1948 War of Independence, the Central Galilee remained overwhelmingly Arab.

To preclude any future attempts to restore the Partition Plan, the Israeli government, in the 1950s and '60s, embarked on a massive development plan, establishing development towns, *kibbutzim* and *moshavim* throughout Israel's periphery, to draw Jewish population to the Negev and the Galilee and settle almost one million new immigrants who were flowing into the young country. Jewish development towns of Carmiel, Upper Nazareth, Shlomi, and Maalot were built among and upon the lands of the Arab towns of Sakhnin, Nazareth and Majd il Krum.

In addition, national development budgets drew industry to these new towns, offering grants up to 40 percent of initial capital costs to factories locating there. Corresponding incentives were not available in the neighboring Arab villages and towns, whose economic situation was no less dire than that of the new Jewish cities.

Building these Jewish towns over the years required rezoning of public lands, expropriation of private Arab lands, and the setting of municipal jurisdictions, all of which contracted the area of Arab town that had stretched across the Galilee, and placed land under the jurisdiction of new Jewish municipalities.

In the mid-1970s, the Israeli government and the Jewish Agency started a program termed "Judaizing the Galilee," designed to entice veteran, middle-class Israeli Jews to settle in the area, in order to help solve the "demographic problem" of having so few Jews in a major region of the Jewish State. The Regional Council of Misgav was established as the municipal framework uniting Jewish hilltop "look-out" *(mitzpe)* settlements, with their attractive, single-family homes. An amoeba of land was carved out from among the Arab villages and put under the jurisdiction of the new

Council, to break up blocs of Arab settlement, and, in the words of an official Galilee regional development plan, "to strengthen the Jewish hold on this region."

In 1976, Israeli Arabs had organized a major protest against the expropriations and redistricting of lands. In this first Land Day demonstration, six Arab youths had been killed by the Israeli police not far from here. It was this event that had spurred Rabbi Bruce Cohen to launch Interns for Peace.

In the context of the unresolved Arab-Israeli conflict, I could understand the government goal of drawing Jews to populate the Galilee. I couldn't understand, however, why that couldn't be done in the context of an overall plan to develop the whole area, so that all the residents, Arab and Jewish, could benefit together?

Descending the hill to return to Tamra, the refrain of a popular Matti Caspi song popped into my head: "Things that you see from there, you can't see from here." People moving into the lovely homes in Mitzpe Aviv had a magnificent view of the Galilee. They looked out over the picturesque village of Tamra, cascading down the hill. But they had no idea how they looked from below.

After months of visiting women, teaching English, and starting an English club for high-school kids in Tamra, Sue and I began exploring the neighboring Jewish town of Qiryat Ata. A few times a week we would ride the public Egged bus to meet with teachers, youth groups, and city officials, in order to build connections and start joint activities between Qiryat Ata and Tamra. We always left early in the morning, when Tamra workers (virtually all men) left for their jobs in the Jewish sector — in Qiryat Ata, in Haifa, and in the industrial area of the Haifa Bay — because in the middle of the day, few buses operated.

In addition to starting a Qiryat Ata high school English club, I tried to get some businesspeople involved in exploring the idea of joint business ventures between the towns. When I raised the idea with Eli, the manager of one of Qiryat Ata's banks, he said, "You came all the way from New York to get me together with businesspeople from Tamra? What for?"

I thought to correct him — I had come from Pittsburgh — but what difference did that make in this rural area where, for Jews and Arabs, America and New York were interchangeable terms?

"Here in Israel, you should be helping Jews, not Arabs," chided Eli. "Besides, I already do business with people from Tamra. The major business-people prefer to have their accounts here, where they can count on discretion. In Tamra, the banker may be their cousin or their neighbor. Once he knows a business' financial doings, he may make a comment to his wife, and in hours, the whole *hamula* knows. Here, we aren't involved in their lives. And what kind of cooperation do we need with Tamra?" Eli shrugged. "*Kabdehu v'hashdehu* — respect them and suspect them — keep them at arm's length. I know; I come from Morocco. You have no idea what they're like. They'll be friendly and hospitable, as long as they think you're strong. But if you're weak, they'll stab you in the back. Just wait for a war, when feelings are running high; you'll see that your work means nothing."

I wondered if he was right about war obliterating our work. In Qiryat Ata and Tamra, life seemed fairly calm. However, in the northern Galilee, just a few kilometers north of us around Nahariya, and in Kiryat Shmona to the northeast, Katyusha rockets shot from bases of the Palestine Liberation Organization (PLO) in Southern Lebanon were falling increasingly often. Residents of northern Israel were spending more and more days in bomb shelters; some had been killed. The Israeli Air Force conducted periodic air strikes on targets in Lebanon. Tensions were rising. The Syrians had moved surface-to-air missiles into the Beqaa region of Lebanon. Were these incidents leading to the kind of situation of which Eli warned?

Returning to Tamra in late afternoon, I watched the last Jewish passenger (other than me) get off the bus outside Qiryat Ata. At an invisible spot, the Egged driver (who turned out to be Arab himself) switched the radio station from the Hebrew to the Arabic channel. The remaining passengers relaxed, lounging on the seats, and speaking more loudly in Arabic. They no longer needed to muster the effort to "fit in" among Israeli Jews in the factories, the construction crews, and the markets where they worked or shopped. How much else went with this play-acting in the presence of Jews?

Suddenly I realized the enormous effort it was taking me to "fit in" in Tamra, especially as a woman. I did it at the price of censoring so many parts of myself. No glass of wine in the evening, out of respect for Muslim law, which prohibits alcohol. No mention of my relationships with men, because deep cultural assumptions did not allow most Tamraites to accept that a woman could have premarital relationships and still be respectable. Although I did not hide my Jewishness, or my identification with Zionism, I did not often discuss it. Living according to someone else's rules was exhausting.

I came home to Sue, hoping for comfort. She was pouring herself a cup of mint tea. "Do you know why I'm really here in Tamra?" she said.

I held my breath, fearing that our paranoid neighbors were right about the CIA.

"I came to find out if my father is right — that we can't live with the Arabs."

Sue's father had emigrated from Eastern Europe to Palestine before World War II. An ardent follower of the great Zionist revisionist, Vladimir Ze'ev Jabotinsky, he had fled to America to escape arrest by the British in the Mandate Period.

Jabotinsky, unlike mainstream Zionism's ideological father, Theodor Herzl (who described Palestine as "a land without a people for a people without a land"), anticipated the opposition of the Arabs living in Palestine when the Jews came. He recognized that Jewish colonization and the establishment of a Jewish national home in Palestine would require that the Palestinian Arabs lose their majority status. Respecting the fact that the Arabs longed for what he longed for — a homeland — he believed that they would fight rather than suffer this loss. The pre-state Revisionist groups staged guerrilla action against both the British and the Palestinian Arab population, to cause them to leave. The current Israeli prime minister, Menachem Begin, was a protégé of Jabotinsky.

"So what do you think so far?" I asked with some trepidation. If Sue left, I'd be here on my own.

"They will never really accept us; and we will never really accept them." Sue sipped from the steaming cup. She looked at my crestfallen face. "Well, you will, and Bruce Cohen and a few others. But, Sarah, most people won't."

Chapter 2
Common Ground?

Sue was right: Our allegiances as Jews were sometimes, perhaps often, polar opposites to those of our Arab neighbors in Tamra. On June 8, 1981, Israeli jets flew 1,100 kilometers over enemy territory to bomb the still-cold core of the Osiraq nuclear reactor being built outside Baghdad in Iraq. It was a spectacular military feat that temporarily halted Iraq's nuclear program, with few casualties. Although Israel was condemned by the UN and the United States for this attack, I felt proud of Israel's daring, of its technological precision and prowess in cleanly taking out the weapons of mass destruction of a formidable enemy.

The next evening, I was sitting with the Canaans, one of my favorite families in Tamra. The young women of the family were sharp and informed, thought about issues and expressed their opinions; I always enjoyed talking with them. They were sitting outside on the *frash* on their porch. Despite their requisite *t'fadalu*, they didn't look so happy to see me this time.

"What right does Israel have to violate another country and bomb it?" demanded Suha, the oldest daughter. "What would you think if the Soviet Air Force flew over Washington and attacked a nuclear reactor there? Is that legitimate?"

To me, Iraq was an enemy state, run by an aggressive dictator who had attacked Iran just a year and a half before and was waging a war that was brutally costly to his people. But to those seated around me on the *frash* in their home in Tamra, Iraq was one of the most technologically advanced and modern Arab states, run

24

by a secular leader who was holding back the growth of religious fundamentalism in the Middle East while building the power of his country. They, Arab Israelis, were proud of Iraq's prowess, while I, an American Jew (not to mention Israeli Jews), was proud of Israel's. These loyalties run deep; they are not the sort of thing one bridges in a women's group or an English club. I could do little with this knowledge, other than recognize it. Quickly, I downed the cup of coffee offered as a farewell, and went home, wondering if I should come back to visit the Canaan women any time soon.

At the end of June, despite our vaguely functional Arabic, Abed, the youth coordinator at the Tamra Community Center, asked Sue and me and Ghaleb to help out at the annual summer camp for kids. There, our status as exotic foreigners allowed us to lead games and songs, pass out chocolate milk, and scream for order without regard to our language skills. Inside the town, there was no public space big enough for a summer camp, so the activities took place on the edge of Tamra, in a small grove of eucalyptus trees, dotted with fig trees, and surrounded by sabra cactuses, to which Tamraites referred to as "Damoun."

"Why Damoun?" I asked the camp director.

"Because that's the name of the Arab village that was here until 1948. It was a small village next to the road, very exposed. During the war, people went to live in the larger towns in the hills — Tamra, Shefa'Am'r, Ibilin. When the fighting stopped and people tried to go back to their homes, they found the area cordoned off by the army as a 'closed military zone.' People watched as their homes were destroyed by the army. Eventually, the area was turned over to the Keren Kayemet, the Jewish National Fund, and these eucalyptus trees were planted to make it into a picnic area. Every year we get permission to use Damoun for our camp."

I tried to imagine the old homes, gardens, and walls surrounding the lone fig trees that remained. The sabras (prickly-pear cactii), once living fences dividing one family's property from the other, now bristled to no avail, lost in the transformation from Arab village to Israeli park. In the midst of stringing up lines of balloons, I felt an emptiness. Where were they now, the Damounites? Some, perhaps, were in Lebanon. Others, I realized, were living in the new neighborhoods of Tamra. I wondered how they felt passing

25

daily the land that was once theirs, seeing their homes destroyed and replaced by a forest?

Growing up, I had donated quarters and dollars at Sunday school, dropping them in the blue metal box painted with a map of the Jewish State, so the Keren Kayemet could plant trees in the barren land of Israel, reforesting areas denuded by Ottoman logging. Now I could never again look at a Keren Kayemet forest without asking the question: Who and what was here before?

Throughout June and July, the PLO, based in Lebanon, shelled the Israeli border towns Kiryat Shmona and Nahariya. Israel answered with artillery and air strikes. Tensions rose as the pace of bombing increased. American envoy Philip Habib shuttled between Israel and Lebanon to broker a ceasefire. On July 24, 1981, after ten days of shelling, an agreement was signed.

In late summer, our months of teaching English, running activities for youth movements in Qiryat Ata, drinking coffee, and sitting on *frash* with the people of Tamra paid off. Ghaleb, Sue and I managed to pull off a three-day scouting camp, in which 150 kids from Tamra, Qiryat Ata, and Haifa cooked, tented and hiked together in the Carmel Mountains.

Initially, the Qiryat Ata scout leaders had been wary of the idea. They themselves had never ventured into Tamra. Only after we had invited them personally to our home were they willing to come. Seeing the Tamra scout troop playing the same games they played with their kids in Qiryat Ata, and visiting the community center and touring the town dispelled their nervousness. I felt then the importance of our living in Tamra, and being women there, which gave us even more credibility. If we felt safe, and moved freely in town, how could a Qiryat Ata male youth leader balk?

Being a woman helped in navigating Arab society as well. Because we were foreign, we could slip in and out of the public space with ease, and the men were less threatened by hearing new ideas from a foreign woman. I also had access to the kitchens and the back rooms that were closed to my male colleagues. And because Dina was right — that women do have power in the household — influencing the experience of other women had great impact.

In Interns for Peace, we did not aim to change attitudes, but to generate meaningful contact, points of intersection in otherwise parallel lives. Through joint activities, people could gain information — not only from the newspapers and from prevalent stereotypes, but from direct personal contact. This was the philosophy behind IFP's work, and I appreciated it.

In the fall, a new group of Interns joined us, including Lani, another Dina, and Arik, all Jews from America, as well as Sabri from the Arab town of Rama in the Galilee. In addition to a respectable-enough reputation and a network of contacts, we now had a real team. We decided to pair all the elementary schools in the two towns during the 1981-2 school year. We divided up the schools among us, and approached the principals. I was assigned the Lochamei HaGhetto'ot (Ghetto Fighters) School in Qiryat Ata and the Tamra C School. Interestingly, while all the schools in Qiryat Ata were named for famous people or events in Jewish history, the schools in Tamra were named A, B and C. The Israeli government would probably not have tolerated the names of the famous Arab heroes Tamra city officials would have chosen for their schools.

Mohammed, the principal of Tamra C, was willing to meet but felt embarrassed about the quality of his school and his teachers. As for the Ghetto Fighters School principal, Gabi — who looked like she could have been a commander herself in the Warsaw Ghetto Uprising — she placed me under interrogation. What is Interns for Peace; what experience do you have; what does the principal of the Tamra school think; what activities would we do? After a couple of discussions like this, I managed to arrange a meeting between Mohammed and Gabi, so they could directly work out their issues.

In the meantime, teachers from Sprinzak School and Tamra B were already getting together to design and prepare their year-long program of meetings. Because the Jewish kids spoke no Arabic, and the Arab kids spoke little Hebrew, joint activities centered on areas that would allow interaction without conversation: sports, art, cooperative games.

In December 1981, and again in March 1982, the fifth grades of Sprinzak and Tamra B got together, almost 200 kids and teachers. Before and after each encounter, Ghaleb or Sabri would work with the Tamra kids, and one of the Jewish Interns would work with the Sprinzak kids, to discuss their stereotypes, fears, and feel-

The Interns for Peace team in our Tamra home: Arik Ascherman, Dina Charnin, Sabri el-Haj, Sarah Kreimer (back), Sue Wish, Lani Levine.

ings about the other group, separately and safely.

In the spring, teachers from Sprintzak and Tamra B began to plan their third encounter — an end-of-the-school-year party June. They put off detailed planning until after the roller-coaster week of observances at the end of April, starting with Holocaust Remembrance Day (Yom HaShoah), then Memorial Day for the Fallen in Israel's wars (Yom HaZicharon), and ending with Israeli Independence Day.

On Yom HaShoah, in Jewish towns across Israel, a commemorative siren goes off at 10:00 a.m. At its first tones, traffic comes to a halt as drivers pull over to the side of the road, get out of their cars, and stand at attention. As the siren's wail washes over the streets, shoppers stop in mid-transaction; coffee drinkers put down their cups and stand by their tables, heads bowed, arms at their sides. Everyone pauses for one minute in solidarity with the collective memory of the Holocaust, the murder of six million Jews, about two thirds of the Jewish population of Europe.

This year, on Yom HaShoah, I was at home in Tamra, discussing the June plans with Ghaleb. Although he had signed up to be an Intern for only one year and would soon be leaving, he identified with the work and wanted the upcoming activities to succeed. When the siren sounded outside Tamra in the distance, I immediately stopped talking and rose to stand quietly in the middle of our living room. Ghaleb sat on the sofa, with a frown. On the street outside, cars drove by, oblivious to the siren's wail. As the seconds ticked by, I grew angrier and angrier. Finally, half-way through the minute, Ghaleb slowly stood up.

After the eerie tones died down, I turned on him. "How could you not stand in remembrance of six million people who were slaughtered? Just because they were Jews? The Holocaust is not part of the Israeli-Arab conflict!"

"I did stand." Ghaleb said in a low voice, his anger rising to his face. "But if you think Yom HaShoah is not connected to the conflict, you are blind. For years in school it was pushed down my throat — the Jews were killed in Europe, therefore the Jews need to have a state. What Hitler did was terrible, but why does my family have to pay the price? Why do we have to have our land taken away for a Jewish State?"

I remained silent, so angry I could not speak.

"Do you think it is an accident that the holidays were arranged so that Yom HaShoah comes first, then Yom HaZicharon, then Independence Day? No! It is a manipulation, in order to justify the State of Israel." Ghaleb banged his fist on the table. "But do you know what we call Independence Day? We call it the Naqba — the catastrophe! Because for us, it was a defeat. We lost Palestine; we lost our land. Some of us became refugees; the rest became third-class citizens of a state we didn't want."

I felt my stomach knotting as Ghaleb talked, but still I found no words.

"So I can stand in remembrance of the millions of Jews and others who were killed by Hitler," continued Ghaleb. "But I cannot rejoice on 'Independence Day.' And I certainly cannot commemorate the memory of the soldiers who fell fighting against my people in 1948!"

My shock and anger melted into dismay at the gulf between us.

We sat in the livingroom a long time, discussing the continued discrimination against Jews by Western nations after World War II, and debating the War of Independence, the refusal of Arab states to accept the UN Partition Plan, and the confiscation of lands from Kfar Kara to build *kibbutzim* in the area.

As colleagues, Ghaleb and I managed to find some common ground. At the end of our discussion, however, I remained with the uneasy feeling that the gap between our two sets of hopes was deeper than I had ever imagined. If this is the best we could do as coworkers, how could any network of common activities begin to bridge such chasms? I could not imagine what would happen to us and our meager bridging attempts in the event of a war.

Chapter 3
Peace for Galilee

It was still oppressively hot at 4 p.m. on Sunday, June 6, 1982, as I woke from a nap on the *frash* in my Tamra home. I sleepily turned on the radio to hear: "Israeli troops advanced in a massive land thrust in southern Lebanon today. Cabinet Secretary Dan Meridor stated that 'Operation Peace for Galilee was launched to place all residents of Galilee beyond the range of terrorist fire from Lebanon. Israel continues to aspire to the signing of a peace treaty with an independent Lebanon.' The PLO continues to shell towns around Kiryat Shmona and Nahariya from bases in South Lebanon. Residents along the northern border are requested to remain in their shelters until further notice."

Tamra was less than twenty miles south of Nahariya. Would PLO shelling reach us as well? I had never been under attack; did Tamra even have bomb shelters? Maybe I should pack my things and get out of Tamra — south to Kibbutz Barkai, where we had done our training. People there would certainly know what to do; they'd been through many wars. I began to sweat in the increasingly sweltering air.

"The government spokesperson reports that Operation Peace for Galilee aims to clear out terrorist bases to create a twenty-five-mile wide buffer zone north of Israel's border. Yesterday, the air force successfully hit targets in southern Lebanon. All planes returned safely to their bases."

Would it be dangerous to live in Tamra now? The warning given months ago by Eli, the Qiryat Ata bank manager, echoed in

31

my mind: "If you're weak, they'll stab you in the back. Just wait for a war, when feelings are running high; you'll see that your work means nothing."

I shuddered, imagining Suha Canaan rising from the *frash* in her home with a smile on her face and a knife in her hand. After more than a year in Tamra, I felt that I had built some trust with colleagues at the community center, with neighbors, with high school kids I had taught, with the Canaan women, the Hijazis, the Diabs, whose homes I had visited hundreds of times. Would all this trust now evaporate? Would it be replaced by suspicion, resentment, hatred? After glimpsing Arab Israelis' deep ties with the Arab world, I wondered: Would their identification strengthen as Israel attacked Arab targets in Lebanon? Would that make us Interns targets for any explosion of anger or frustration against Jews or Israelis? It only took one crazy or enraged individual . . .

Dina, Sue and Lani walked in, as phrases like "thousands of troops," "heavy shelling," and "fierce fighting" poured out of the radio. Lani ran over to get Arik and Sabri, and we held an emergency staff meeting. It took little time to realize that we had no idea what to do. I suggested consulting with Munir Diab, head of Tamra's community center, who had invited Interns for Peace into Tamra in 1978.

Stepping out of our house into the scorching air, I looked up and down the main road with trepidation, watching for some expression of hostility. Across from our home, Abu Musa stood behind the counter in his hardware store, as usual. In her doorway up the street, Im Anan swept dust out the door. A few high school kids, in uniform blue shirts, sauntered home, ignoring us. Everything looked normal; I felt no unusual tension in the air. As we walked down the street, I wondered if I had heard correctly that our country was now at war, twenty-five miles away. We reached the community center without hearing any of the usual offers of "*tfadalu*, welcome!" but without incident.

Nayla, the secretary, waved us into Munir's sparse second-floor office. Sabri and Dina carried in extra plastic chairs. Smiling as usual, Munir greeted us with the usual *"Salaam aleikum, tfadalu"* (Peace be with you, welcome), as he offered us little cups of sweet Turkish coffee from a plastic thermos on his desk and made the usual inquiries as to our health.

After our own polite replies of *"El hamdil'alla,"* (Thank God), Sue opened directly: "Israel is at war in Lebanon; are we safe here?"

His round face permanently cheerful, Munir looked at each of the six us, in turn. He had coached each of us in delicate situations in the past. He had opened doors for us, had publicly entrusted the safety of kids at the community center to us. He spoke without hesitation: "The war is not taking place in Tamra; you see what it is like here. No harm will come to you; please stay with us in our community."

I was touched by Munir's request. Despite my fear, I trusted his judgment.

"But there are 18,000 people in Tamra; what if one person gets crazy?" asked Lani, expressing, as she always did, what other people were feeling and afraid to say.

"You are our guests. It would be an *i'ib,* a stain on our honor, if you were harmed in Tamra."

"What if there is bombing? Where are the shelters?" Lani continued.

Munir laughed. "There are no bomb shelters in Tamra. The government never built any here, nor in any other Arab town. The PLO knows this is an Arab village. Besides, we are out of range of the Katyushas."

"What about our work?" asked Arik.

"Wait a few days," counseled Munir. "Then we'll see."

The conversation with Munir left me feeling vulnerable, off-balance. With difficulty, I had just begun to understand some of the sensitivities and codes of daily life in Tamra. But what were the rules in wartime? I had no experience on which to draw; I had to rely on the judgment of others.

We called Rabbi Bruce Cohen and Farhat Aghbariya, the directors of Interns for Peace, to get their advice. They echoed Munir's analysis, and encouraged us to stay in the field. "But it is up to each of you," they concluded. "If you choose to leave, we will honor your decision."

Each of us called a couple of good friends. I talked with Devorah, my kibbutz mother. Her voice was tight, as she told me that her husband, Zvi, had donned his uniform and gone off to his unit. "Why don't you come back to Barkai?" she offered. "You could stay in our house."

We all pondered our options. After a brief group discussion, each of us made the decision to stay. Even if we could not do our regular work, we wanted to stay with the people of Tamra and Qiryat Ata, whom we had come to know.

I was aching to disprove Eli's prediction that the thin veneer of ties and trust, maintained in daily life, disintegrated in wartime, exposing the true, deep and opposed loyalties of Arab and Jew. If I assumed that he was right, his words would become a self-fulfilling prophecy. If, on the other hand, ties held between Arabs and Jews in wartime, I would have my own first-hand evidence to contradict his.

On Monday, Sue, Sabri and I went to Qiryat Ata, to find out what was happening there. As we rode the bus past the cucumber fields of Tamra, I wondered if people in Qiryat Ata were maintaining the same veneer of normality, as in Tamra. The moment I stepped off the bus, I knew they were not.

We stood alone in the main square of the town. Eerie silence hung in the air, as in the yellow moments before a storm. Sidewalk tables stood fresh-wiped and empty in front of Melech HaFelafal. The waitress gazed into space. Store doors gaped open on the main street; no one entered. Walking to Sprinzak School, we passed an old woman waiting for the bus, and two teenage girls arm-in-arm, not speaking. Since entering Qiryat Ata, I had seen only women. As if in a horror movie, I felt that the earth had opened and swallowed all the men, leaving the women to walk the streets alone.

Opening the heavy doors of Sprinzak School, I was met by an odd hush in the usually tumultuous halls. In the principal's office, a radio buzzed constantly, a mix of nostalgic Israeli folk music, and the business-like tones of newscasters who were prevented from reporting the news that everyone craved: What was happening in Lebanon? How many casualties, and who were the victims? How long would the war continue?

We asked to speak with Ya'akov, the principal. "He's been called up," answered his secretary, "but we've asked for him to be released. I hope he'll be back in a few days."

In the teachers' room, instead of the usual chatting and gossiping people sat separately, listening to the radio, scanning a newspaper, staring into space. After several truncated attempts, I gave up trying to start conversations with the teachers I knew. *We have to see . . . I hope everything will be all right . . . It can't be like Yom Kippur . . .* Their short, distracted answers told me I was talking with people who were far away, reliving earlier wars, earlier wounded and dead. I felt trapped in a tragic drama, with a script that I was powerless to change. Suddenly, Chaya, the assistant principal, spotted Sabri, and came striding over. "You're one of the Interns for Peace, aren't you?!"

I thought she was going to start screaming at him: *What are you doing here, gawking? Go back to your village and leave us alone!*

Instinctively, I stepped closer to Sabri. Chaya continued breathlessly. "You used to coach a soccer club at your community center, didn't you? Could you teach phys-ed here at Sprinzak until our sports teacher, Avi, comes back from Lebanon?"

Sabri stared at her, a blank look on his face. He, an Israeli Arab, a Moslem from Rama Village, a Palestinian, was being asked to teach Jewish kids as a substitute for their regular teacher, who was fighting Palestinians in a war in Lebanon?

"I could do it," Sabri spoke slowly. "But . . . Well, you know I'm an Arab, don't you?"

"Yes, I know. But we are desperate. We have asked the army to let our principal return; we think he'll be back in a few days. We don't have enough teachers to run all the classes, and there are no substitutes. Every school is in the same situation. Do any of you teach math?" she said, looking hopefully at Sue and me.

"No," I answered. "But we could teach English."

"Great!" said Chaya. "Come to the principal's office; we'll look at the schedule."

As we looked, I quickly figured which days I could commit to being in Qiryat Ata. Receiving my assignment, I thought of the Hebrew word, *l'alter*, to improvise. No one had asked for our qualifications; no one cleared this plan with the Department of Education. We were in the throes of a giant, society-wide improvisation.

I asked Chaya to reconsider about Sabri. Maybe one of the kids' fathers, *chas v'halila* (God forbid), would be wounded in the war; how would the child then feel or act, taking sports with Sabri? As she went to discuss the idea with some veteran teachers, Sue asked Sabri if he wanted to take a day to consider the offer.

Without hesitation, Sabri shook his head, warming to the absurd challenge.

Chaya returned to confirm her proposal. Sabri, Sue and I arranged to come together on Mondays and Wednesdays to teach at Sprinzak School.

That evening, I sat with one of the teachers, Paduya, and her two kids, at her Qiryat Ata home, as she scanned the TV news for pictures of her husband, Yigal, and her brothers, listening for hints of their fate. She was tense, sitting cross-legged on the flowered couch, but then smiled in recollection of an incident from the Yom Kippur war, just nine years earlier. "I hadn't heard anything from Yigal for days," she said. "I hadn't seen him for a couple weeks, but I knew he was serving in the Golan. It was his birthday, so I baked a cake and drove up to find him." Paduya's grey eyes sparkled as she ran her hands through her wavy hair. "At each army blockade, I asked about his unit, and they let me through."

I had seen Paduya managing classes of forty kids, and I could imagine 18-year-old soldiers responding instinctively to her no-nonsense tone.

"I think it was almost midnight when I found him. I stayed overnight in his tent, and went back the next day."

I marveled at her guts, and at the informality and the close, personal nature of war in this strange country. War, to me, conjured up pictures of Vietcong in jungles, of marines fighting anonymously, thousands of miles away. Once again I felt how little I knew or understood of life in Israel.

The next week, Ya'akov was released from his reserve duty and returned to take charge of Sprinzak School. The kids, meanwhile, loved their sports classes with Sabri. He was a great coach, laughing and joking with the boys while working them hard. No one mentioned the absurdity — and the beauty — of an Arab Israeli teaching Jewish kids whose fathers were fighting other Arabs just twenty-five miles away. But after a few days, and a few comments about "getting those Arabs" in Lebanon, even Sabri couldn't stand the dissonance and stopped volunteering.

Many men, including Paduya's husband, were still not home, but the statistics dribbling in from the front gave the illusion of control. After a week of fighting, Israeli troops had reached the

Lebanese capital of Beirut and were fighting in the surrounding hills. For the first time, Israel was conducting a war not primarily against an Arab country but directly against the PLO, which had set up bases among hundreds of thousands of Palestinian refugees in the towns and camps of southern Lebanon, especially in the area around Beirut. Almost 200 Israelis had been killed, and more than 1,000 had been wounded. The Palestinian/Lebanese body count was unclear, but it was being reported as in the thousands. Over 500,000 were homeless.

With their country fighting their people, Arab Israelis faced a deadly dilemma. If they identified with the Palestinians in Lebanon, they were traitors to their state; if they identified with Israel, they were traitors to their Arab nationality, perhaps even to their own families. The refugees in southern Lebanon were the families of those Palestinians who had fled the Galilee in 1948, in the war declared by the Arab states upon Israel's declaration of independence. At the end of that war, Israel had sealed its borders. Those who had fled the fighting, some 700,000 people, were not allowed to return to their homes.

The next day, Nayla, the secretary at the Tamra community center, invited me to her home. Drinking tea in the livingroom of the simple house in which she had grown up, she told me, "I am 34 years old, the same age as the state. I have grown up as an Israeli; I know nothing else. But I have grown up as an Arab as well. My cousins on my mother's side live in a refugee camp not far away, in Lebanon. In 1948 their parents fled the fighting. They went to stay with relatives in Tyre, just a few kilometers north, until the fighting stopped."

Nayla's dark eyes were sad, but her voice continued without anger. "We stayed here; my parents could not bear to leave their home, even if it seemed dangerous. Besides, the *mukhtar* (village leader) of Tamra had promised the commanders of the army that there would be no armed resistance in Tamra. Families from the surrounding villages even came to live in Tamra during the war, because it was quiet.

"A few months later, the war ended, and my aunt and uncle wanted to come back home. They tried, again and again, to cross the border, but each time they were turned back by the soldiers.

Three generations of women in Tamra, including Sarah and her mother.

Israel had closed the border. So, my cousins, my uncle, my aunt, they could not come back. Their house — the one above us on the hill —" she turned and pointed through the window — "it lay empty for years, with all their furniture, silverware, pots, even their clothes, still in it."

Sitting on the sofa in her parents' home, Nayla looked directly at me. There was urgency but no malice in her words. She wanted me to understand, but unlike the Canaan sisters, she did not hold me responsible. "My cousins are still there, in Lebanon," she said. "Now Israel is bombing all around Tyre, even Beirut." Tears pooled in her eyes, and Nayla plucked a tissue from the decorated box on the table. "I am scared for them. You know, I have never seen my cousins . . . " Nayla buried her face in her hands.

I tried to imagine her situation by conjuring up an image of the U.S. bombing a Jewish neighborhood of Montreal. It was too absurd; I could not imagine the fear, the anger, the fundamental lack of safety were my own government to bomb my cousins. What emotional gymnastics are required to continue living in such a situation? What greater convolutions are needed to enable voting for, and paying taxes to, such a government?

Powerless, torn by Nayla's words and by the confusion of trying to identify with people on both sides of the conflict, I put my arm around her, trying to bring some human comfort in a situation that neither of us could affect.

By mid-June, life had settled into a nervous pattern. Our Interns team returned to the school principals to discuss whether to carry out the final joint activity of the year. All three Tamra principals and their teaching staffs were in favor of going ahead. What did they have to lose? Even in "normal" times, Israeli Jews have mixed feelings about their Arab neighbors, not fully accepting them or trusting them. Now the level of mistrust was stifling. A joint activity would be a breath of fresh air.

Arriving at the Ghetto Fighters School, I watched 6- and 7-year olds walk, then run, through an air-raid drill. They were dead serious, knowing that they may need this drill for real in the coming days. Their teachers strode next to them with clenched faces. For many teachers, this was their fourth or fifth war. I thought of neighboring Tamra, which had no bomb shelters and no air raid drills, as if bombs and rockets would know not to fall on an Arab village in Israel.

Katie, the fifth-grade teacher who had been working with us, strode toward me with a stern look. "We have decided to cancel the final activity."

"Why?" I asked, wanting to engage her in discussion.

She turned on me in rage. "My husband is in Lebanon; God only knows what's happening to him! I can barely concentrate on normal teaching. Do you expect me to receive kids from Tamra here and be hospitable to them? This is a war! What if one of the kids, or one of the mothers, talks about wanting to kill Arabs? Do you want that? No, we can't possibly carry out this meeting now!"

The look in her eye, the panic in her voice, silenced me. Katie left no room for discussion. Gabi, the principal, not ready to overrule her teachers on this issue, told us that we would have to end the school year without the final encounter.

Lani, Dina and I met up in the center of town to exchange reports. The school that they had been working with had refused as well. I felt depressed. We had all worked so hard, and learned so much; now, it all meant nothing.

We went to join Sue at the last school, Sprinzak. When we arrived, Leah, the teacher who had been responsible for the school exchanges, came over and asked, "What is happening in Tamra? They are in such a difficult position; do they want to continue meeting?" Hearing that they did, Leah smiled with relief. "You know, the war isn't here, between Tamra and Qiryat Ata; we're all still neighbors. As an educator, I want to teach my kids that even though we're at war, they don't have to hate their neighbors."

Ya'akov, the principal, saw us, and invited us into his office. He agreed with Leah. He knew that he would take flak from parents about this decision, but he was ready.

So in the third week of Operation Peace for Galilee, almost 200 fifth-graders of the Tamra B School and Sprinzak Elementary met in Qiryat Ata for a day of skits in simple Arabic and Hebrew. The kids taught one another songs, ate humus in pita, and drank chocolate milk out of little plastic bags. At 1:00 they all sat on the ground to listen to the final exchanges of thanks and good wishes.

Possibly just twenty five miles away, their unknown Arab cousins were engaged in combat against their Jewish fathers or brothers. Yet here, on a sunny day in June in the schoolyard of Sprinzak School, the kids of Tamra and Qiryat Ata were being normal 10-year-old neighbors. I do not remember any of the speeches made that day. But I remember the two principals, Khalil and Ya'akov, smiling side by side on the makeshift podium, looking out over the kids and teachers.

As the Tamra kids got on the bus to go home, Ya'akov and Khalil embraced. They had maintained their relationship and that of their schools in the midst of a war. They had not allowed the stereotypes and the traumas of their communities to dictate their own decisions and actions. They had made a choice and written a new script for themselves and for hundreds of people around them.

It seemed that Eli's prophecy would not come true after all.

Chapter 4
Respect Them and Suspect Them

As Israeli troops surrounded West Beirut in early July and shelled the city, the Israel-Lebanon border became oddly porous. In fact, the Lebanon War brought more contact between Palestinian citizens of Israel (that is, Arab Israelis) and Palestinian refugees in Lebanon than had thirty-four years of relative peace. From the shores of the Mediterranean, edged by the rubble of Sidon, the Arabic service of Israeli Television broadcast the greetings of Palestinians from Lebanon to long-separated relatives in Israel. I sat on the *frash* with women friends in Tamra as they peered, weeping, at the TV looking for lost family members and friends among the parade of refugees who stepped up to the camera.

Tamra residents began receiving letters and news of their relatives in Lebanon through Israeli Druze soldiers or Israel Defense Forces (IDF) doctors. After years of silence, one family suddenly got a note: "We are all fine. Your cousin's daughter, Layla, had a baby last month. Our house has not been badly damaged; we hope to move back soon. Ahmed's sons, Aziz and Mohammed, were taken in for questioning."

The family of a Tamra doctor temporarily took in a Palestinian boy from one of the camps, who had ended up in Haifa's Rambam Hospital for a kidney transplant.

One day, as I entered the community center, Nayla pulled me aside. Her face was glowing. "My aunts are here! They came a few days ago from Tyre; I don't know how they got through, but they're here in Tamra. It's wonderful to see them! They can't stop

41

talking with my mother. They cried to see the old house, to meet all the cousins and nephews and nieces who were born since they left. And they can't believe the changes in the village since '48 — the electricity, the water, Kupat Holim clinics, new schools, new shops, new roads and homes."

A few days later, Nayla sat listlessly behind the reception desk, barely listening to the kids for whom she usually had infinite patience. "My aunts went back to Lebanon," she told me, her eyes brimming with tears. "I miss them. You know, when they were here, I kept thinking — what would my life be like if my parents had fled, and I had grown up there, in the camps in Lebanon, in the civil war? I may not have finished high school; I probably wouldn't be working. It made me feel so Israeli."

At the same time, the Lebanon War also pushed Arab Israelis to identify increasingly as Palestinians. In mid-July, as Israeli planes bombed Palestinian targets around the Lebanese capital and the IDF placed an economic blockade on West Beirut, our Interns team was asked to come on as counselors in a Jewish-Arab summer camp being held at the Hadassim boarding school. In the afternoons, after swimming, sports and regular camp activities, we led dialogue groups between the Arab and Jewish kids.

In one session, everyone was asked to choose from a list of twenty words those with which they most identify: Israeli, Arab, religious, artist, Jew, Palestinian, sensitive, immigrant, daughter . . . human being. George, a quiet, hazel-eyed, Christian Arab from Jaffa, picked "Palestinian" and "Israeli."

"How can you be both?!" demanded Rafi, a tall, dark-haired Jewish boy from Haifa. His father was stationed in Lebanon, where he was most likely fighting Palestinian militias.

"Because I am both," answered George, offended.

"Why didn't you choose 'Arab' or 'Christian'?" I asked.

"Well, usually, I would say 'Arab,'" George began, not looking at Rafi. "But when Palestinian refugees are being killed in Lebanon, I feel like a Palestinian. If my parents hadn't stayed in Jaffa in 1948, it could be me up there."

I thought how easy it was for me to relate to George's dual empathies. As an American Jew, I had never identified more with Israel than when it seemed to be losing the Yom Kippur War in 1973. Yet I could also understand Rafi's confusion. Was he supposed to relate to George as a friend, as a fellow-Israeli, or as part of the Palestinian enemy? How, for that matter, should I relate to George, or to my neighbors in Tamra? By the end of the workshop, I was exhausted from the effort of maintaining double vision in order to help the kids handle this cross-eyed reality.

Before the war, our Interns team, in cooperation with the Tam-ra and Qiryat Ata municipalities, had prepared a four-day summer work-camp for the forty graduates of our two English clubs. In Qiryat Ata, the Arab and Jewish English-club graduates were due to paint playground equipment in neighborhood parks. In Tamra, where there were no parks, the group was due to construct a playground in an empty lot. The teens would work in the morning, get to know the community together in the afternoon, and sleep at one another's homes in the evening. But as the war continued, I could not imagine that parents would allow their kids to visit, much less sleep over, in one another's communities. We decided to postpone the work camp from July to August, in the slim hope that something would happen to relieve the atmosphere.

Throughout July, Israeli troops held the hills surrounding Beirut and shelled Palestinian neighborhoods in the Lebanese capital from ground, air and sea. Israeli civilian protests against the war grew, as military action deviated sharply from the stated purpose of clearing out a twenty-five-mile buffer zone north of Israel's border.

The number of participants in the Interns work-camp dwindled from forty to thirty to twenty. I had a sinking feeling that Eli's warning would prove true this time: "Just wait for a war, when feelings are running high; you'll see that your work means nothing."

Although the atmosphere had decidedly not improved, we could no longer postpone the work-camp. We were now down to ten participants, five on each side. I felt like Abraham in dialogue with God about how many righteous citizens of Sodom were enough to stay God's decree to destroy the city. God had decided that ten was His minimum, and in the end, He couldn't find even that many.

"It hardly seems worth it," said Sue, as we tried to decide what to do.

I disagreed. "In this atmosphere, every connection is important. And don't forget, there may be ten kids, but that means fifty family members, and hundreds of neighbors who see the kids working, and some kind of connection between the municipalities. As long as we have something that looks and feels like a group, let's go ahead."

After much discussion, we decided to give it a try. Holding the work-camp became a personal challenge, and we met, or spoke, with the kids and their parents daily, to maintain the level of energy.

On August 4, the Israel Defense Forces cut the flow of electricity to the 500,000 residents of West Beirut, where the Palestinian population and the PLO strongholds were located. On August 12, three days before the work-camp was due to begin, Israeli planes and gunboats bombarded the Lebanese capital for eleven hours.

Meira, the mother of one of the Qiryat Ata girls, called us at the community center to tell us that she was not letting her daughter come to Tamra. "She can work in the camp on the days when they are in Qiryat Ata. But I won't have her sleeping at a stranger's home in an Arab village while a war is raging less than 100 kilometers from here."

"I understand how you feel," I began, and wondered how many times I had said these words in the past year, in conversation with hundreds of Arabs and Jews: *You can't trust the Arabs . . . I hate the Jews . . . Who are you to tell us what can be done?* I was supposed to understand and work with all of these sentiments. Now I had to empathize with Meira.

"Meira, I understand you're worried," I continued, in as reassuring a tone as I could muster. "How would it be if we all stay together in a school at night? We can bring sleeping bags and sleep on mats on the floor. Then we'll have all six Interns together with the kids twenty-four hours a day."

Somehow, this idea seemed to ease Meira's worries. After much discussion, she agreed to let her daughter come to the camp.

On August 15, 1982 four Jewish teenagers from the English club in Qiryat Ata came to Tamra to join their five Arab compatriots. Over the next two mornings the kids, together with all the Interns, cleaned, graded and removed rocks from an empty lot in the Hejazi neighborhood to get it ready to serve as a playground. In the afternoons, we toured the town in mixed groups, as a way of getting to know each other and the local community.

I went with three of the kids to meet Abu Salah, one of Tamra's elders, and drink coffee in his sitting room, the *diwan*. Seated on the floor, wearing slacks, a button-down shirt and a *keffiyeh*, his dark eyes crinkling at the corners as he smiled, Abu Salah told us what it was like in Tamra in 1948, "when the Jews came."

He described it as one more passing event in his long life in this land — somewhat like Ottoman rule, the coming of the British in 1918, or their departure in 1947. I could imagine someone sitting on the floor in this *diwan* in another fifty years, hearing of the passing of "the Jews" — the latest of the string of invaders who come and go above the heads of the villagers. Although Abu Salah could not have been more charming or cordial, I left his home with the cold feeling of being a mere breath of wind passing through an ancient grove of olive trees.

After two days in Tamra, our crew moved over to Qiryat Ata, where we sweated in the early morning heat, sanding and painting seesaws and swing sets. In the afternoon, I went with my team to hang out in the town square. At Melech HaFelafel, we struck up a conversation with Sami, a thin, mustached, grey-haired gentleman. He was leaning on a cane, sipping a glass of tea with mint. As soon as he realized that some of us were from Tamra, he switched from plodding, accented Hebrew to fluent Arabic. Yasser translated as Sami told of fleeing anti-Semitic riots in his native Iraq to come to Israel in the 1950s. He described his love for cosmopolitan Baghdad, where he had been a merchant, and the humiliation of the *ma'abarot*, the transit camps of young Israel, where he had nothing and was treated as an illiterate by the Ashkenazi representatives of the Jewish Agency.

In this exchange, I realized that it was not only Israeli Jews who knew little about Arabs, but also Israeli Arabs who knew little about Jews. Here was Yasser, an Arab, translating the Arabic of Sami, a Jew, and learning about anti-Jewish discrimination in Iraq. People in Israel live in multiple intersecting circles, sharing commonalities yet residing far from one another.

At the end of the four days, our compact crew went to the nearby Qiryat Yam beach to relax together before parting ways. We were the only mixed Arab-Jewish group on the beach. After defying social convention together, visiting one another's homes, lugging boulders, sleeping on the floor, we had become a team, in that intense and intimate way forged out of being together twenty-four hours a day, on a "mission."

Just seventy-five miles north of us, along the shores of the Mediterranean, another mission was taking place; Beirut was under siege. As we were building playgrounds together, Israeli planes and artillery were destroying the Palestinian neighborhoods of West Beirut in an effort to drive the PLO out of Lebanon.

One of our Qiryat Ata kids saw some friends lounging on the beach and went over to say hello. He stood, out of earshot, gesturing and arguing. After a few minutes, he came back to our group, agitated.

"What happened?" asked Yasser.

"These friends of mine — they asked me who I was with. So I told them, and they said, 'What are you doing hanging around with Arabs? We're fighting a war; they're on the other side.' I told them they don't know what they're talking about. You know, when you people asked me to join this work-camp, I didn't really want to go. But I liked our English club, and I'd never been to Tamra. I never even talked to an Arab. Now, Yasser's eaten at my house, and I've eaten at his. We sweated together. I met his brother and his mother. Tamra is a real place to me now; I have friends there. I can never say the things about Arabs that I used to say without even thinking."

Lying on the sand, in the long rays of the late afternoon sun, I felt a sense of victory. I wished Eli had been there to see Yasser beaming. True, four days can't change the reality of forty years, and nine teenagers would not change the relationships between two cities. Still, the experiences of the summer had changed me. They had shown me that feelings of suspicion or resentment were no more real than feelings of empathy or understanding between Arabs and Jews. We are not fated only to "respect and suspect" one another; it is possible to build meaningful cooperation between a group of Arabs and Jews, even during a war. And no longer was I a member of the audience in this drama; I had become an actor.

On August 23, 1982 Christian Phalangist leader, Bashir Jemayel, was elected as Lebanon's president, declaring his intention to free Lebanon of Syrian forces and hinting at willingness to sign a peace treaty with Israel. Jemayal had led his Phalange militia in fighting both PLO and Syrian forces in Lebanon. By

August 30, in a deal brokered by the American government, the PLO leadership, together with over 14,000 PLO fighters, had been evacuated from Beirut to Tunis, where they established a new base of operations. It looked like Israel had won a highly strategic victory, albeit at a high price: 344 Israeli soldiers had been killed in the war, as well as over 6,000 Lebanese, mostly civilians.

On September 14, Bashir Jemayel was assassinated in a massive bombing of Phalange headquarters in Beirut, apparently by Syrian operatives, possibly in league with other rival forces in Lebanon. Israeli troops entered the Lebanese capital, ostensibly to ensure calm.

On Friday, September 17, I went with a friend to the Negev development town of Dimona to celebrate Rosh HaShanah, the Jewish New Year, with his family. Because they were a traditional Jewish family, electricity was not used on the holiday; radio and TV were silent until the end of the New Year on Sunday night.

After three stars came out, signaling the end of the holiday, we turned on Israel Radio news to hear: ". . . hundreds of Palestinians believed massacred in the Sabra and Shatilla refugee camps south of Beirut." Over the past three days, we learned, Phalangist militias had carried out a massacre in the Palestinian refugee camps of Sabra and Shatilla, murdering hundreds, or even thousands, of civilians. Israeli troops, guarding the camps, had reportedly let the Phalangists in to conduct "mopping up" operations. Israeli soldiers had continued to stand guard on the hills surrounding the camps, sending up flares at night to light the Phalangists' operations, and listening to the shots.

I felt sick. These reports came from Israeli sources, yet I could not believe that the IDF, which prided itself on its "purity of arms" and on being an army of defense, was now apparently an accomplice to a widescale massacre of men, women and children on foreign soil.

I returned to Tamra the next morning with trepidation. Descending from the bus at my usual stop, I felt an odd silence in the air. Walking along the narrow, curving roads, I examined the faces of passersby, trying to gain a sense of the atmosphere. Normally, as we walked by, people stared openly at us, smiling and saying *"Shalom!"* or "Hallo!" Now, most people avoided eye contact or glanced at me with suspicion.

The words I had heard so often from Israeli Jews, and dismissed, echoed in my head: *You can see the hatred in their eyes . . . you can't trust them . . . they will smile and drink coffee with you, and when you turn, they'll stick a knife in your back.*

Hungry for someone to talk to, I stopped at the Canaan household before going home. When Suha opened the door, her jaw went tight. She stood for a moment in the doorway, blocking my entrance. But shutting the door in my face would have meant a humiliating violation of etiquette — not toward me, but toward her family's good name. She stepped aside, and I entered, feeling uncomfortable.

We'd barely sat on the *frash* inside, when she stated, "You Israelis are murderers!"

"But, Israelis didn't commit the massacre, Phalangists did," I protested, with a knot in my stomach.

Suha had never addressed me in the plural before. In the past, we had disagreed, but I had always been Sarah, not a representative of the Israeli people or government. Now, even though I was not Israeli — I had lived in Israel less than two years, as a tourist — I felt that if I separated myself out, I would be running away from some collective responsibility.

"But you let them in," she said. "You protected them; it was all planned in advance, coordinated. Two days after [Phalangist leader] Bashir Jemayel was murdered, Israel let Phalange troops into a Palestinian refugee camp. What did you think would happen? You wanted a massacre, and you let the Phalangists do it for you! You killed my cousins!"

Ashamed, confused, feeling my gaping lack of knowledge, I mumbled a quick "I don't really know what happened," and, rising from the *frash*, excused myself. I strode home, asking myself: How much had Israeli commanders known? How much had they coordinated the operation? How much had the government authorized? Whatever the truth, I could understand that Israeli Arabs felt that their state placed little value on their lives or the lives of their people.

Numb, I opened the door of our home to find Sue, Lani, Sabri and Arik huddled in a circle on the *frash*, looking worried, talking urgently. I wondered where Dina was.

"I don't want to stay here; the energy is too weird," said Lani, who never minced words. "People are wounded, anything can happen."

"No one will hurt us; we're here on the invitation of the local council and the community center," Sabri argued.

"Yes," I said, "but if someone lost an uncle or a cousin in Shatilla, I don't think he'll be thinking of the local council; he'll just see Jews, or Israelis. Or Americans — they don't come off so well right now either. Hey, has anyone seen Dina?"

"I think she went to the community center," Sue reported. "But she's been gone a long time." That wasn't like Dina, but we had no phone with which to call. "Im Musa told me that we shouldn't stay in our houses tonight," Sue added. "She didn't think anything would happen, but just in case, she invited us to spend the next couple nights at her house."

Our neighbors assumed, as we did, that even if people wanted to harm us, they would not violate the hospitality of another family's home in order to do so. The image of the strangers in Lot's home in Sodom popped, unbidden, into my head.

Suddenly, Dina walked in, her face white. When Lani put her arms around her, Dina began sobbing, her body shaking. After long minutes, she gathered her breath, and gazed around at us. I looked at her face, her arms — no bruises, no blood. Thank God.

"On the way back from the community center," Dina said, her eyes red, "I passed the Communist Party headquarters. It was packed, and more men were arriving, milling around on the street. Someone from inside the building called me over, and asked if I wanted to speak about the massacre in Sabra and Shatilla. I told them how sorry we feel for the people who were killed. But I was the only woman in sight; it was a Party meeting; I felt uncomfortable.

"Suddenly, a young man stepped in front of me, yelling at me for speaking Hebrew. He pushed me. I tried to keep walking, but more men pressed around. I couldn't get away." Dina's breath came in small gasps. "I was scared. I called out — 'You have to help me!' Some men opened a way for me. I squeezed out, and started running."

For the first time since living in Tamra, I was frightened. Dina had just been assaulted for being a Jew. On the street, people looked at me with hatred. Women whom I had known well over the past year saw Israel as the enemy and counted me in that camp. Once again, I thought of Eli's warning: Respect them and suspect them; if you're weak, they'll stab you in the back. Maybe we really were in danger; maybe it was foolish even to consider staying in Tamra.

On the other hand, people who barely knew us had braved the gathering mob and saved Dina. Our neighbors were offering us their children's beds to sleep in. If we left now, I would feel that I was giving in to extremists. I would feel as if we were abandoning our community, our friends, our work, in a time of great need.

We decided to go to talk with Deputy Mayor Mohammed Canaan, a leader of Hadash, the Communist Party in Tamra, to tell him what had happened and get his advice. As we entered his office at the municipality, the group of men gathered around him fell silent. Quickly, the men dispersed, and we were left alone with Canaan.

He stood up, his tall frame bent slightly, and motioned us to chairs. He had already heard of the incident. "How are you?" he asked Dina, as the janitor brought tea on a tray. "You walked by Party headquarters just as the Young Guard was in the heat of a debate. There were some hotheads . . . I am sorry this happened."

Sabri looked down at the large desk in front of us, and picked up a flyer, printed in black and red. It called for "foreign elements" to leave Tamra.

"We found this circulating today," Canaan explained. "It is an affront to the people of Tamra, and an affront to the local council. The municipality is putting out its own flyer in reply, explaining that we invited Interns for Peace volunteers, and that we stand behind the program. It's important for you to stay."

Both his words and his decisive tone touched me. Perhaps the young women in the Canaan extended family, his *hamula*, were taking out their anger verbally on us, but he and the Council were publicly standing by us.

"Are we in danger?" asked Sue. "Maybe we should leave, until things calm down."

Mohammed Canaan's young face looked lined. "No, I don't think you're in danger. But perhaps you should take your neighbors' offer to sleep at their homes for the next few nights. Just in case."

50

For the next few days we stayed with our neighbors and tried to go back to the rhythm of life in the village, but without success. We kept our eyes and ears open for hints of violence. In nearby Nazareth, during a protest against the Sabra and Shatilla massacre, Israeli Arab demonstrators threw rocks at the police, and were shot. In other parts of the country, Arabs blocked major intersections in protest.

On Saturday night, September 25, a group of us from Interns for Peace participated in a demonstration in the Malchei Israel Square in Tel Aviv, protesting the government's deception and conduct in the war, and calling for the resignation of Defense Minister Arik Sharon and Prime Minister Menachem Begin. With 400,000 people, it was by far the largest demonstration ever held in Israeli history.

As a result of the public outcry, a government commission of inquiry, the Kahan Commission, was established to investigate the events leading up to the Sabra and Shatilla massacre. Within months, the Commission found that that Arik Sharon was unfit to serve as Israel's minister of defense. He was found to have been indirectly responsible for the massacre, and directly responsible for misleading the Israeli public and leaders. Under the guise of establishing a twenty-five-mile buffer zone, he had led the military to devastate West Beirut in order to oust the PLO from Lebanon and aid in the installation of a friendly Christian government that would make peace with Israel. Following the Commission's recommendation, Sharon resigned.

On November 11, 1982 an explosion at Israeli military headquarters in Tyre, Lebanon killed seventy-six Israeli soldiers and military personnel. Soon afterward, most Israeli troops were pulled out of Lebanon, leaving behind a contingent of regular soldiers to serve alongside the Israeli-trained South Lebanese Army in the buffer zone.

By the time I left Tamra, in December 1982, the new town of Mitzpe Aviv had been pretty well completed, and Jewish families were moving in, unaware of how they were seen by the Arabs down the hill. The pioneering work we had done during the war in Lebanon had helped to create human ties at a time when commonality was under attack. In the coming years, thousands of Israeli Arab and Jewish schoolchildren, parents, teachers and principals would go through meetings on the model we had built in Tamra.

Our experiences in Tamra and Qiryat Ata had affected us all deeply. Arik decided to become a rabbi, and went on to build the courageous organization, Rabbis for Human Rights. Dina went back to the U.S. to work in the New York office of Interns for Peace. Sabri became a community center director in Rama. Other Interns went on to build the Israel-Palestine Center for Research and Information (IPCRI), to address housing inequities in mixed cities throughout the country, and to catalyze community-based child development programs in Arab villages and development towns.

My experiences in Interns for Peace convinced me to stay in Israel and continue working for an Israel I could be proud of. Crossing the seam between Jewish and Arab societies, I had gained the basis for understanding both. I saw that, despite the pain, the despair, the conflict and the injustices, Jews' and Arabs' conceptions of one another could change through well-constructed action, even in the midst of a war. There was no magic, but there was the power of possibility.

My experiences in Interns for Peace convinced me of something else as well: that well-constructed encounters would not change the situation of inequality in which Arab citizens live. When our English club graduates from Tamra went out to look for work, they would find that the English-club graduates from Qiryat Ata could get jobs in the government-owned Electric Company that they could not get. When they went to apply for a mortgage, they would find that their Jewish friends from Qiryat Ata qualified for a government subsidy, while they did not qualify. When they had kids, they would find that their Jewish friends received a higher level of government child allowances than they did. And in order once more to see their relatives, the Palestinian refugees in Lebanon, they would have to wait for another war — or an historic peace.

Chapter 5
There's No Place like Home

When my father met me at the Pittsburgh airport, I knew something was wrong. I had gone home for a visit to my parents before making *aliyah* — immigrating, or emigrating, depending on your perspective, to Israel.

"You should be prepared for a shock," he told me in his no-nonsense way. "Mom doesn't look well. She isn't eating much these days, and she's very thin. I'm glad you're home."

In 1973, a tumor had been removed (along with a breast), but the cancer, alas, had lurked in her bloodstream and traveled to her lungs. Still, when my parents had visited me at Pesach just seven months earlier, Mom had looked good. She had traipsed around to Kibbutz Barkai, to Safed, to Tamra, visiting the friends I had made in the last two years.

Not wanting to impinge on my plans, my parents had not told me how badly Mom was doing. Now, seeing her at the kitchen table — gaunt arms and thinning grey hair recalling images of Holocaust survivors — I was shocked. The mother I had known all my life had disappeared and been replaced by a frail, sick woman. Immediately I knew I would not soon be returning to Israel.

In order to give structure to my life, I enrolled in a master's program in public policy at Carnegie-Mellon University. Then I turned to the task of helping my father and the home hospice service care for my mother.

Despite her physical weakness, Mom's mind remained sharp. She continued to analyze the news and criticize the country's leaders — as well as my decision to leave the American, liberal tradition in which I had been raised, in order to move to a country based on religious and ethnic nationalism. "How could you throw all this away?" she chastised me. "And for what? Your grandparents came to America as refugees, and were accepted as full citizens, regardless of their being Jewish. Now you want to live in a country with no separation of church and state, set up to prefer Jews over Arabs?"

I tried to explain what I loved about Israel: the closeness of people, the willingness of strangers to help one another out of a solidarity long gone, or never existing, in America; the intrepid energy of improvisation; the stubborn pursuit of impossible dreams; the creation of a home for Holocaust survivors, spewed from European civilization; the strong social welfare system in Israel, which provided good health care to rich and poor, Jew and Arab; the sense that I, as an individual, could make much more of a difference in a young, dynamic Israeli society than in the huge, intractable systems of America.

None of these arguments touched my rational, skeptical mother, who hated not being in control. In her twenties, she had given

Back in the day: The Kreimer family, circa 1960.

54

up pursuing a career in the field of psychology, feeling she "didn't know enough." After marrying my father and having the requisite two children, she had longed for more than the *Leave It to Beaver* vision of domestic happiness in the 1950s. When I had entered kindergarten in 1960, she had returned to the university to earn a master's degree in library science. She became responsible for cataloguing at the Carnegie Libraries of Pittsburgh, a career she could manage.

In the winter of 1983, Mom and I collapsed an entire adult life together into four months. In the face of death, she let go of her intellectual force field, allowing herself a softness, against which she had defended herself for all the years I could remember. We laughed and read op-ed pieces in *Time* magazine. I massaged her feet, while she mused: "I've had a good life; I'm not sorry for anything. I have had a wonderful marriage with your father for over thirty years, and I have two wonderful children I'm proud of."

My tears brimmed over immediately, and made their way down my face. Why did she have to be dying for me to hear that?

"Mom, I wish you could meet my future husband, and see my children when they're born."

She looked at me. "Who knows? Maybe I will."

Shocked, I looked to see if she were delirious, or kidding me. Her green eyes were clear and serious. I knew she didn't think she would recover from the cancer. "Do you believe in life after death?"

My mother the skeptic stated: "I believe in infinite possibility."

She died at age 54, on the third day of Pesach, 1983. She had wanted to make it to the seder, to celebrate with all of us, together, one last time: Dad, my brother Seth, his wife Nancy, their baby daughter, and me. And she did.

Pesach, the holiday of rebirth and freedom, overflowed with sadness and abandonment. When everyone went home, Dad and I cleaned out Mom's closets. She and I were about the same size; but there was something creepy about putting on her clothes so soon after her death.

"Try it on," my father urged, as I fingered a lovely orange flowered blouse. My father was sad but not sentimental.

When I slipped on the blouse, his eyes widened. "That looks so much better on you than it ever did on Mom!" We both laughed, and I culled out a few of the shirts I liked best.

I had a year to go to finish my degree before returning to Israel. Living with Dad, I relished having an adult relationship with him. He invited friends over for dinner, something Mom had never really liked to do. Through his contacts in the steel industry, where he was an arbitrator, Dad got me in to tour one of the last remaining steel mills in Pittsburgh. From time to time, Dad visited coal mines and steel mills, believing it was important to see and feel the situations the workers were in, as he judged their grievances. Sometimes, over dinner, he talked through some of his bankruptcy cases — at this stage in his career, all complex cases involving the reorganization of companies with substantial debt.

"I don't fool around with negotiations. No one wins that way; it just wastes time. I look for the deal that will serve everyone's interests best — my clients', as well as the creditors'. Then I put it on the table, and we argue about that. Nine times out of ten, the parties accept it, with minor changes."

I longed for my father to come over to Israel with his no-haggling approach, so antithetical to the Middle East, and counsel those negotiating Israel's conflicts.

With no one to argue against my making *aliyah*, I began to argue with myself. There was something unfathomable about my choice to live in Israel. I had none of the feelings that my Zionist friends had of feeling estranged in America and at home in Israel. In America, I had always been able to be myself — whether boycotting grapes with my temple youth group to support the migrant workers who picked them, or doing Alinsky-style community organizing in Providence, Rhode Island, or hiking the Appalachian Trail. My sister-in-law, Nancy, was a Reconstructionist rabbi, a career impossible to maintain in Israel, with its state-supported Orthodox rabbinate. I respected her, and resonated with the Reconstructionist view of Judaism as a civilization. Sometimes, I toyed with the idea of becoming a rabbi myself.

Ideologically, I was really more of a Bundist than a Zionist. As a student at Yale, I had studied the Jewish socialist movements in Europe, and was captivated by the Bundists, who were scorned by the Zionists in the 1890s. To me, their efforts to create a socialism that recognized cultural identity synthesized a vital middle road between the rigid universalism of the Communists, who insisted that religion was an opiate of the masses, and the ethnic national-ism of the Zionists, who advocated that Jews leave their countries of origin in order to establish a separate Jewish state. The Bund, moreover, had included a higher proportion of women activists than either the Zionists or the Communists.

In writing my senior thesis on the Jewish Bund, I fell in love with the feisty veterans I interviewed, who had escaped the Nazi occupation and ended up in the Workman's Circle Multi-Care Center in the Bronx. I was especially fond of 88-year-old Miriam, who as a child in Poland had run secret messages from leader to leader in the Bundist underground. She recalled one of the Bund's basic messages to the workers: "The sun belongs to all of us."

Clearly (as much as any major life decision is clear), my choice to make my life in Israel was not rational. It probably stemmed from a desire to make my own way, out of the orbit of the strong expectations with which I'd grown up. There was also something tantalizingly romantic about being part of an overarching nation-building enterprise for which friends and strangers continually told me I was needed, and I did feel that I had some uniquely suitable combination of skills and temperament that allowed me to be effective on the troubled seam between Arabs and Jews in Israel.

On March 15, 1984, just after Seth and I had stopped reciting kaddish for our mother, Dad, who had gone on a cruise in the Caribbean, where he had been swimming and snorkeling in a long-awaited vacation, died of a massive heart attack. In a morbid déjà vu, Seth and I once again sat *shiva* in the home in which we had grown up. Hundreds of people came to pay tribute to a man who had earned broad respect in his communities.

From the Jewish community came colleagues who had served with him and learned from him in the organizations he had led: the Jewish Community Relations Council and Congregation Ro-def Shalom. From the legal community came judges and lawyers who, whether arguing with him or against him, respected his in-tegrity. Union leaders, industry officials, and fellow arbitrators came to express their sadness at the loss of a colleague who had adjudicated, with impeccable fairness, thousands of disputes in the region's coal and steel industries.

Dad had loved solving problems. When Seth had come to be Boy Scout age, Dad had started a Boy Scout troop. When urban blight had hit the heart of the Jewish community where he had grown up, he had helped found the Squirrel Hill Urban Coalition, which revitalized the neighborhood's central business district. When he had seen people with no recourse to legal help, he had started a mediation service at the bar association.

When I was growing up, Dad had been my greatest fan and defender — driving me to school when I was late, supporting my various ventures and adventures, stocking the refrigerator with my favorite foods when I came home from college. He had been proud of my work in Tamra, and could understand my attraction to Israel. Now that he was gone, who would give me that support? At night, when all the mourners went home, and the house was quiet, I lay sobbing in the bed in which I had slept for twenty-eight years.

At the end of the *shiva* week, Seth, Nancy and I numbly cleared out the closets, gave Dad's clothes to the Women's International Zionist Organization, and put the house on the market. Well-kept by our family for decades, it sold quickly, and I toiled with friends and relatives, cleaning out the last physical remains of the home that had been my base all my life. Over the summer, which I spent with Seth and his family, I thought often of Dad's history as a young labor arbitrator, learning from one of the pros in the business, Lou Garrett. After a number of cases in which Dad had consulted with Garrett, he came one day to get advice on a particularly difficult matter. Spelling out the claims on both sides, Dad asked Garrett, "What do you think?" Garrett answered, "I think it is in good hands."

Over the last years, Dad had often used that line when we had come to him for advice. Now, orphaned and bereft, as I returned to Israel to begin building my new home, I wondered: Were my hands good enough?

II. At Thirty: Attaining Strength
(1985-2000)

Chapter 6

Let Sleeping Dogs Lie

If you want truly to understand something, try to change it.
— Kurt Lewin, founder of social psychology

Ilan, director of human resources at Matta Foods in Hadera Israel, was intrigued. In his forties, from Yemenite Jewish background, Ilan spoke with the ease of someone who has dealt with myriad human foibles. He told of a production unit in which he was about to make Ahmed, an Arab worker, the team leader.

"Suddenly, all sorts of petty issues are landing on my desk. People who've worked together for years are complaining about each other. They're having trouble meeting their production schedule. I believe that Ahmed is the right person for the job, but other employees aren't accepting the idea. Can you help me with this?"

I desperately wanted to say yes. I had been waiting and working toward this very moment, ever since Rabbi Bruce Cohen had asked me to return to Interns for Peace to develop its new Industry Project. I was thrilled to be back with old friends, working in the field. With enthusiasm and naiveté, Bruce and I were seeking improve workplace relations between the thousands of Israeli Arabs and Jews employed together on a daily basis in factories and hospitals throughout northern Israel.

Week after week, in the summer and fall of 1985, I had driven through Israel's periphery, visiting directors of human resources in

61

some of Israel's largest companies that had been plunked down in development towns in the 1950s and '60s: Strauss Dairy in Acco, Delta Textiles in Carmiel, Elite Foods in Upper Nazareth, HaEmek Hospital in Afula. Director after director had told of problems in Jewish-Arab relations in the workforce: *Can't get Jews to work night shift; they're uncomfortable with so many Arabs. High turnover . . . arguments . . . Jewish workers won't accept Arab shift manager . . .* Time and again the conversation had ended abruptly when I proposed trying to improve the situation. *Let sleeping dogs lie,* these managers would say. *When people walk into the door of this plant, I want them to know there are no Jews or Arabs here, just employees.*

After thirty-seven years of citizenship, Israeli Arabs were still seen as security risks, not only in Israel's defense industries, but also in key civilian industries. I was surprised to find, for example, that no Israeli Arabs were among the thousands of workers in the government-owned Israel Electric Company, for "security reasons." Even more surprising: Few Arabs were employed by Israel's leading dairy and food producer, Tnuva, which was owned by the socialist *kibbutzim* and *moshavim*. On the other hand, Israel's hospitals were virtual oases of cooperation, in which Arab and Jewish doctors, nurses and technical personnel served hundreds of thousands of Jewish and Arab patients and their families every day.

When I had left Pittsburgh to return to Israel in September 1984 — this time making *aliyah* — I felt at a loss in so many ways. Often I would wake from a dream conversation with Mom or Dad as it evaporated into the sunlight of another Mediterranean morning.

Aiming to grapple with the Israeli context in my studies, I had arranged to take my final public-policy courses at Tel Aviv University. Israeli inflation was galloping at a treacherous 400 percent. As prices rose daily, I found it easier to focus on the frustration of not being able to compare the price of laundry detergents than to feel the trauma of the other drastic changes in my life. In my public-finance class, the other students, adept at improvising through yet another crisis in Israel, seemed effortlessly to factor in the inflation to all the standard equations we were learning, while I was perpetually baffled.

To keep me company in my fourth-floor walk-up near the

beach in Tel Aviv, I took a cat, Pushkin. It seemed par for my course at this point in my life when she fell off the balcony railing, using up one of her nine lives as she plunged to the garden below. Amazingly, she landed on her feet, literally, and emerged bruised but not broken. Survivors, Pushkin and I kept each other company, recovering.

One stifling July morning in 1985, just as I was about to finish my master's degree in public policy, I woke up to the news that four people — Prime Minister Shimon Peres, General Secretary of the Histadrut Federation of Labor Yisrael Kessar, Governor of the Bank of Israel Moshe Mandelbaum, and the president of the Manufacturers' Association — had signed agreements, overnight, that froze wages, prices, and interest rates. Their midnight attack almost immediately slashed inflation from 445 percent to about 20 percent. In that moment, I learned what I had failed to grasp in the classroom: that public policy in Israel is intensely personal.

Now Ilan's straightforward question faced me with the responsibility of affecting real people and a real business, and suddenly I wondered: What if all those other personnel directors were right? I had no experience working in factories. What if our intervention would ruin years of working relations?

Taken by Ilan's candor and willingness to tackle the problem head-on — "Can you help me with this?" — I plunged ahead. "I think so," I said, swallowing my trepidation.

Immediately after, I called Sue Wish, my compatriot from Tamra, with whom I had faced so many impossible situations in the past. Sue had married her Israeli boyfriend, and was now living in Hod HaSharon and working as an occupational therapist. "You can do this, Sarah. You may need to tool-up, but remember: you are not better than anyone, and no one's better than you."

With the backing of Bruce and Farhat Aghbariye at Interns for Peace, I gathered a Jewish-Arab team, graduates of Interns for Peace and/or of Tel Aviv University School of Public Policy: David, a labor lawyer, Ramzi and Abed, organizational consultants, and me. We crafted a training program, designed a working model, and went back to Matta Foods armed with a theory for improving intergroup relations.

Every Tuesday afternoon, in the empty lunchroom of the

Matta factory, we pulled metal chairs around one of the formica-topped tables and gathered to discuss Jewish-Arab relations with the production team of the cheese department. Well-schooled in the what-is-the-problem-we-are-all-Matta-workers approach to life in a mixed workforce, both Arab and Jewish employees spent weeks telling story upon story of good relations.

Arab employees told of working extra shifts for weeks during the 1973 Yom Kippur War to make up for the absence of their mobilized coworkers. One told of becoming a driver in the service of the Israel Defense Forces when his private truck was drafted into military service during the war. (All vehicles in the country were liable to be drafted for noncombatant functions.) Jewish employees told of inviting Arab coworkers to ceremonies of *bar mitzvah* and *brit milah.*

We had agreed with Ilan to have six meetings. By the time four went by, nothing seemed to have changed: no issues raised, no arguments, no conflicts. Our theory posited several stages in the development of healthy minority-majority relations: from cordial contact, to the minority exerting its identity and the majority feeling threatened, to an eventual renegotiation of intergroup relations on a more equal footing. We were stuck in the cordial contact stage: Everyone was enjoying the chance to chat and take a break from work on company time. Truth was, despite our theory, I was afraid to push to more open conflict.

Finally, at our fifth meeting, I remarked, "There's a lot of tension between Jews and Arabs outside the door of the factory. What seeps into Matta?"

Silence.

Zhenya, an older woman, took a breath and, looking at her hands, muttered in a heavy Russian accent, "When there's a terror attack, I wonder: What are the Arabs here thinking?"

A young Arab man, Abed, nervously drumming his fingers on the table, blurted out: "Do you think I like people being killed? But I'm worried about other things that happen every day. A lot of the Arab employees have been working here for years, but none get moved up into managerial positions. Why not?"

"If an Arab became head of a department at Matta," said Chaya, a feisty, dark-haired Jewish woman, "wouldn't he favor the Arab workers?"

By the end of our sixth session, very few tough questions had been raised. I wondered if the intervention had been worth the effort. When our team met with Ilan for a debriefing, however, in his modest office with molded plastic chairs — which looked like they'd come straight from a kibbutz general assembly — he was smiling.

"Well, I appointed Ahmed as unit head, and he's doing fine. I've stopped getting all those picayune problems. The department is meeting its production schedule. So it looks like whatever you did worked."

Miraculously, reality had followed theory. When Ilan had proposed moving an Arab into a position of authority, he had disrupted the cordial-contact stage, empowering the Arabs and threatening the Jews. Breaking the unspoken agreement — that raising Jewish-Arab differences and tensions was dangerous and therefore forbidden — had enabled people to talk about some of the issues that worried them as Arabs became more visible and more equal. In this factory, where human relations were basically healthy, that had been enough.

Walking from Ilan's office, along lanes shaded by ficus trees, I realized that helping Israeli Arabs and Jews pierce some of their ethnic and national boils had empowered me, as well. So many conflicts had been swept under the rug in my home. Even in these last years, my mother had hidden her cancer from her coworkers, from her own mother, and, for a time, from her children. She had refused to allow any of her own friends to visit her as she lay sick in bed for months. And when I was a kid, I had never seen her in an open and fair fight with my father. When they'd had serious disagreements, they dealt with them after we were asleep, so as not to "fight in front of the children."

Throughout 1986-7, the Interns for Peace Industry Project replicated this model in factories and hospitals throughout northern Israel, where thousands of Israeli Jews and Arabs worked together daily under assumptions that mirrored the society outside: *We can work together as long as you play by my rules. Give up your identity at the door. Don't speak Arabic. Don't expect to get into management.* Raising and examining some of these assumptions in order to begin improving Jewish-Arab relations within existing factories and workplaces was valuable work.

However, when Arab workers picked up their identities at the factory gates at the end of the day, they went home to surrounding Arab towns and villages where unemployment was significantly higher, and average monthly income lower, than in neighboring Jewish towns. Arab towns such as Tamra or Nazareth grew in size, without developing an economic base or urban infrastructure. Instead, industrial areas and educational and government institutions were developed in Carmiel, Upper Nazareth, Safed, and others of Israel's Jewish cities, not in Arab towns.

As long as the Israeli national interest was defined almost exclusively as the Jewish national interest, these realities wouldn't change. Few people saw the picture that I saw it, or understood that in a country of four million people, where the major resources were human resources, neglecting the development of one of every six Israelis was not in our society's best interest.

In December 1987, the dogs started waking up.

Chapter 7
Janus in Jerusalem

On December 8, 1987, an Israeli truck plowed into a group of Palestinians from Jabalya refugee camp in Gaza Strip, killing four and injuring seven. Coming on the heels of a Palestinian's fatal stabbing of an Israeli businessman in Gaza, rumors spread through Gaza that the truck incident was retaliation. Demonstrations broke out, first in the refugee camps of Gaza, next in the West Bank, and then spreading to East Jerusalem. Day after day, Palestinian teenagers threw rocks and Molotov cocktails at Israeli soldiers, who shot back or chased them through village streets. Communiqués by the Palestinian Unified National Leadership of the Uprising appeared as flyers on the streets, calling for general strikes, boycotts of Israeli products, and refusal to pay Israeli taxes — challenging, in other words, the basic assumptions of Israeli rule over the West Bank, East Jerusalem and Gaza.

When I founded the Center for Jewish-Arab Economic Development in Tel Aviv at the end of 1987, I was unaware that this was the beginning of the Palestinian *intifada*, which would continue over the next six years and segue into the Palestinian Authority and the Oslo agreements.

On a crowded and winding Nazareth street, about a hundred yards from Mary's Well — where, in Greek Orthodox tradition, Jesus' mother-to-be received word of the Immaculate Conception — I found a storefront with grimy windows and a small, homemade sign: Alpha Omega. Inside, amid beat-up wooden tables strewn with wires and chips and late-night coffee cups, Imad Younis sat alone with a computer, his dark close-cropped hair visible above the computer screen.

As soon as he noticed me, Imad jumped up and strode over to shake hands. Lean and fit, in pressed shirt and jeans, he had a ready smile, although his eyes looked tired. He explained in simple terms the electronic Multi Channel Processor (MCP) he was developing to measure the activity of a single brain cell by electronically amplifying the electric signals it gives off. At every step of the way, he had tested his equipment with Israel's leading brain researchers — at Hadassah Hospital and the Weizman Institute — who eagerly awaited his new machine. In fact, they had already placed their orders.

In order to produce the MCP, Younis needed to hire engineers, but his new company, Alpha Omega, could offer neither competitive salaries nor job security. Younis turned to a few fellow Arab graduates to join him part-time without giving up their hard-earned engineering jobs in veteran Israeli companies. His one-room space was also too small, and Younis desperately needed some working capital to build the business.

"I applied to the Upper Nazareth Incubator," he related in a matter-of-fact tone, as he served freshly-brewed coffee in small cups. "It offers exactly what I need: low-cost space, access to financing, business and legal advice. You know, in the whole city of Nazareth, I can't find a lawyer who knows about international patents." Imad leaned back, and disappointment flitted across his composed face. "After I filled out all the forms for the Incubator, they asked me how many Russians I employ. I told them truthfully — none. A few weeks later, my application was rejected."

In the 1980s, civilian technological industries had just begun to sprout in Israel. Few Israeli Arabs attended Israel's prestigious computer engineering program at the Technion. Fewer still succeeded in landing jobs in engineering, a field dominated by the powerful military industries, from which Arabs were excluded.

Imad Younis, a Nazareth-born Arab Israeli, was one of the chosen few. Upon graduation, he was accepted as an engineer in the research and development department of Fidelity Medical Services. However, in 1988, to the great chagrin of his father, who urged him to stay in the promising professional position he had reached, Imad left the company and sold his car in order to gain the capital needed to pursue his dream of launching a technology start-up. Many young Arabs in Israel looked to Imad as a role model and tracked his career as an indicator of their own future opportunities.

The Incubator Program of the Ministry of Industry had recently opened in the neighboring Jewish town of Upper Nazareth, offering an ideal solution for Alpha Omega. Open to promising Israeli entrepreneurs, it was designed to infuse Israel's nascent civilian high-tech sector with capital, and to provide technical assistance to talented engineers who may have winning ideas but know little about business. Spurred by the arrival of thousands of engineers as part of the massive immigration of the late 1980s from the former Soviet Union, the ministry viewed the program as a way to initiate new technological businesses by, and for, the new immigrants.

Many young Israeli Arab engineers and students saw Imad's rejection from the Business Incubator in Upper Nazareth, and few Arabs afterwards applied to the government incubators, as they anticipated a situation they knew from so many aspects of life in Israel: that the program was meant only for Jews.

I was visiting Imad as head of the new non-profit I had founded, the Center for Jewish-Arab Economic Development (CJAED), which aimed to encourage Jewish-Arab economic cooperation and to advance economic development in the Arab sector, on an even playing field. In our belief that truncated Arab development harmed Israel's economy, and that Arab citizens should have an equal place in Israeli society, CJAED challenged assumptions that had long maintained domestic quiet in Israel.

Arnon Gafny, governor of the Bank of Israel in the late 1970s, now chair of Koor Industries, Israel's largest industrial conglomerate, agreed to head my new enterprise. Koor was just starting to develop partnerships with Israeli Arab investors to divest itself of some of its low-tech enterprises in food, textile manufacturing, construction, and retailing. Such partnerships could take advantage of cheap labor in Arab villages, of growing capital among a small number of Arab entrepreneurs, and of steadily increasing consumer power in the Arab sector.

With Gafny's backing, we gathered a strong group of Arab and Jewish business leaders. Gafny insisted on including a curious additional participant: Uri Pinkerfeld, a short, stocky, plain-speaking *kibbutznik*. A *sabra*, born in Jerusalem in 1928, Uri had joined his *kibbutznik* when he graduated from high school. "Most people want to be upwardly mobile," Uri joked, eyes twinkling in his weather-beaten face. "A farmer's son becomes an architect. In my case, it's the opposite: My father was an architect, and I became a farmer."

In the British Mandate years, he had joined the core group that set up Kibbutz Revadim in Gush Etsion. In the War of Independence, Uri had served in the Palmach, the elite fighting unit of the Haganah, and witnessed the fall of Gush Etsion to the Arab Legion. When the armistice lines were drawn, leaving Kibbutz Revadim's houses and fields in the Jordanian-occupied West Bank, Uri helped re-establish it in its current location, not far from Ashdod.

Uri's passion and charisma pushed him beyond the fields of Revadim. He became active in the Kibbutz Artzi movement, for which he was chosen to be general secretary. More recently he had been working with the movement's sister political party, Mapam, to improve conditions in Arab villages, many of which bordered Kibbutz Artzi *kibbutzim*, and to strengthen ties with the Arab population — because, Uri told me, "It's the right thing to do." Over the years, I came to rely on Uri, with his immense wisdom and practicality, as a socio-political north star.

At CJAED, we told the story of the truncated economic development of Israel's Arab sector, and the loss this brought to the country as a whole. We hired Arab and Jewish researchers to work under the direction of Professor Zvi Sussman, former research director at the Bank of Israel. Their report identified tremendous economic potential in the Arab sector and a high cost to Israel's economy because of the lost potential. Furthermore, it recommended policies for realizing the latent potential.

I had few illusions that these recommendations would be picked up and implemented by the Likud government led by Yitzhak Shamir, but the report, and the involvement of prominent Israelis in our Center, started to make visible the economic situation of Israeli Arabs, and to show that their loss was our loss, that their well-being was a critical element of our national equation.

I realized that if we were to develop Arab-Jewish partnerships, we ourselves needed to be an Arab-Jewish partnership. A colleague suggested that we involve Mustafa Abu-Rumi, an energetic and talented urban and regional planner whose family — the finest producers of *labaneh* (yogurt cheese) and other cheeses in the Galilee — I'd met in Tamra.

As he and I traveled around, we met entrepreneur after entrepreneur who took the hand he or she had been dealt and played it with finesse. We soon realized that CJAED was too small and young to change Israeli development policy, but it could support business development in the private sector through loans, consultation and networking. We raised money and negotiated with Barclays Discount Bank to start a loan-guarantee fund. We hired a dedicated economic consultant, David Azran, to run the loan program and provide economic advice. David, who had grown up Jewish in Morocco and immigrated to Haifa with his family in the 1960s, saw Jewish-Arab cooperation as natural, and his work in the Center as a contribution to building the country.

One day, Mustafa, David, and I were invited to Nazareth by Diab Mahroum, the great-great-grandson of the founder of Mahroum Sweets, renowned bakers of *baklawa, knaffe* and other Arab pastries since 1890. Diab wanted to expand the business beyond its traditional base of Arab customers and the daily flow of Christian pilgrims who stopped on their way to visit Nazareth's world famous Church of the Annunciation. The family knew how to produce quality products, but they lacked knowledge and connections in marketing beyond the Arab sector.

David contacted a colleague who was the supplier of food products to Israel's national airline, El Al. Would he consider buying *baklawa* instead of the bland chocolate mousse served on international flights? The buyer came to Nazareth to meet the family and taste the products. After a number of meetings, tours through the factory, discussion of prices, the buyer agreed that, if Mahroum could meet the regulations for producing kosher products, El Al would buy their line of *baklawa*.

Within weeks, Mahroum opened a second factory in the

neighboring Jewish town of Upper Nazareth, hired a rabbi to supervise the keeping of kosher regulations, and began producing a line of kosher *baklawa* and other sweets for the Jewish market. Within a year, the new factory was marketing not only to El Al, but to Jewish-owned restaurants throughout the north. In addition, their experience with El Al gave the Mahroum family a foothold to begin exporting to Europe and America.

One steamy Tel Aviv morning in September 1988, as I was about to enter a long line to board the #4 bus to work, carrying a heavy picture to hang in my office, a tall, slim, reddish-haired man gazed curiously at me, as children do before they've learned that it's impolite to stare. When I returned his gaze, he smiled slightly, and motioned me into the line in front of him. I noticed his strong, graceful hands.

"Pretty hot today," I started off lamely, trying to jump-start a conversation with this intriguing stranger.

"Yes," he agreed. "Not like in Scotland."

With one sentence he had transported us from this run-down bus terminal, which stank of urine, to a land of lakes and bagpipes.

I looked carefully at his face as I gave my "elevator speech" about working for Jewish-Arab economic cooperation and development. I braced myself for the typical reaction of skepticism, derision, or disinterest. Without a pause, Shuki (as he introduced himself) asked how we found the businesspeople and how we got them together. He seemed surprised and amused when I didn't recognize the name of the large (and apparently well-known) *kibbutz* in which he had grown up — Afikim — and explained that, although he was working as an engineer, he was spending more and more of his time tutoring kids in math.

After sharing that bus ride, we continued to meet, with increasing frequency. I learned of Shuki's childhood on *kibbutz*: his freedom to wander the fields, catching lizards and frogs; the stifling conformity of "the group"; his desire to sleep in his parents' home and not in his bunk bed in the children's house; his raids on the *kibbutz* kitchen; the deep camaraderie.

I loved his impish humor, his patience, his ability to "see" me emotionally in a way that my family never had. Within six weeks,

Shuki proposed, and we decided to get married in June 1989.

Two months before the wedding date, he was called to *miluim*, reserve duty, in Bethlehem. The Palestinian *intifada*, which had begun in Gaza in 1987, was raging. In response to Palestinian youths hurling rocks and firebombs at Israeli soldiers patrolling the West Bank, Defense Minister Yitzhak Rabin had called on soldiers to "break their arms and legs." Shuki, an officer, was put in charge of a jeep crew patrolling the city.

As I said goodbye to the gentle man who had donned army fatigues and become a soldier, I was hit with my impotence and the impotence of generations of Israeli women, indeed women everywhere, in the face of the military. I was proud of my husband-to-be, manly in his uniform, going off to defend me on the homefront, and at the same time repelled by what he would be asked to do as a soldier defending Israel's occupation in the midst of a popular uprising. From either perspective, Shuki was entering a world I did not know, and in which I had no place. A picture flashed briefly through my mind of Shuki lying dead or wounded on a Bethlehem street, of my preparing for a funeral instead of a wedding.

"Be careful," I muttered lamely, as we kissed goodbye.

With *sabra* confidence, he assured me: "I know how to take care of myself."

A week later, sitting in my apartment in late evening, I heard my cat Pushkin scratching to be let in. Stooping to pat her as I opened the door, I was surprised to see not the cat, but a pair of dusty brown boots, in which stood Shuki, grinning and sweaty. "I had the evening off, so I came to see you."

Over dinner, Shuki described the last few days with sad eyes. "It's an impossible job. We drive around the city and Palestinian kids throw rocks at us. The other day, my soldiers were about to shoot at one of the kids. I ordered them to stop. The soldiers are not much older than the kids in the streets.

"Today was the worst. We had to clear away a pile of burned tires from a road leading to the school. IDF procedure requires us to have Palestinians move them, so there's no incentive to booby trap these things." Shuki took a long drink of water. "School had just let out. I stopped a man walking near a group of kids, requested his ID, and asked him to clear away the pile. As he stooped to begin the work, I realized that he was a teacher at the school. Standing there with my gun, I imagined the tables turned, and me forced to clear away tires, humiliated in the eyes of my students." Shuki rested his forehead on his hand, shutting his own eyes. "I was ashamed," he said quietly, from behind his hand.

That night, in bed, Shuki was particularly gentle and attentive. Enjoying his every touch, I imagined those same hands holding a gun, and his soft voice commanding soldiers and civilians. The contrast was baffling and exhilarating. After he slipped out of bed at dawn, I laid under the covers, aching for his return. Two weeks later, Shuki finished *miluim*, and the experiences in Bethlehem were locked away in a safe recess of memory.

We were married on June 29, 1989 on a grassy hill at Kibbutz Barkai, where I had done my training for Interns for Peace almost a decade before. My family came from America, Shuki's from Israel, and our friends, Jewish and Arab, from Tamra and Jerusalem, from Umm el Fahm and Tel Aviv, to share our joy.

Shuki and I moved to Bat Yam, a small town just south of Tel Aviv, where we could afford to rent a sweet, two-bedroom house built in the 1950s. The wooden doors and window frames fit loosely, appropriate to the mild Mediterranean climate and to the approximate nature of everything in Israel. No one here used

Sarah and Shuki on their wedding day.

double glazing or other ways of sealing windows. So when the order came from the Israeli Home Front Command in the fall of 1990 to seal off a room in the house — using plastic sheeting taped over the windows to make it impenetrable to nerve gas, in case of an Iraqi Scud missile strike on Israel — I turned to Shuki and laughed.

On August 2, 1990, Iraq had invaded Kuwait and annexed it, taking control of the country's vast oil fields. When diplomatic talks with Saddam Hussein's regime failed to bring an Iraqi withdrawal, economic sanctions were imposed and international tensions grew. U.S. President George H.W. Bush organized a Western and Arab alliance to back military action to restore the status quo ante, and on November 29, 1990, they received the go-ahead from the Security Council of the United Nations to "use all necessary means" to cause Iraq to withdraw from Kuwait.

I couldn't imagine being under missile attack from a country 500 miles away, and I couldn't imagine defending myself with duct tape. I was pregnant, due to give birth in January 1991. The whole situation seemed absurd.

I thought of those ridiculous retention drills in Sterrett Elementary School in Pittsburgh in the 1960s, when we lined up against the internal walls of the building with our faces to the wall and our hands covering our heads — to "protect ourselves" in case of a nuclear attack from the Soviet Union during the Cold War. But Shuki was an Israeli, and being under attack was no fantasy for him. At the height of the Yom Kippur War in 1973, he and his soldiers had been bombed in Sinai while waiting to cross the Suez Canal to bring supplies to Israeli troops moving to encircle Egypt's Third Army. Unable to sleep, he had crawled out of a suffocating bunker to spend the rest of the night between trucks of food and fuel. As dawn broke, an Egyptian plane dropped a bomb directly on the bunker, killing those who had stayed inside.

We decided to seal our bedroom, using plastic sheeting and packing tape from the local hardware store. It was the most hopeful of the three rooms in the house. I was 35, nine months pregnant, incomparably happy — and growing terrified.

We already had our gas masks, packed in cardboard boxes, complete with needles and vials of atropine as an antidote to nerve gas in case the plastic sheeting didn't work. Shuki made sure

I tried on the mask and knew how it worked. We took pictures of each other; mine turned out looking like a World War I soldier about to give birth.

Our Bat Yam was a forgotten, podunk town with no strategic significance, except to the thousands of Russian immigrants who found that here they could be near centers of work in Tel Aviv and still afford the housing. What were the chances that here, of all places, an Iraqi Scud would land?

We listened and watched on TV as George Bush got his coalition in order, warned Saddam Hussein, and, on January 17, 1991 commenced bombing. The next night, I was startled from deep sleep by a noise.

It was the phone: "Sarah, are you all right? Hussein just launched a Scud to Israel!" My friend Marilyn was on the line from the U.S. She had seen the pictures on CNN of Saddam launching a missile attack.

Shuki turned on the radio.

"Nahash tsefa, nahash tsefa!" came the announcer's voice, giving the code words, "Viper snake! Go to your sealed room and put on your gas mask."

My stomach dropped, and at that moment I realized the origin of the expression "scared shitless." I ran to the bathroom. A picture of writhing Kurds in mud houses in northern Iraq flashed into my head, but I banished it.

How could my life end now? I thought. It seemed to be just beginning.

As Shuki and I huddled together on our bed, staring at each other through the eyeholes of our gas-masks in our increasingly stuffy sealed bedroom, we simultaneously heard and felt the shattering boom of a rocket landing and the wail of an air-raid siren. Where had the missile landed? How long did it take for nerve gas to travel? The radio played patriotic old Israeli folk songs, a sure sign of war.

Finally, we heard the voice of army spokesperson, Nahman Shai: "A missile has landed in the Tel Aviv area. It contained a conventional warhead. There were no casualties. You may leave your sealed rooms. Drink water."

Shuki held me in his arms, and I trembled with both relief and fear.

Night after night, sitting helplessly in our ridiculous sealed rooms, as missiles fell in the Tel Aviv area, we came to welcome Nahman Shai's *yiddishe-mama* advice to "drink water." Indeed, there was little else we could do.

One morning, I received a call from Diab Mahroum, the *baklawa* producer from Nazareth. Knowing we lived near Tel Aviv, Diab invited Shuki and me to come to live with his family while the war continued. I was touched by the offer, not only because I knew it was genuine, but because he was saying, in a simple human way: *I am with you. We are in the same boat; I want to help you.*

Although we didn't take Diab up on his offer, Shuki, an expectant and protective father, decided to get us out of Bat Yam. He called a distant relative who was out of the country and offered us to stay in her penthouse suite in the Sheraton Plaza Hotel in Jerusalem. There we felt calm, confident that Saddam would not risk striking Jerusalem's Old City and Al Aqsa Mosque, the third holiest site in the Muslim world.

Life assumed a bizarre rhythm. Israelis worked somewhat normally by day, when the Iraqis refrained from missile attacks lest their launchers be discovered. By night, we bunkered down in our homes, listening for warning sirens.

But Diab's was not the only, nor the dominant, voice among Israeli Arabs. As the Allied forces continued bombing Iraq, and Saddam Hussein continued firing missiles into populated areas of Israel, I drove, quite pregnant, to Wadi Ara to visit Abu Bassam and discuss his participation at a conference on Jewish-Arab cooperation in the olive oil industry — a conference that we had continued to plan, despite the war. I found him leaning on his cane, drinking coffee under a gnarled olive tree outside his hillside oil-press above Umm el Fahm.

He smiled around missing teeth, and waved me to a stool next to him. I noticed his quick eyes, surrounded by the deep lines of his weathered face. Abu Bassam saw everything. I enjoyed talking with him, because he took a broad range of issues into consideration and often came up with surprising conclusions. Not by accident had he bought machinery for a modern press, becoming the first Arab olive oil producer to market his cold-pressed oil under a kosher label in Israeli supermarkets. Before getting down to business, we chatted about the olive crop, his sons and grandchildren, the political situation.

"*Wallah,* Saddam is a real leader," Abu Bassam told me, looking directly into my eyes.

I returned the gaze, wondering what I was supposed to do now.

"Bush is trying to grab the oil, but Saddam is defending himself, like a man," he said. "Bravo for him!"

I could feel Abu Bassam's personal pride in Saddam as an Arab leader standing up to the West — and to Israel, the West's proxy in the Middle East. The PLO had chosen to side with Saddam against the U.S.-led military coalition, causing hundreds of thousands of Palestinians working in Kuwait to be thrown out of well-paid professional jobs. In the West Bank and Gaza, Palestinians cheered and danced on rooftops as they watched Scud missiles falling on Israeli cities. Although I thought the PLO had made a tactical error in its political alliance, I could understand the sentiment of those millions of Palestinians living under Israeli occupation that "the enemy of my enemy is my friend."

Despite clear discrimination, however, Arab citizens of Israel were not living under occupation. If Abu Bassam identified so deeply with the leader who was sending missiles to hit me, how did he feel about me? How, for that matter, did I feel about him? Which was the "true" face of this man, the one revealed by what he was saying now, or the one reflected by his close business dealings with Israeli Jews over the years? Maybe, as I had seen in my workshops with factory employees, Abu Bassam had no true face, but managed daily life in Israel by living like Janus, the god with two faces.

Looking out over the forested valley of Wadi Ara and the Arab city of Umm el Fahm perched above it, I felt betrayed: by people with whom I had worked, and by my own perception. Beneath my feet, I felt a deep gulf opening between what I saw and what seethed under the surface for hundreds of thousands of Arab citizens. I felt the rift between my expectation that it was possible to create civic equality in this country, so that everyone could win together, and Israeli Arabs' deep longings and connections, not with Israel or with Jewish fellow citizens, but with the Arab world and its leaders.

I left without asking Abu Bassam to join the conference.

On February 4, 1991, after thirty hours in a Jerusalem hospital named Misgav Ladach — literally, Refuge from Suffering — I gave birth to my first son, Shai. Eight days later, at the height of the Gulf War, the *brit,* the circumcision, was held at the small nearby Reform synagogue, Har El. The room was packed with people from all over Israel, many carrying their gas masks in the brown cardboard boxes afforded by the Home Command. As the rabbi spoke of birth and new beginnings, I wondered how many people were dying in Iraq, and how many would die in Israel. I remembered my mother's words as she lay dying, when I mourned her inability to meet my future husband and children: "I believe in infinite possibility." And in that moment, she was with me almost tangibly in the room packed with family and friends.

The joy and the sadness, the thirty-hour birth, the fear of being gassed, my love for Shuki and for this unknown child who had grown inside me over the past nine months, flowed together and burst out in a stream of tears. Perhaps all of us in Jerusalem, in Israel, lived like Janus, always looking with two faces, both forward and back, toward birth and toward death.

The rest of the *brit* is lodged in my mind as a jumble of colors and kissing, photographs and bewilderment, a noisy celebration of my son's birth, of new life born into a loving community of friends in the midst of a war. At "home" that night in the suite, as the sirens sounded and we ran to the hotel's sealed room, I realized that the *brit,* attended by Mustafa and David and by the Center's board members and clients, had also marked a celebration of my nascent organization, which might also be a home of sorts, a place of shared and infinite possibilities.

Yet as I left the hotel's sealed room with Shuki and my week-old son, and once again heeded Nachman Shai's advice to drink water, I knew, in the pit of my stomach, that I could not protect Shai, my new son, against the dangers of the world into which he had been born.

Chapter 8
The Past No Longer Matters?

The Gulf War ended as quickly as it had begun. The lightning victory for the West and allied Arab states triggered long-term political shifts in the Middle East.

In March 1991 Shuki, Shai and I moved back to our home in Bat Yam. I returned to work, pumping breast milk and traveling throughout the country. The Center's loan fund and economic consulting were beginning to jump-start small businesses in scores of Arab towns. We found our efforts gaining an inadvertent tail wind from Likud government policies, which liberalized Israel's economy, breaking the strictures of Israel's socialist legacy and opening opportunities for entrepreneurship.

In October 1991, the United States and the collapsing Soviet Union convened an unprecedented conference in Madrid, where reluctant leaders from Israel, Syria, Jordan, Lebanon, as well as a Palestinian delegation, talked directly for the first time about Arab-Israeli peace. A multilateral process continued among the parties, even as the Soviet Union dissolved into fifteen post-Soviet states.

Since 1977, and during all my years in the country, Israelis had preferred the more economically liberal and politically conservative Likud to the socialist-leaning Labor Party of the Ashkenazi elite. Asked once in a random political opinion poll whom I would like to see as minister of justice, I threw out the most far-fetched answer I could dream up — Shulamit Aloni, strident head of the tiny Ratz faction, which fought for myriad unpopular causes, from separation of religion and state to an end to the occupation. "Of course," I said apologetically to the pollster, who was trying to keep a straight face, "that will never happen."

When I went to the ballot box on June 23, 1992 — five months pregnant with my second child — to vote for the 13th Knesset, I had few expectations that the new government would be different from the old. In the morning, I was surprised to find that Labor had squeaked through to a narrow victory in the polls. Over the coming weeks, Prime Minister Yitzhak Rabin formed a lean coalition with Shulamit Aloni's Meretz (a combination of Ratz and the old socialist *kibbutz*-based Mapam movement), Shas, and the Mizrahi religious party.

Aloni was appointed not minister of justice but of education.

When Rabin broke with the past by including the Arab parties — not in the government itself, but in the government's narrow voting bloc — I was amazed. Until then, Arab parties had never entered the power equation of the ruling coalition of Israel. Now, for the first time, issues of concern to Arab citizens were included in the government's platform, and Arab Knesset members were appointed as deputy ministers for health and agriculture. For the first time, I and my colleagues at the Center found ourselves communicating with Arab citizens placed in ministerial advisory positions. Until then, such advisors on Arab affairs were "Arabists," Jews trained in and connected with the security services. Their job was to filter out the requests of the "unwanted" Arabs and to reward jobs and contracts to the "good" Arabs, those willing to cooperate with the party and the system.

The new Arab professionals viewed their role as facilitating, rather than manipulating, the overall advancement of Arab towns, entrepreneurs, farmers, women, and youth. In this, they sought the advice of the Center for Jewish-Arab Economic Development. The Ministry of Industry accepted our recommendations and recognized sites in twenty-one Arab towns for development as industrial zones, which enabled factories to move out of residential areas and expand. The Ministry of Economy launched a program to hire Arab professionals in government ministries. The Ministry of Tourism agreed to join the Center's pioneering survey of potential tourist sites in Arab towns in northern Israel, then made a historic decision to rezone priority areas to include Arab towns. With the resulting government assistance, a nascent bed-and-breakfast industry sprouted in homes in Arab towns throughout the Galilee, drawing Israeli Jews as guests.

After years of swimming against the current, I felt overwhelmed by the speed with which we were suddenly moving through bureaucratic waters. As the mainstream embraced our work, I was both excited at the Center's growing success and afraid of being swamped by the force of these turning tides.

In the midst of this exciting turmoil, on October 15, 1992, I gave birth to my second boy, Liad. Arriving precisely on his due date, Liad slipped out so easily that Shuki and I immediately began planning for our third child. Charming and cheerful, Liad was undaunted as I strapped him in his carseat and dragged him all over the Galilee. I was breast-feeding between meetings with Arab mayors, entrepreneurs, and government officials. I was coming home, exuberant and exhausted from my life of "having it all." Carried along on the flow of success and estrogen, I barely took the time to wonder how I could continue keeping so many balls in the air.

Soon, inundated with requests from Arab mayors seizing opportunities to develop their towns, Mustafa Abu Rumi left his position as my associate director at the Center to devote himself to his urban planning office. In his stead, Helmi Kittani, a highly recommended mid-career banker who had organized an impressive entrepreneurship training course for us, joined the Center's staff. The board of directors, itself a mixed group of Arab and Jewish businesspeople, proposed that the Center practice what it preached and become truly a Jewish-Arab joint venture. They wanted Helmi to be named not associate director but co-director with me.

Ideologically, I welcomed the step. I knew it was right for the Center to stretch itself to a new model of joint management. Helmi and I brought vastly different networks of connections, complementary professional skills, and different national identities. But truly, I felt nervous. I could understand something of the dread felt by those new brides in Tamra on the eve of their arranged marriages. I knew only good things about Helmi as an individual, but there is a world of difference between collegial cooperation on a project and allowing a relative stranger to become the new stepfather of the organization that had been my baby. Besides, could I really share power with an Arab man, older than I, a father of six, used to being in charge at various branches of Bank HaPoalim? Would I have to fight for my place in an organization I had conceived of and built?

I consulted with Shuki, knowing what he would say, and needing to hear it: "How can you run an organization that demands equality in our society without taking the risk to share power and responsibility in this one small organization?" Then I swallowed my trepidation and agreed to the match.

Although not tall physically, Helmi, at 44, was a man of stature in his community. His ability to listen, to make quick decisions, and to take responsibility for those decisions, drew people to rely on him instinctively. My reliance on Helmi, however, was not instinctive. Over the coming months, part of me stood aloof, observing him and his choices, as we analyzed and reacted to the myriad situations the Center faced. Should we work independently or with the Ministry of Tourism in examining the potential for new tourist businesses in Nazareth? Helmi wanted to bring the government in. Was a certain Bedouin entrepreneur a good choice for a joint venture partner? Helmi checked out the man through his wide networks. How much of our budget should we allocate to training women to manage businesses? Helmi and I agreed that women were key to the Arab economy.

Sensing my unease

Sarah Kreimer and Helmi Kittani, featured in *Link* magazine, June, 1996. Photo by R. Kapitchinsky.

about giving up financial control of the organization, Helmi turned down my polite offer to become a co-signatory on its bank account. "When the time is right, we'll do it," he remarked, in a seemingly off-handed way.

One day, at the end of a meeting at the office, Helmi unwrapped a pita sandwich that his wife Jamila had made him. (I usually raced out in the morning and bought a sandwich at a lunch counter in the middle of the day.) He laid the paper wrapping neatly on his desk, leaned over it, and took a bite. "I was the first Arab manager of the Shore Branch of Bank HaPoalim in Netanya," he told me. "I decided to set up meetings with the local business leaders, to get to know them. I would walk into the office for my appointment, and say: I'm Helmi Kittani, manager of the bank. For a moment there would be a bewildered silence. Sometimes they would even ask, 'Isn't that an Arab name?'"

Helmi paused to smile. "If Moshe and Avraham can manage banks in Nazareth and Baka al Gharbiye, why shouldn't Helmi or Mohammed be in charge in Netanya, Herzliya and Tel Aviv?"

In fact, with his light brown hair, square jaw, and fluent Hebrew, Helmi could easily pass as Jewish. In the 1970s, few Arabs were in management positions in Israel's banks, certainly not in Jewish towns. Neatly gathering up the corners of his napkin and throwing it away, Helmi continued describing to me the convolutions of "making it" as an Arab in the Jewish State. "You know, when people, Israeli Jews, wanted to compliment me, they would say, 'You don't look like an Arab.'" Hearing those words coming from his own mouth, Helmi burst out laughing, then paused a minute, checking my face, before continuing.

"When I was approached about running the Center, I hesitated. After managing a bank, where I was responsible for millions of shekels, I thought: why would I want to be 'number two' at small non-profit? It was my grandmother who encouraged me to take the job. She knew that I didn't want to go on giving business loans the rest of my life; I wanted to advance the economic level of Arab towns, and integrate them into the economy of the country."

I was taken aback by this latter disclosure. My own grandparents and parents had died years before. I had gotten used to making decisions alone. Now, my work partner, an Arab man, was telling me that he consulted his 90-year-old grandmother about his life decisions.

"She reminded me of an Arabic saying that she quoted often," Helmi continued. "'The inheritance of your father can be divided between you and your brother.' You know, in the 1950s, the State of Israel took many of our family lands and established Moshav Maor on them. My grandmother would invite the Yemenite Jews who settled there to drink coffee with her. I couldn't understand that; they were living on our land, and she was drinking coffee with them. So my grandmother told me: 'In the end, either we live together in this country, or we die together. And I prefer to live.' And I," he concluded with a smile, "prefer to help us all live better."

I was touched by Helmi's openness, by the notion of a grown man taking advice from his grandmother, and by his willingness to let me into his life.

Months later, I met that grandmother. She was sitting cross-legged on a *frash* on the cement floor of her dark, one-room home, on the ground floor of Helmi's house. She was clothed in a loose white flowing *thobe*; wisps of white hair escaping from under a white *hijab* tied lightly over her head. I bent to greet her, and was surprised to be pulled down by her strong, bony hands. *"Ahalan wasahalan,"* she greeted me in a thin voice as I sat, facing her. She had few teeth left in her mouth, but her wizened face was elegant. She asked me a few questions about my children and my husband, which I answered in rudimentary Arabic. But when she focused her watery blue eyes on me, I felt that she understood exactly who I was.

Our Center grew. In addition to our loan fund and business consulting, we added a training unit and a project to strengthen community economic development of Jaffa's mixed Jewish-Arab commercial district. As our organization continued to achieve individual successes throughout the country, we realized that we needed to expand our reputation, as well.

Ruth Dayan, first wife of Moshe Dayan, was one of our board members, and offered to ask her brother-in-law, Ezer Weizman, recently chosen as President of Israel, to address the our fifth annual membership meeting. The public blessing of Ezer Weizman, the flamboyant fighter pilot, former defense minister and key negotiator of the peace agreement with Egypt, would bring publicity, honor, and status to the Center and our mission.

Over the years, Weizman had personally helped hundreds, perhaps thousands, of people — Arabs and Jews — slice through bureaucratic brambles to reach the proper official ensconced in one or another government "castle." In his role as minister for minority affairs, he had managed the near-impossible, dismantling the infamous Area Nine army firing zone in the heart of the Galilee and allowing thousands of acres of prime agricultural land to return to the use of the Arab owners from whom it had been seized decades earlier for military use. When the President's Office accepted our invitation, we were ecstatic.

Two days before the conference, Shlomit, the Jewish woman who staffed our community development project in Jaffa, asked me what I was wearing to the event. I hadn't given it a thought. On the spot, with the practical good sense of a woman who had inherited and built up a family textile business, she spirited me out of the office and drove me to the boutique section of the Mashbir department store. There she picked out a suit and presented it to me to try on. Looking at myself in the mirror, I felt magnificent. The tailored, grey-striped suit, with an alluring slit up the back of its full-length skirt, emphasized my height, making me look both feminine and commanding.

"It's too fancy," I protested. "And too expensive; I'll never wear this again."

"It's just right," pronounced Shlomit, paraphrasing the Yiddish blessing my grandmother used when we bought new clothes: "Wear it in good health!" Then she added words my grandmother had never said: "You deserve it." Tears sprang into my eyes at the sudden and long-awaited praise. Shlomit continued, oblivious. "You've worked hard, and now the President of the State is honoring your work. Enjoy it. You will have many chances to wear it in the future; you are just beginning."

On July 14, 1993, President Ezer Weizman — tall, lanky, a bit stooped, and grinning — strode into the conference hall of the Tel Aviv Hilton Hotel at the Center's annual meeting. On his way, he stopped to greet and joke with every person he knew. No one cared how long it took Weizman to reach the podium. I relished every moment of the honor and excitement of being recognized by the President of Israel.

Greeting Israeli President Ezer Weizman at the Center's "coming out" party.

Presiding over this giant coming-out party, I was thankful that Shlomit had taken charge of me. Surveying the audience, the smiling faces — every eye riveted to President Weizman making his way attentively through the hall — I felt the warmth of recognition radiating throughout the place. Ezer Weizman, the man, and President Weizman, the state's leading citizen, was honoring not only our organization and its activists, but the idea underlying our work: the importance of the Arab sector, of Arab citizens, and their potential role in Israel as a whole. That recognition was like water in the desert.

Hundreds of businesspeople, Arab and Jewish alike, drank in his words: "We must, as quickly as possible, find ways to build cooperative relationships between Jews and Arabs. To create business ties — not just to Cairo — but to Damascus, to Amman, to Baghdad. And if Israelis can travel to Cairo on business trips, why can't they come to Baka el Gharbiye, to Umm el Fahm, to Nazareth, and other towns inside Israel? All this is possible, in spite of the fear."

As he spoke, President Weizman must have known what we,

the Israeli public, discovered, without warning, a month later. On August 29, 1993 the Israeli Cabinet revealed that secret negotiations had been conducted over the past months in Oslo, Norway, resulting in a formal Agreement of Principles between the Israeli government and the Palestine Liberation Organization, the PLO.

In defending the agreement to the Knesset, Prime Minister Rabin declared: "Every change has its risks, but the time has come to take a chance for peace . . . With the rise of Khomenism in the Arab and Moslem world, including among Palestinians, the dividing line is between those who favor talks for negotiating settlement, and those who oppose them. The past no longer matters."

This made me ecstatic. Instead of trying to prove we have no partner for peace, our government was negotiating vigorously to bring about peace. Instead of selling us "spin" about what is needed to gain security in this Land, our leaders were exposing hard truths — about compromises, about withdrawing from territory in order to give a chance to reach an agreement.

No longer would my friends be arrested for wearing t-shirts stenciled with the Israeli and Palestinian flags, or for meeting with PLO representatives. No longer would our government be ruling over another people with no end in sight. No longer would there be one law for Jews and another law for Palestinians in the territories; rather Israel, the Jewish State, would follow the ethical commands of the Torah: "There shall be one law for you, for the stranger and the citizen, for I am God, Lord of you [all]" (Leviticus 24:22).

Two weeks later, on September 13, 1993, Yitzhak Rabin and Yasser Arafat signed the official Declaration of Principles on the White House lawn. I watched them on TV while nursing Liad and wishing that Shuki, who was teaching, could be with me to celebrate this historic break with the past. Along with millions of Israelis, I held my breath as Rabin hesitated, almost repulsed, before shaking the hand of his bitter enemy, Yasser Arafat. Certainly, Rabin, who had ordered Israeli soldiers to break the arms and legs of rock-throwing Palestinians in the *intifada*, had not embarked on this path for love of Palestinians. Nonetheless, Arafat, the man who had vowed to push the Jews into the sea, who symbolized hatred and rejection of the very notion of Israel, in that instant became our negotiating partner for bringing peace in this contested land.

Over the next weeks, popular conceptions in Israel shifted with shocking rapidity. Instead of anonymous figures in *kaffiyehs* portrayed in news photographs captioned, "Palestinians plan retaliation," newspapers featured shots of Palestinian leaders with names and neckties: "Ahmed Qrei (Abu Ala) meets advisors."

I was deeply moved by the official letter that Arafat sent to Rabin as accompaniment to the declaration they had both signed. Although Arafat was no Anwar Sadat — and we had yet to see whether he would keep his word — in this simple letter, the PLO gave Israelis what we have long craved, recognition and legitimacy, from those who had sworn to throw us into the sea. "The signing of the Declaration of Principles marks a new era," the letter said. ". . . I would like to confirm the following PLO commitments: The PLO recognizes the right of the State of Israel to exist in peace and security. The PLO accepts United Nations Security Council Resolutions 242 and 338. The PLO commits itself . . . to a peaceful resolution of the conflict between the two sides and declares that all outstanding issues relating to permanent status will be resolved through negotiations . . .The PLO renounces the use of terrorism and other acts of violence and will assume responsibility over all PLO elements and personnel in order to assure their compliance, prevent violations and discipline violators . . .The PLO affirms that those articles of the Palestinian Covenant which deny Israel's right to exist, and the provisions of the Covenant which are inconsistent with the commitments of this letter are now inoperative and no longer valid."

The opening of a political process with the Palestinians led us at the Center to ponder the extent to which we should be involved in fostering economic ties with Palestinians in the West Bank and Gaza. On the one hand, broadening the circle of economic cooperation made sense: Economic advancement for Arab Israelis was linked to the peace process, which would lower barriers and fears, as we had begun to see, and move us towards a regional economy in which Israeli Arabs held the distinct advantages of language, culture and family ties. On the other hand, Arab Israelis on our board feared neglecting the core mission of the Center — economic development and equality within Israel — in favor of the "sexy" mission of advancing peace through economic ties.

I suggested that we run some pilot programs, based on developing three-way cooperation among Arab Israelis, Jewish Israelis, and Palestinians from the West Bank and Gaza. In the fall, with the help of Samer Haj-Yehia, a young Arab Israeli studying for his Ph.D. in finance at Hebrew University, we discreetly opened an entrepreneurship course for Palestinians in the Jerusalem area. The course attracted a strong group of potential entrepreneurs, who were pleased with what they learned.

For years, "cooperation" had taken place naturally and quietly in two major industries, construction and textiles, with Palestinian subcontractors providing cheap labor for Israeli companies. On the heels of our initial success with training, Helmi and I pondered the possibility of arranging a public business conference to bring together Palestinian and Israeli businesspeople working in the same industry. Our idea was to try to raise the cooperation to the level of joint ventures, in which partnership would be more equal and encourage the growth of a more independent Palestinian economy next to Israel's. Israeli businesspeople and business associations were excited about the possibility. Large sectors of Palestinian society, however, remained wary of open cooperation with Israelis, lest it lead to "normalization" and acceptance of the daily limitations that remained in place under the occupation. Some leading Palestinian economists advocated separation of the Israeli and Palestinian economies, to allow for independent economic development rather than a further subordinate intertwining.

Advertently or inadvertently, the growing Israeli government policy of closures along Israel's border brought about such separation. In March 1993, in response to a wave of Palestinian terror attacks, the Israeli government broke with its policy of free movement from the West Bank and Gaza into Israel by setting up checkpoints on main roads. These served to regulate and even close off access for Palestinians trying to get into Israel proper. While businesspeople usually received entry permits, many workers did not. The closures brought massive Palestinian unemployment in their wake. Later, Rabin would say, "We need to bring thousands of foreign workers to reduce the number of Palestinians walking around in our streets."

Individual Palestinian businesspeople were caught between the desire to expand cooperation with Israeli businesses and the lucrative Israeli market and the fear of retribution for unacceptable "collaboration." Helmi and I drank scores of cups of coffee and found many cordial and interested Palestinian businesspeople, but each meeting ended with polite smiles and noncommittal words that told us that none of them would accept an invitation to a public conference, much less help us organize such events.

Just as we were about to give up, some friends introduced me to Abdel Fatah Darwish, a Palestinian economic journalist in East Jerusalem. We met in his dark, cubbyhole office in a once-grand old home off Nablus Rd. Although in his early thirties, Darwish, with his dark mustache, premature balding, and slightly formal way of speaking, projected the air of an older man. The sparkle in his eyes was boyish, however, as he spoke of his mission to put out *Al Raed*, an independent Palestinian economic journal, in an atmosphere of highly politicized partisan thinking.

Born in Jerusalem, Darwish had received his M.A. in economics from Sindh University in Pakistan, and had worked for five years as the economic editor for *Al Qabas Daily* in Kuwait. At the end of the Gulf War in March 1991, however, Darwish had been expelled from Kuwait, along with most of the 400,000 other Palestinians who had made up much of the country's professional and business class, after the Palestinian leadership had sided with Saddam Hussein and his invasion of Kuwait. The newly restored Kuwaiti government made it clear that Palestinians were no longer welcome in the country, and the Kuwaiti and Saudi governments both cut their financial support to the PLO and Palestinian institutions. The expulsion from Kuwait was a blow to the Palestinian economy, for many expatriates had sent their sizeable earnings back to parents and children in Jerusalem, the West Bank and Gaza.

Darwish had returned to his family in Jerusalem and, using the insights gained in the various countries of the Middle and Far East over the years, become an entrepreneur. He fervently believed that a modern Palestinian economy could not be developed without mutually beneficial economic cooperation with Israel. "Anyone who says otherwise is fooling himself," Darwish said with a scowl, drawing on a cigarette. "Israel is the most developed economy of the Middle East, and it is next door to us. Cooperation for business development is not collaboration," he added. "It is necessary to build our own economy." He squashed his cigarette butt into a full ashtray. "Do you know that we need to add nine thousand jobs to our economy each year just to provide work for young people graduating from high school?" He tapped a fresh cigarette out of a half-empty pack, lit it, and looked me in the eye. "How can we do that alone? Will Jordan help us? Egypt? They can barely manage their own economies."

After hours of talking about our lives, our views, our dreams, Darwish concluded, "I would be pleased to cooperate with you and your Center. Why don't we put on a small conference here in Jerusalem — maybe in the construction sector? I will bring the Palestinian businesses; you bring the Israelis." We shook hands, and I left the office, elated.

Helmi and our Board were pleased to move forward on the idea. Over the coming days, I met with the Israel Manufacturers' Association and the Association of Building Contractors. They were willing to invite their members to such a conference, as long as we designed the program together with them to deal with *tachlis*, that is, practicalities, not politics.

Despite Darwish's confident words, Helmi feared that he was taking significant personal risk to convince Palestinian business-people that economic cooperation was not "collaboration." Not a few Palestinian "collaborators" had been killed in the last months. Together, Helmi and Darwish went to speak to key Palestinian political and economic players, to introduce the Center, clarify intentions and sensitivities, and get their backing. One of these key players was Saeb Bamya, deputy minister for international co-operation in the new Palestinian Ministry of Trade and Industry.

Slight, bespectacled, with a quick smile and a quicker wit, Saeb was one of the "Tunisians" — the PLO expatriate leader-ship, headed by Yasser Arafat, which had grown up first in Jordan, then relocated to Lebanon, then was expelled to Tunisia at the end of the 1982 Lebanon War. With the signing of the Oslo accords, this Palestinian refugee leadership was allowed back into the West Bank and Gaza to run the new Palestinian Authority. Tensions arose, however, between the "Tunisians," who parachuted into leadership positions from abroad, and local Palestinian leaders, who had lived with Israelis and under Israeli occupation, had led both the violent and nonviolent actions of the *intifada*, and had paid a personal price in Israeli prisons over the last years.

Saeb, an erudite and savvy economist, aimed to work with the local business leadership, building on local capability. He spoke plainly and consistently, whether in private conversation or at a podium. From the beginning, he brought the top PLO leadership to back him in pursuing a policy of economic cooperation with Israel as a pillar of Palestinian state-building.

"For us Palestinians," Saeb explained, "separation is a nightmare, linked with unilateral policy, and we don't like it. There are three pillars needed to move forward toward peace: security — for both sides — economic growth and development — for both sides — and a political horizon. If this occupation will continue, there will be no peace. Yes, terror is the enemy of the economy, and terror is the enemy of the Palestinian dream. But poverty and unemployment are the best environment for terror. And Israeli measures taken against the total Palestinian population in the name of security give direct support to terrorists and extremists. Israel is, and will continue to be, our most important trade partner. I see only the option of cooperation. But we have something to say about the terms."

In all the years I worked with Saeb, he never wavered from this belief, at what personal risk, I never knew. His steadfastness held tremendous power. Even in the darkest hours of the conflict — and they would come — he worked for business cooperation, for fair trade agreements, for workable security arrangements that would allow Palestinians and Israelis to continue commerce with some degree of parity.

He treated me as if I were key to bringing the Israeli side around. When I got discouraged, I would come to Saeb, and he would look me in the eye and say, "Sarah, we are in the same boat. We must not support the extremists among us."

It was not always the extremists, however, who tried to rock our small boat. A week before the "Building Peace" conference was due to take place, an ad appeared on a prominent page of the *Al Quds* Arabic daily calling on Palestinian businessmen to boycott the upcoming conference because it was taking place in the Hyatt Hotel, built on confiscated Palestinian land in East Jerusalem. Darwish suspected that ideology was not the only motivation behind the attack. Now that the rules of the game were changing, various players were trying to establish a better competitive position. Consulting urgently with Saeb and other leading figures, Darwish paid personal visits to scores of key businesspeople and set the young staffers at Al Raed to work making hundreds of phone calls. Helmi and I breathed not a word of the trouble to the representatives of the Israeli Contractors' and Manufacturers' Associations, who had recruited their members.

"Building Peace" drew almost two hundred Palestinians and Israelis from the area's construction industry. Although little publicized, it marked the first Palestinian-Israeli business encounter to take place after the signing of the Oslo accords. Our Center, slim and agile, was able to serve as a modest vanguard, pushing past old boundaries, helping to break old patterns, and creating a future that moved on a trajectory different from that of the past.

Chapter 9
Each of Us Is a Small Light

I looked over the chocolate birthday cake at Shuki, with his receding chestnut hair, as he intently coached Liad to blow out his first birthday candle. Shai, round and dimpled and 2 years old, jumped about with excitement, and we all sang "Happy birthday to you!" in Hebrew and English. As I made a quick wish for our lives to continue just as they were now, Shuki looked up. We smiled at each other before the candle flickered and hissed out.

It was October 1993, and my dreams, both political and personal, were being realized. Israel was moving toward peace with the Palestinians, albeit haltingly. Some of the Center's proposals for a more equitable and prosperous society were being implemented. I had two beautiful children with a man I loved deeply. Often, I came home to our two-bedroom apartment in Tel Aviv to see Shuki lying on the rug in the living room, bald and giggling, with Liad clambering over his knees.

Shuki, too, was pursuing long-incubated dreams. After years of ambivalence about abandoning his career as an engineer, he had enrolled in a mid-career teacher-training course. Despite warnings about frustrating bureaucracy and low pay for teachers, he wanted to teach mathematics in the public schools, to help kids of all backgrounds overcome deeply ingrained messages that they were incapable of understanding math. He believed that breaking those stereotypes about math could unlock many other capabilities as well. Shuki had the uncanny skill of seeing through people's defenses and relating to the vulnerable and able person inside.

One day in November, he called me from the doctor's office. "Meet me at Ichilov Hospital," he said in a flat tone. "The imaging department. Dr. Cohen wants an immediate CT brain scan."

Over several weeks, Shuki had noticed that the fingers of his right hand were not responding as usual. At first, he paid little attention, thinking the problem would go away as inexplicably as it had come. But as the days passed, writing had become increasingly difficult, so Shuki had gone to see a neurologist.

It was after dark when the technician finally took Shuki for the CT. As the machine probed the inner recesses of Shuki's head, I sat on a molded plastic chair in the waiting area, exhausted from days of breastfeeding, running around the country, and mediating between Shai and Liad, who lately had started fighting. I was too tired to think. Half an hour later, Shuki returned to the waiting room, eyes bloodshot behind his horn-rimmed glasses.

Within minutes, a young doctor called us into his office, a poorly lit cubicle. Sitting down on one of the two chairs in front of his desk, I felt out of place. *We should be home with our kids.* My attention was riveted to a light board on the wall to his left, illuminating a dark X-ray sheet filled with rows of tiny pictures of a brain.

"There is a small growth of some kind here," he said, pointing to a blob on one of the little brains. "It's pressing on the area that controls movement in your right arm. It is fairly accessible, so I would recommend surgery as soon as possible, to have it removed. It may be an abscess. However, since you have a history of melanoma, we can't rule out the possibility of metastasis."

Staring at the multiple pictures of Shuki's brain with the blob, I felt cold. Yes, it was probably an abscess. I turned to Shuki, who sat unmoving next to me, his brain tucked invisibly inside his skull, his right arm hanging listlessly by his side. "I knew this might happen," he mumbled, so low that I wasn't sure I had heard him.

Shortly after we had met, Shuki told me that he had suffered from skin cancer and needed to be very careful about exposure to the sun. Every six months, he went for a comprehensive check-up. About two years ago, a second mole had been removed and found to be cancerous. However, Shuki took all possible precautions, and neither of us spent much time worrying about the various what-if scenarios.

96

Now the what-if scenarios were racing out of the past to over-take us. I felt numb, then nauseous.

Over the next weeks, unable to concentrate, Shuki cancelled meetings with many of his students. One evening, he shouted at Shai in a tone I'd never heard before. I rushed to intervene. Shuki stormed into the bedroom. Shai sobbed in my arms, his whole body shaking as he took in little breaths. As the sobs subsided, Shuki came back and stood in the doorway, mortified at his own lack of control. He walked over and knelt down to meet Shai at eye level, not knowing what to say. With my arm around Shai, kneeling close to Shuki, I explained in as matter-of-fact a tone as I could muster, "Shai, Abba isn't feeling well. He's very upset about that. He didn't mean to yell at you."

Shuki looked into Shai's brown eyes and said simply, "I am sorry." Then he rose silently and left the room. Shai gazed after him, his little breaths still coming unevenly.

The doctors scheduled Shuki for surgery on Wednesday, December 15, the seventh day of Hanukkah — holiday of lights and miracles, commemorating the Maccabees' victory over the Romans and the little jar of oil, sufficient only for one day, that fueled the holy lamp in the Temple for eight days. I clung to the hope that the surgeons would remove a benign growth and restore the miracle of healthy life.

The evening before, the kids and I had gathered with Shuki's sisters, Yael and Nira, and his brother, Moti, in the third-floor lobby of Ichilov Hospital. As a substitute for the good health they longed to bring, all had brought piles of sweets for Liad and Shai, who danced and tottered happily around the hospital halls, munching away. Together, we lit the menorah with forced jollity, singing Hanukkah songs about hope, about kindling lights and banishing darkness: "My candle, my candle, my little candle . . . Each of us is a small light; all of us together are a great light."

Amidst the kids' random motion, Shuki sat on one of the orange plastic waiting-room chairs as the locus of our activity. Liad, his strawberry-blond fuzz of hair keeping him easily visible, tottered out to explore the lobby, cheerful as usual, and then back to Shuki for a refueling of comfort. With his good left arm, Shuki gathered Liad onto his lap, holding him quietly. His right arm hung limp by his side. Tomorrow morning's intravenous vent was already prepared and taped to the back of his hand.

Shai, enchanted with the piles of chocolate that were, as he repeatedly reminded his brother, "Mine!" brought candy after candy to Shuki to open for him. Shai didn't notice how deftly Shuki used his left hand and his teeth to peel off the wrappers. He just knew that his father would help him.

Afraid that he would wake up from brain surgery a "vegetable," or unable to speak, Shuki next asked me to film him delivering a message to the boys. Looking like a prisoner on death row in his mustard-colored hospital pajamas, he measured each word, speaking thoughtfully to some future version of our little boys. He made two abortive attempts to describe how he and I met at the Tel Aviv bus station, how we married on Kibbutz Barkai, as the prelude to Shai and Liad's life. Then, as he always did, he cut straight to the point.

"Tomorrow Abba will go in for very important surgery. Important for his life . . ." He paused. "Important for your life." A thought flickered through his eyes, and he laughed, his face lighting up with momentary humor. "I hope I will come out alive."

Shuki kept speaking calmly, focused directly at the camera, as Shai munched chocolate on the floor by his feet. The relatives began packing up around us. "Shai and Liad, I love you. I will always love you . . . I simply love you."

Then the tears sprang into his eyes, and he stopped speaking. Shai, who heard the familiar words, "I love you," turned his face up to Shuki and responded instinctively, "I love you!"

Tears stung my eyes too. I was still focused on the glimmer of hope that we had: that the answer could be hopeful, that the operation was taking place at one of the best hospitals in the world . . .

As I snapped off the camera and detached it from its tripod, I felt drained. Despite the brave façade, Shuki was preparing for death. His dark assumptions wormed their way into my psyche. What if something were to go terribly wrong the next morning, and we would never be able to have a conversation again, never be able to embrace? What if the operation was successful but the tumor was melanoma and not an abscess? I wanted to run over and hold Shuki in my arms, to feel him holding me one last time before his surgery. But my husband was already far away, unreachable. He had gathered his strength, focused his generous attention on the kids, and delivered his message, and now he had with-drawn within himself, as he had learned to do long ago in the children's houses of Kibbutz Afikim, in order to be "alone" in the constant presence of other people.

I tried kissing him. The kiss landed on his cheek as he turned away and walked slowly on slippered feet into the ward.

I stood for a moment, insulted and abandoned amid diaper bags and tired babies, among forced songs and unspoken dread. Heavily, I gathered the kids and the chocolates and the stroller, and trudged home in the dark, drained of dreams and expectations.

The next morning, Nira, Yael and Moti sat together outside the operating room, buried two floors underground, in case it needed to function in a national emergency. Yael had risen early to be with Shuki as the barber shaved his head and the nurses prepared him for surgery.

Hour after hour we sat in the windowless room, waiting, star-ing at the television set droning on in the corner. We spoke every now and then to relieve the tension, repeating the same meaning-less phrases over and over again: *It's probably an abscess . . . The doctor said it would be a long operation; they have to open up the cranium . . . Dr. Vaknin is the head of the department, one of the best surgeons in the world . . .*

The book I had brought lay limply in my lap; I was unable to concentrate even on Grace Paley's short stories.

Finally, Dr. Vaknin strode out of the operating theater to in-form us that he had been successful in removing the growth, and that, as soon as Shuki woke up, he could be taken to the ward. I didn't ask if he would wake up able to talk, to recognize his chil-dren, to move his arm.

In an amazingly short time, an orderly wheeled Shuki from surgical recovery, and Dr. Vaknin swooped in, demanding of Shuki, whom he knew was a math teacher, "What's the quadratic equation?"

Without surgery, I could not remember the quadratic equa-tion! How could Shuki, still groggy from anesthesia, be expected to respond?

"$(A + B)^2 = A^2 + 2AB + B^2$," Shuki whispered, a weak smile flitting over his lips.

"Okay, you can take him up to the ward," said the surgeon, also with the hint of a smile.

I was ecstatic.

Within hours, Shuki was fully conscious, sitting up, smiling and talking, relieved and thrilled to be alive. Were it not for the bandages around his head, I would never have guessed that he had had neurosurgery earlier in the day.

The next morning, Moti stayed up in the ward with Shuki, while Yael, Nira and I walked down to Dr. Vaknin's office to receive the pathology results. Each of us sat stiffly in simple straight-backed chairs across from Dr. Vaknin, severe behind a polished, overpowering desk. The surgeon, dressed in white shirt and tie, with an impeccably trimmed goatee, looked with piercing eyes at each of us in turn; then got straight to the point.

"The tumor was a metastasis of melanoma," he stated with the hint of a French accent. "I could not remove all of it without hurting healthy tissue. In such cases, I prefer quality of life over a possible lengthening of life."

Struggling to translate his words into human terms, I vaguely grasped that the doctor had chosen to leave a piece of the tumor, in order to allow Shuki to function normally for this next period, instead of removing all he could see and crippling Shuki's use of arm or leg.

Vaknin's voice continued; I tried to catch up to the flow of information. "Once melanoma metastasizes to the brain, there is little treatment available. I will recommend radiation, but after that, it is just a matter of time."

The clock on the office wall ticked, echoing in the silence. I didn't want to ask the obvious next question.

Dr. Vaknin did not wait to be asked. "Life expectancy at this stage is, on average, six months."

"Six months!" I echoed. I had expected to hear "years." What life could be lived in six months? Shuki and I had just started our family; Shai and Liad were still babies; Shuki was studying to be a math teacher; our marriage was just four years old.

How could it be six months? Dr. Vaknin had said "average." *That means some people lived for years. Besides, he is a surgeon, not an oncologist. We can get a second opinion. Maybe there are alternative treatments. Sometimes there are miracles.*

Dr. Vaknin assured us brusquely that he would give Shuki the same information he had given us. We rose, and left the office in silence. Only outside in the corridor did we turn to look at one another, worried, pale, shocked. I wished we were huggers or criers, but we were not. Yael stared down the hall, her arms crossed over her chest; Nira's usually smiling face was limp. Clutching my knapsack, I felt alone in my dread of the future.

Although Shuki knew of his diagnosis, he chose, at first, not to relate to it. He was delighted to have awoken from surgery with all his faculties. Once again, he had use of his arm; two weeks after the operation, he was picking the kids up and swirling them in circles. After weeks of worry and anger, he felt healthy and grateful, and pleased to be going home.

A couple weeks after the surgery, Shuki and I both awoke just before dawn to find Shai and Liad curled up in our bed. With an elfish glint in his eye, Shuki pulled me gently out of our bed to the boys' bed in the next room. We laid down on their futon on the floor, drawing their little blankets over our large bodies, enjoying the warmth of a full-body embrace. Slowly and mindfully, we made love with the joy of our early courtship, relishing every moment.

After a December visit from my brother, Seth, and his family, Shuki began turning inward. He relinquished more and more of his future-oriented activities, his studies and his tutoring, and stayed close to home. Even there, he found it harder and harder to listen to Shai and Liad, to answer their pleas for the little playdough figures he crafted so deftly, to meet their never-ending demands for attention.

As the weeks passed, Shuki focused more and more of his stubborn intensity on various alternative treatments — from diets of vitamins and foul-tasting juice made from grasses, to a regimen of saunas and cold showers, which he dreaded— all designed to extend the period of quality life. I tried to be supportive, but my own mother's skepticism ran deep in my psyche. Shuki felt it and resented it, pulling farther away from me. Almost unconsciously, I, too, pulled away from him, focusing more of my attention and emotion on Shai and Liad, who needed it and returned it so naturally.

Shuki underwent one last medical treatment: radiation. When

he lost his hair, he looked, for the first time, like he was sick. As he began losing weight, I realized that it was time to start preparing the boys for what lay ahead. Liad did not have enough words to hold a complex picture. But Shai did. One night, I told Shai that Abba was very sick, and the doctors didn't know what to do.

Without hesitation, he offered: "They should go and learn!"

"Yes," I agreed, tears springing to my eyes at the confident logic of a child, for whom the world is packed with hope. "They are trying, but they may not be able to learn fast enough to help Abba."

The answer seemed to be enough for him, and I did not volunteer additional information. After Shai fell asleep, I stayed awake a long time, staring at the blond curls framing his cherub face, his arms splayed out in trusting abandon. How long would he be able to maintain his blessed innocence in the face of what was about to happen to him, to all of us? How could I possibly protect him? I buried my head in a pillow, sobbing with the sadness and helplessness. I wanted to turn back the clock, to live once again in our happy days together before Shuki's disease . . .

While I was dragged deeper and deeper into the darkness of a narrowing cave, my colleagues at work were building a bright future with an ever-widening horizon. Deals and options developed daily; the Center's staff worked long hours to keep up with the pace of opportunities.

On the heels of "Building Peace," Helmi charted a conference for the textile industry, and received signs of interest, not only from Palestinians, but from Egyptians as well. The interest flowed into a stream of inquiries, and Helmi hired Lisa Fliegel, a red-haired journalist, artist, and organizer, to coordinate the conference, "Weaving Peace."

How could I continue to direct the Center? I could barely get myself to leave the house to go to work. I could neither fathom nor predict the course of events with Shuki. How long would he be at home; how long would he be capable of interacting with me and the kids, how long would he be taking care of himself? I had no idea how the kids would react along the way, or what would be demanded of me.

Torn by the contradictory trajectories of my life, I walked into Helmi's office. "I've decided to resign as co-director," I said. "I can't concentrate; I don't know how long this period will go on. The Center can't afford to be held back now."

Helmi fixed his light brown eyes on my face, and without hesitation said, "If you leave, I leave."

I was shocked. If we both left, our work would disintegrate.

"We're in this together," Helmi said. "Right now, your job is to take care of Shuki and Shai and Liad. Do what you need to do for them. I will take care of the Center. You are the co-director of the Center, and when the time is right, you will come back and do the job the way you always have."

The tears I had been holding back for days began streaming down my face. "Thank you," I stammered. Embarrassed, Helmi walked out to get me a tissue. When he returned, I knew that I didn't need to finish my sentence, to tell him how overwhelmed I was by the depth and breadth of trust, partnership, and friendship that had grown between us.

As the weather warmed and spring breezes rustled the trees, I tried to keep the household running, to make Tu B'Shvat baskets of fruit and Purim costumes for the kids, and every now and then to make dinner. At Shai's third birthday in early February, Shuki, Liad and I went to the Little Butterfly Kindergarten to celebrate. When we walked in with the requisite chocolate cake and birthday candles, Shai was grinning and prancing with excitement. The kindergarten teacher danced Shai through a number of hoops on the floor, as the children sang, "Hop, hop, tra-la-la, I've grown up another year!" I watched Shuki staring at Shai, filling himself with this 3-year-old image of joy that would have to substitute for years of future images he would never see. With Liad on my lap, I felt I would explode from the agony of holding together the sorrow of Shuki's approaching death and the hope of the boys' young lives.

By March, Shuki lost his appetite and his patience. His brother Moti came to live in our home to help Shuki with daily chores. As he shut door after door on his hopes and dreams, Shuki took out his anger on me. Nothing I bought him was right; nothing I did was acceptable. One day, at his request, I went to the tax authority to renegotiate his payments on his self-employed file. When he learned that I followed the representative's advice to close the file, Shuki began screaming at me: "You've ruined everything! How could you? You idiot!" He continued with such vehemence that the veins throbbed in his temples, and his brother had to restrain him.

Frustrated and humiliated, too confused to cry, I began to shake uncontrollably. I was furious, but what right did I have to be angry at Shuki, when he was the one dying? I could see him struggling to continue living in the shadow of his death sentence.

I wanted desperately to help, to listen, to share the burden in some way, but Shuki had increasingly lowered some invisible curtain, cutting me off from his thoughts and feelings. When I tried to touch him, he drew away. I felt hurt, resentful, inadequate, and exhausted, always exhausted — physically, mentally, emotionally. I was trying so hard to keep everything together for the kids, for Shuki, for myself, and no one seemed to appreciate me, nor my efforts.

Finally, when he could no longer stand the dissonance of the kids' exuberant growing up and his own daily dying, Shuki decided it was time to go to the hospice. Moti, Yael and Nira took turns staying there with Shuki, along with a group of dedicated friends. The kids and I visited every day or two. No matter how he felt, Shuki would always perk up and pay attention to the kids when they arrived.

As Pesach neared, however, Shuki asked to receive higher and higher doses of morphine so that he would be less and less aware of what was going on around him. He had only three requests: that people be with him twenty-four hours a day, that he be buried on Kibbutz Afikim near his father, and that he be awake enough to celebrate one last Pesach seder with the family.

When we arrived on Pesach eve, Shuki was seated in a wheel chair, his head lolling from the weight of the morphine. I gazed at him in horror. We had come to celebrate the holiday of the liberation of the Jewish people from the slavery of Egypt, the holiday of God's miraculous renewal of the earth in spring — and Shuki was trapped in a world of death and morphine. How would the kids relate to this bent shell of a man whom their father had become? Shai, holding my hand tightly, looked cautiously around the hospice to find his father, hesitating as his gaze rested on Shuki. Liad, however, broke loose and toddled toward Shuki, eagerly calling, "Abba, Abba!" He settled himself comfortably in Shuki's lap in the wheelchair, smiling and happy. With his child's eyes he saw neither the wheelchair, nor the gaunt frame, nor the morphine-glazed eyes; he saw his father, the man who had loved him from the day he was born, the man who had played with him and sung to him, the man who had run after him and made him laugh. He saw his father from the inside.

In a room laden with sadness and endings, Liad had cut through the outer wrappings to find his father, and snuggled close, reveling in what he had now. That gentle moment would have to last a lifetime, for never again did he see his father.

At 5:00 a.m. on April 14, Moti called to say that Shuki had died. I rushed to the hospice. When I entered Shuki's room, Moti tactfully slipped out, leaving me alone with the body that had housed my husband. Shuki lay pale, inert, but still warm, his once-vibrant body suddenly small amid white hospital sheets. I wanted to touch him, to kiss him, to caress him, but I was horrified by the cadaver that lay in place of the man I had loved. Shuki had reached the ultimate "turning inward."

What had happened at that miraculous moment when body and soul parted? Where had he gone? Shuki had believed in reincarnation. Would I yet meet his soul in some other form, at some other time?

I stood in the mysterious presence of what was left, a spent body, a transformed soul. And memories: his gallant smile on the day we met at the bus station; his gentle hands on my body the first night we made love; the joy in his eyes as he lifted my veil under the *chuppah* at our wedding.

I began to cry. Never again would Shuki see or hold Liad or Shai. Never would his wise hands help them build a kite. Never would I be able to turn to him and say: *I can't do this anymore, will you take the kids out for a walk?* Never would I come home to him at the end of a day, to be comforted when I felt inadequate or overwhelmed.

The tears turned to sobs and the sobs to dry heaves. I choked on the pain and fled to the bathroom, so I wouldn't wretch on the now-cold body.

I don't remember how I told the kids, or how we got to Kibbutz Afikim, but I remember walking to the newly dug grave with Shai, and together laying down the last picture he had drawn for his father: a black panther. I remember that Liad had chicken pox and cried a lot. I remember feeling powerless to juggle everything so that I could give Shai and Liad the attention they needed, not only from their mother, but in place of their father, who was now relegated to the past.

Chapter 10
Glimpse of the Promised Land

Beyond the hills and the desert,
Say the legends, there is a place
From which the living do not yet return
And it is called the Red Rock.

—by Haim Hefer, sung by Arik Lavie*

I asked our taxi driver to pause on the Jordan Valley ridge just north of Beit Shean, before descending to the newly opened Sheikh Hussein Border Crossing, where we would be welcoming the Jordanian textile delegation arriving for the Center's "Weaving Peace" conference. Below us stretched the Jordan Rift Valley, where the narrow Jordan River wended its way through a green-brown patchwork of banana, date and wheat fields of *kibbutzim* on the Israeli side, and of private farmers on the Jordanian side. Across from us, the Jordanian hills rose in brown and barren mirror image of the hills on which we stood.

As we drove down the narrow road, I peered through the cold drizzle for signs of an international terminal. All I saw was a white trailer standing alone in an empty lot and a narrow road winding past it to a barrier. Across the valley, the road climbed an identical

---

* The Red Rock is a folk-ballad of the 1950s, describing the daring journey of three Israeli youths who sneak across the Jordanian border to visit the legendary Nabatean city of Petra, where they are discovered and killed. The song was banned by Israeli authorities shortly after it became popular, for fear that it would encourage similar attempts.

slope toward the Irbid area of Jordan. When the taxi drove off, I wondered for a brief moment if we had come to the right place. Our steps crunching the gravel, we walked to the trailer, on which a fresh white sign with blue letters in Hebrew, Arabic and English declared: "Jordan River Border Terminal — Welcome to Israel."

Here, on December 20, 1994, Helmi, Lisa Fliegel, Ruth Dayan — founder of the Maskit network of handicrafts stores, ex-wife of former Defense Minister Moshe Dayan, and Center board member — and I awaited the arrival of the first Jordanian business delegation to Israel.

The idea of inviting the Jordanians had been born half a year before, when Helmi, Ronit and I had crowded around a small black radio on the Center's reception desk, listening to a live broadcast of a second ceremony on the White House lawn. This time, Israel and Jordan were signing a declaration to establish peaceful relations, making Jordan the second Arab country to recognize Israel and to open diplomatic ties.

"History is made when brave leaders find the power to escape the past and create a new future. Today two such leaders come together." President Clinton paused here for effect. Helmi and I looked at each other; his eyes were glistening. He had relatives living in Jordan. "On this morning of promise, these visionary statesmen from ancient lands have chosen to heal the rift that for too long has divided their peoples. On both sides of the River Jordan have lived generations of people who thought this day would never come."

A dull pain throbbed behind my eyes. Shuki was one of those people; I ached to call him and share his joy. Growing up on Kibbutz Afikim, whose fields ended at the Jordanian border, Shuki had spent many nights in bomb shelters. During Israel's War of Independence, his sister, Yael, had been transported with other *kibbutz* children under cover of darkness over back roads to Haifa, to escape the advance of the Jordanian army. During the War of Attrition, terrorists would sneak across the Jordan River to carry out attacks in the *kibbutzim* and towns of the region. As an IDF soldier, Shuki's brother Moti had crossed into Jordan to ambush these terrorists before they could cross into Israel.

Often Shuki had wondered if there would ever be peace with

this forbidden country, so geographically close. He had longed to meet a Jordanian civilian, to travel to Amman and Jerash, to explore Petra, the ancient city carved into the red rock of the desert. Now others would visit the lands on which he'd gazed all his life.

The next day, Lisa Fliegel, the relentlessly energetic journalist-organizer the Center had hired to coordinate the textile conference, bounced into the office with an idea. "Let's put on our textile conference for Palestinians, Israelis, Egyptians and Jordanians! We'll make history, as first Israelis ever to host a Jordanian business delegation to Israel."

Over the months that followed, Lisa enlisted every leading Israeli businessman and businesswoman involved in textiles and fashion to be part of the Center's Middle East extravaganza, "Weaving Peace." Dan Catarivas, head of the new Middle East department of the Israeli Ministry of Industry, was pulled into the vortex, bringing with him other key government officials. Egyptian textile companies we had met in Cairo at a European Mideast conference agreed to come. Lisa's contacts in Jordan came through with the Al Hayat International Trading Company, run by a Palestinian entrepreneur living in Jordan, Mohammed Atiyeh, who worked with a woman business consultant, Ola el-Masri, to put together a delegation of the ten leading Jordanian textile manufacturers.

Our Palestinian colleagues, Abdel Fatah Darwish and Saeb Bamya, organized an impressive Palestinian delegation from both the West Bank and Gaza. Then Lisa came out with her next whopper. "Let's have a fashion show! You know, with models and music and a runway, and they'll show the latest designs from each country. It'll get great publicity; it will make the conference an 'item.'"

Now, shivering in the December rain, I thought of Shuki, grow-ing up in the shadow of these Jordanian hills, from which enemy soldiers had shelled *kibbutz* fields in the valley. Were he alive, he would have joined us here, excitedly awaiting the arrival of the first Jordanian business delegation to cross this bridge into Israel. In so many ways, Shuki had died too soon.

I stood without him in the raw and fickle December air. One moment, dark clouds gathered, and we were drenched with rain; the next moment, the clouds broke and scattered, and the sun splashed the mountains on either side of us with clean light.

Suddenly, against an ominous blue-black sky, a rainbow appeared, arching over the valley. I pulled back my hood to enjoy its momentary glory. As light rain caught in my hair, I breathed the blessing, traditional upon seeing a rainbow: *baruch ata adonai . . .* blessed are You, Lord our God, King of the universe, who remembers the covenant, is trustworthy in His covenant, and fulfills His word. The blessing recalls the first rainbow sent by God as a sign of His promise to Noah that He would never again destroy the world by flood: "This is the token of the covenant which I make between me and you and every living creature that is with you, for perpetual generations. I have set my bow in the cloud, and it shall be for a token of a covenant between me and the earth."

Helmi, Ruth, Lisa and I stood together, rapt with the beauty shimmering above us and gratified that we were living in a time of receding floodwaters, fresh covenants, and new plantings under hopeful skies. I hoped that not only God, but the Palestinians, the Jordanians, and our own government would remember their agreements for generations to come, and that the blessings of these days would not be as transitory as the rainbow, which even now faded into the darkening sky.

The Nazarene Tours bus we had ordered to pick up the delegation pulled into the lot beside us. Some called to us from the trailer, and we turned to see a Jordanian bus dropping off a group of about twenty dignified, well-dressed people, who began walking the hundred meters over the bridge, rolling their voluminous luggage toward the Israeli side of the border. I picked out Ola immediately, a slim, dark-haired woman in spike heels, who walked with the assurance of one who is accustomed to getting her way with people.

Although none of us had met in person, after weeks of frantic phone calls, battling bureaucracies, overcoming official and unofficial obstacles, and coordinating what to say and not to say to the media, we felt like we were reconnecting with long-lost friends. One by one, we introduced ourselves with warm handshakes and ritual kisses on both cheeks.

Inside the trailer, the Jordanians opened their huge suitcases of samples for the Weaving Peace Exhibition; the Israeli customs agent shook his head. "This is a tourist crossing. We have no customs regulations; no merchandise can cross here."

Knowing that the economic protocols to the Israeli-Jordanian peace agreement hadn't yet been signed, Dan Catarivas' representative, sent to iron out these issues, took the official aside. I watched while they argued and conferred and placed a few key phone calls. Soon, with promises to display but not sell their wares, the Jordanians crossed into Israel and boarded the Nazarene Tours bus.

Riding south through the Jordan valley, we talked incessantly, trying to piece together our pictures of life "on the other side." I sat next to Ra'ed, a tall, impeccably dressed manufacturer of denim fabric. As we neared Jericho, he peered out the window, and remarked in British-accented English, "We must be nearing Jerusalem."

"Yes, how did you know?" I asked, surprised.

"I have agricultural land in the Jordan valley. The color of the earth changes in the central region, in the area between Amman and Jerusalem."

Indeed, the two sides of the Jordan River were once joined in one land mass. Millions of years ago, the earth's tectonic plates had shifted, and the crevasse that opened between them, stretching from Syria to Africa, became the route of the Jordan River and the lowest spot on earth.

Once again, I realized how close we are to one another, and how artificial the boundaries. Just hours before, waiting in the rain, Ruth Dayan had told us of traveling the region with her father before the founding of Israel in 1948, when the borders were open and trains ran freely from Damascus to Haifa to Cairo, on rail lines built to serve first the Ottoman, then the British, empire.

After a two-hour drive, we pulled up to the Hyatt Hotel in Jerusalem to find Haim, our public-relations man, arguing heatedly on the phone with the chief of police for the Jerusalem district: "What do you mean it is illegal to display the Palestinian flag in Jerusalem? Israel already signed a peace agreement with the PLO last year! . . . The agreement doesn't allow Palestinian Authority presence in Jerusalem? Do you know what I had to go to, to get this flag in the first place; you can't find them in this country! . . . No, we can't display the Egyptian, the Jordanian and the Israeli flag and just forget the Palestinian flag . . . Yes . . . yes . . . Okay, I can do that. Thank you."

Haim turned to us with a grin. "He said there are no clear regulations about displaying the Palestinian flag in Jerusalem, so the police are not going to confiscate it. But if anybody ever asks us, we never talked to the chief of police."

"Weaving Peace" erupted into a full-blown festival, orchestrated by an ecstatic Lisa Fliegel, who never stopped moving, introducing people, providing materials, arranging interviews. Conference sessions highlighted economic trends in the regional textile industries. During breaks, portly men held smoky conversation about labor rates in Amman and restaurants in Tel Aviv. Hundreds of businesspeople packed into the product exhibition, fingering Jordanian denim jeans, Israeli wool-blend suits sewn in Gaza, and Egyptian cotton fabric.

The conference climaxed in the evening's fashion show. A hush fell over the hall of four hundred people as the lights dimmed. Then rock music blared out, and spotlights played over the crowd, coming to rest on three glamorous, dark-eyed models strutting up the runway in designer dresses fashioned from flowing embroidered Bedouin gowns. Male models stepped out in sleek men's suits, striding and turning in time with the heavy beat. For the finale, the crowd exploded in applause and laughter, as Israeli Minister of Economy and Trade Shimon Sheetrit was invited onstage to shake hands with a fashion model dressed in designer army fatigues and a *keffiyeh* to mimic Yasser Arafat. When the lights went on, I looked around to see a room buzzing with hundreds of Jordanians, Israelis, Egyptians and Palestinians — talking, joking, and drinking together, swept up in the energy generated by the show.

Throughout the evening, Helmi appeared at table after table like the proud father of the bride, injecting a key sentence in Hebrew, joking in Arabic, deflecting a barbed political comment. His ease in this multicultural crowd stemmed from years of gracefully negotiating two or three cultures on a daily basis, from managing bank branches in Jewish Netanya and Arab Kalanswa —and from years of attempting to discern the fate of unseen relatives in Jordan and Syria. It stemmed also from the tutoring of his widowed grandmother, who provided advice to women in surrounding villages, and negotiated with the Israel Lands Authority to maintain family property. "Weaving Peace" created a momentary home for Helmi,

On the runway at the "Weaving Peace" fashion show, 1995.

a safe haven that few could inhabit, at the crossroads of the cultures in which he had schooled himself throughout his life. I felt proud to be his partner in expanding the Center to an international scale.

The following morning, Helmi and I met groggily in the lobby of the Hyatt, waiting for the Jordanians to come down to board the bus for a tour to Israeli textile plants. Taking a long drag on a cigarette, he mused, "I was thinking of what my grandmother used to say: 'It is our fate from God — that we [Arabs] and the Jews be together — alive or dead. We will either live together or die together. And I prefer to live.' Last night, I got the sense that we really may live together — in dignity."

Gratification poked through my exhaustion. We were creating and facilitating not only an event, but a hope. Throughout the day, that nascent hope grew, as Israel's leading textile manufacturers hosted Jordan's business elite, providing technical production overviews and generous meals. At Bagir, an executive spoke with the Jordanian denim manufacturer about options for joint ventures. At Delta Textiles, industrialist Dov Lautman took aside Omar Salah, who, tailored and trim at age 28 and with a face like Michelangelo's David, looked more like one of the models from the fashion show than like an industry tycoon. Salah had just returned from studying and working in the United States, and with his family had founded the Century Investment Group.

We did not realize that Salah had maneuvered his way across the border previously, and had already met with Lautman. Only a year later, when they announced the opening of the first Israeli-Jordanian, jointly owned textile plant in the new industrial zone in Irbid, Jordan, did we realize that we had witnessed the making of a historic deal. Century went on to become one of the largest employers in Jordan, with 6,000 workers and joint venture deals with The Gap, Victoria's Secret and Cannon — and Delta Textiles ultimately closed many of its sewing factories in Arab Israeli towns and moved production facilities to Irbid, where labor costs were cheaper.

"Weaving Peace" brought us inquiries from other industry leaders in Israel, as well. The Center for Jewish-Arab Economic Development was soon asked to bring a Jordanian delegation to join the upcoming Israeli high-tech conference, "The Borderless World," in January 1995. Once again, Mohammed and Ola succeeded in organizing an impressive delegation, this time of young software engineers and information technology entrepreneurs who had studied business and engineering in London, Texas, and California, and worked in Siemens or Sandisk before returning to Jordan to create a new industry. After the conference, they asked to visit the bars and beaches of Tel Aviv. Surprisingly, they had also heard of the recent opening of Jerusalem's Malcha Mall, billed as one of the biggest shopping malls in the Middle East. For me, as well as for them, it was a first visit.

After purchases of frilly lingerie and gaudy jewelry for wives and daughters, we stopped in Café Hillel, where I had a long conversation with Hatem, a member of the business delegation from Jordan who owned an IT firm. Struggling to hear each other over the din of a thousand shoppers, he and I got onto the subject of borders and boundaries. "Today's borders are a colonial fiction," he stated matter-of-factly, taking a sip of espresso. "They were carved out by the British and the French after World War I." Reaching for a paper napkin, Hatem took out a pen and sketched a map of the Middle East, explaining the logic of the current borders, which divided religious and ethnic groups to allow foreign control, and cut oil-rich areas of the Gulf into multiple sovereignties. Suddenly, amid coffee cups and clamor, Saddam Hussein's 1991 claims, as he invaded his neighbor — that Kuwait was really Iraq — took on a different weight.

Over the coming months, the Center organized a "Plasto-Peace" conference for the plastics industry, as well as "A Taste of Peace," a major food-industry conference. Israeli companies eagerly followed up the contacts made through these affairs. After years of maneuvering around the Arab boycott — lifted following the Oslo accords — they felt suddenly free and were excited to forge ahead, spurred by a growing vision of the "New Middle East" and by the whiff of new markets, new capital, and new labor forces, as well as incentives for joint ventures from the European Union and the United States.

Jordanian businesspeople, on the other hand, were more circumspect. They struggled, both internally and in their society, between economic interests and historical pain. A majority of the Jordanian population was Palestinian, families of refugees from the war of 1948, and Palestinians also made up a disproportionately high percentage of the business community. Intense popular opposition accompanied the Jordanian government's signing of the peace agreement with Israel, which was still seen as a country born out of dispossession of the Palestinian people. While we Israelis saw the expanding network of connections as part of the "dividends of peace," most Jordanians saw it as a despised *tatbi-*

yeh, "normalization" of relations with a country that continued to subject Palestinian cousins, brothers and sisters to occupation in the West Bank and Gaza, and discrimination within Israel proper.

In addition, entrenched interests in Jordan as well as in Egypt feared being swamped by Israel's booming economy. While Israel's 5.3 million people were dwarfed by Egypt's galloping population of over 60 million, Israel's economy had grown to roughly the size of Egypt's, each with a GDP of about $100 billion.

When Israeli companies' initial attempts to build on the introductions to the Jordanian companies floundered, they realized they needed help in brokering the connections, and requested that Helmi accompany them to Amman to continue their business explorations. When he entered Jordan, Helmi felt that he was in a place both new and familiar. Although he had never visited the country, he had family there, cousins, aunts and uncles, nephews and nieces, whom he had met over the years in the West Bank. Instinctively, he understood the dual codes of conduct, and was able to traverse the worlds. He could defuse cultural and political landmines — whether it was an Israeli offering a subcontracting arrangement that hurt the pride of an independent Jordanian textile company, or a Jordanian making a misguided comment. The Israeli businesspeople felt that he was Israeli; the Jordanians saw him as Arab. His ease in negotiating the cultures of the Middle East and in helping forge joint business ventures vindicated our original hypothesis about expanding the Center's work to the international arena: that Arab Israelis can catalyze Middle East business.

Helmi's Arab-ness came naturally, from home, but his Israeliness was hard-earned. Over decades at Bank HaPoalim, he had listened keenly to the people around him, inviting colleagues to his home, and initiating personal conversations, especially with his mentor and supervisor, Shraga Litsburg, who was a Holocaust survivor. In those conversations, Helmi recalled, "I saw his sadness and his difficulty in remembering. I learned so much from him — about Jewish culture in Europe, about the Holocaust, about the transport of Jews from all over Europe, about Christian families, who, despite their fear, hid Jews. This gave me hope — that in every difficult situation, it is always possible to find people who are sane, who you can count on, who together with you will work for change, and will not allow every catastrophe to occur.

"We had discussions — how much should we fear that something like that will happen again? Can weapons of mass destruction be used? Is the Dimona nuclear reactor the instrument that will prevent the destruction of the Jews? How can we ensure that the Golem won't rise against its master, that the Jewish people won't turn into a people of destruction? These were emotional, difficult discussions, but we went into them openly.

"These conversations helped me understand the real fears of the Jewish people; and to distinguish them from artificial fears, used for political purposes. With those who really are afraid, you have to sit and understand and convince them that your intention is not the destruction of Jews but the creation of conditions that will not allow such crimes to be committed again — not against the Jewish people, and not against another people, through the Jewish people. These were difficult intellectual conversations, with ordinary people whom I worked with and became friends with."

The opening of borders in the Middle East opened mental borders within Israel, as well. The Israeli Ministry of Tourism joined the Center's initiative to support a growing number of bed-and-breakfast inns, starting in the Arab villages of the Galilee. Jewish families from Tel Aviv began to vacation not only in kibbutz guest houses but in the homes of Arab families in Coucab, in Sakhnin, in Arrabe. Other government ministries began to address long-invisible problems and worked to equalize regulations and budgets so that National Insurance payments, and federal allocations to municipalities, would be provided at similar, sometimes equal, rates to Arab and Jewish citizens.

High-tech entrepreneur Imad Younis once again applied for a research and development grant from the Israeli government. This time he received it. In order to qualify for the maximum grant, however, Alpha Omega needed to be in a Priority Development Zone, as defined by the Ministry of Industry. Despite its high rate of unemployment, Arab Nazareth was not designated as such, so Alpha Omega moved to the Industrial Zone of the neighboring Jewish town, Upper Nazareth, next door to the Business Incubator from which he had been rejected five years earlier, purportedly because he had no Russian immigrants on his team.

I visited Imad in Alpha Omega's new home, which was bright

and spacious and allowed, for the first time, a separate office for the CEO. As he took me around to meet the staff, Imad grinned frequently.

"I want to introduce you to our newest engineers — Vladimir and Alex." As Alpha Omega had grown and sought to hire engineers, it had

Imad Younis, founder of Alpha Omega.

attracted some of the new Russian immigrants who had struggled, often unsuccessfully, to be accepted into Israel's mainstream high-tech firms. Ironically, Alpha Omega had fulfilled exactly the criterion that had resulted in its rejection from the incubator — by becoming perhaps the most ethnically integrated technology business in the Galilee.

On May 4, 1995, I stood once again on the edge of the Syrian-African Rift, overlooking the Sea of Galilee and beyond to the hills of Jordan and Syria. It was Israel's 47th Independence Day, and Liad, Shai and I had come to Kibbutz Kinneret to celebrate with Shuki's sister Yael and her family.

Actually, we had come the day before to commemorate Shuki's first *yortsayt*. Standing among gravestones in the *kibbutz* cemetery, in the heavy Jordan Valley heat, I smelled the dry earth and fertilizer, while time collapsed; I couldn't grasp the concept of a year.

A year: the difference between being alive and dead. The difference between borders being closed and open. Three hundred and sixty-five days of changing diapers. For Liad, the year was a lifetime. Now he was 2, his strawberry blond hair tousled as he toddled around so serious and confused.

Just over a year ago, Shuki had found a baby bird on the sidewalk and brought it home. He'd nursed it with milk and bread, kept it in a box, and taught it how to fly from his finger in the living room. One evening, he'd put the box outside the window, and in the morning, the bird was gone. I always imagined it had flown away.

I missed Shuki so desperately, so helplessly. Nothing I could do would bring him back. He had not lived to see peace with Jordan. He had not lived to realize the promise of a lifelong partnership with the mother of his children.

Now it was time to celebrate, and we milled around with the members of Kibbutz Kinneret on a grassy knoll. Long tables were set with blue-and-white paper cloths and plastic chairs crowded alongside. Colored lights winked on above our heads as the sun set. Before digging into the food, hundreds of children, parents, grandparents fell silent, then stood to sing the national anthem, *"HaTikva,"* "The Hope." Alongside *kibbutzniks* who had fought battles with Jordanian and Syrian soldiers, who had tilled fields under fear of firing from the Golan, I sang "Our hope will not be lost, the hope of two thousand years, to be a free nation in our land, the land of Zion and Jerusalem."

Holding Liad's and Shai's small hands, I let go of the ambivalence I often felt in singing those lines, knowing that our hope was realized at the price of the Palestinians' loss of hope. Now that a new fabric of agreements and relations with Arabs was being woven, Israel was becoming more fully a free nation in our land — free of isolation, free of the threat of war, free of our own occupation of three million Palestinians on the West Bank and Gaza, which sapped our political and moral resources. After years of wandering in a political desert, Israel was moving toward a vision of the Promised Land with which I could identify: a Jewish homeland making peace with its neighbors and reconciling its relations with its own Arab citizens, so that they, too, could be active partners in shaping the nation.

I felt proud to be Israeli. I felt proud to be adding my energy and skills to the huge efforts of our nation's leaders, who were taking significant risks to move our country to peace. Looking down at Shai and Liad, I felt proud to be raising them, albeit alone, in a society that was pursuing a difficult path of justice and hope.

Chapter 11

Assassination

And I will establish my covenant between Me and thee and thy seed after thee in their generations for an everlasting covenant. And I will give to thee, and to thy seed after thee, the land in which thou dost sojourn: all the land of Cana'an, for an everlasting possession.

— Genesis 17:7

The actions that gave me hope for Israel's future were sapping the hopes of other Israelis — those who believed in the biblical promise of *eretz yisrael hashleima*, the Greater Land of Israel.

Their assumption was that Israel's victory in the 1967 war was a sign of Divine intervention, and a partial fulfillment of God's promise to Abraham, as written in the book of Genesis. This promise focused on the heart of the area won by Israel in the 1967 war, named Judea and Samaria in the Bible but known internationally as the Israeli-occupied West Bank. Settling this land was seen to be the fulfillment of Divine commandment, a path toward redemption of the Jewish people, a sacred, historic duty, and the ultimate realization of the Zionist enterprise. Relinquishing this land to Palestinian sovereignty, on the other hand — even in the context of a peace agreement — was considered to be anti-Zionist, traitorous, even blasphemous. Rabbi Avraham Shapira, the venerated head of the religious Zionist Mercaz HaRav Yeshiva, taught that no action of a human, democratically elected government should be allowed to interfere in the unfolding of the Divine will to return the biblically promised Land to its people.

The Rabin government's pursuit of agreed-upon borders for Israel rested not on a biblical mission but on a strategic understanding that the real security risks to Israel arise from powerful surrounding countries such as Iran and Iraq. In order to form regional alliances to meet those risks, it was necessary to resolve the Palestinian-Israeli conflict. That resolution required historic reconciliation: that the Zionist movement make its peace with Palestinian national aspirations and vice versa, and that the two national movements arrange to split sovereignty over the Land — for the good of future generations of Israelis. So the Israeli government was systematically abandoning the settlement movement and the dream of the Greater Land of Israel.

The settlers did not take this threat lightly.

The only settler I saw regularly, my bank teller, Shmulik, was a rotund, balding immigrant from South Africa. Every time I came to make a transaction, he told me about the Palestinians from the neighboring village, Mashha, whom he had brought to work that morning. "We have good relations with our neighbors," he assured me, his one wisp of hair waving emphatically. "They are *miskainim* (unfortunates); they have no transportation, no jobs nearby. I always pick up a few of the men waiting on the road, and bring them to Tel Aviv where they can find work."

"Aren't you nervous that one would be a suicide bomber?"

"No," Shmulik smiled, passing me a bank form. "I've known them all for years. Some of them built my house in Sha'are Tikva."

"What would you do if Sha'are Tikva were slated to be turned over to the Palestinian Authority?" I asked, signing the form.

"Oh, it won't come to that," Shmulik replied.

How could he be so confident? I wondered, hoping and believing that he would be proven wrong.

As I traveled around the country in fall 1995, I began to see posters on billboards depicting Yitzhak Rabin in a Palestinian *keffiyeh*. I understood the feeling behind the photomontage, but found it offensive, a humiliating distortion of the man and his motivations. Rabin, a military hero, saw peace with the Palestinians and Syrians as a strategic asset for Israel. As chief of staff during the Six-Day War in 1967, Rabin had led the Israel Defense Forces (IDF) to their astounding victory over the armies of Egypt, Syria and Jordan, gaining the very territory that he was now using as a bargaining chip for peace. As minister of defense when the *intifada* broke out in 1988, Yitzhak Rabin had publicly ordered soldiers to break the arms and legs of Palestinian rock-throwers. A man who had dedicated his life to defending the State of Israel could hardly be seen as a weak-kneed quisling of the Palestinians, and certainly not as a traitor.

When walking in Jerusalem with my friend and first roommate in Israel, Orly, in late September, I saw a poster of Rabin dressed in a Nazi SS uniform and felt enraged. Orly, a "salt-of-the-earth" *sabra* who had voted against Rabin in 1992, felt trapped between extremes. "Rabin's idea — giving land to that terrorist Arafat — scares me, Sarale. They will be right next to us then; and who can count on them? But what *chutzpah* to show the prime ninister as a Nazi! Those settlers are fanatics."

Despite the increasingly violent opposition, both Israeli and Palestinian, Prime Minister Yitzhak Rabin and Palestinian President Yasser Arafat signed the Oslo II agreement in Washington on September 28, 1995. In contrast to the Oslo I framework agreement, ratified by an optimistic and overwhelming Knesset majority two years before, Oslo II was received with trepidation. It committed Israel to painful withdrawals from West Bank territories occupied for almost thirty years. Israeli troops and civil administration were to be redeployed out of seven Palestinian cities, and the Palestinian Authority would take on their management and policing. Israel would be leaving part of the Land.

On October 5, the night of the Knesset ratification debate, I watched the broadcast of an opposition rally in Jerusalem's Zion Square. Likud leaders Ariel Sharon and Bibi Netanyahu overlooked the crowd from the wrought-iron balcony of the Ron Hotel, waving to the angry thousands gathering under the banner, "Rabin — Arafat's dog." Watching Netanyahu relishing the invectives of "Nazis, Collaborators, Judenrat" shouted against Rabin and his cabinet, I felt my stomach knotting.

Inside the Knesset, Oslo II squeaked by with a one-vote majority. Only the support of Israeli Arab parties saved the government from parliamentary defeat.

Where were the voices in favor of the peace process? Where was my own voice?

When I heard that Rabin's old army buddy, "Chich" Lahat —

former Tel Aviv mayor and Likud member — would take the lead in organizing a mass demonstration in support of government policy and against the growing violent atmosphere, I was relieved. In a bold gamble, the organizers chose as the venue Tel Aviv's Malchei Israel Square, site of Israel's largest civil demonstration to date, 400,000 in protest Israel's of collusion with the Lebanese Christian militias in the Sabra and Shatilla massacre. In this place, a showing of less than 100,000 would signal that the current government and the peace process were trapped in a dangerous tailspin of declining support. Yet how many people would come out of their homes, not in protest but in favor of the government's controversial policy of withdrawing from territory?

It was dark and chilly outside as I prepared to take 4-year-old Shai and 3-year-old Liad to the peace rally on November 4, 1995. I didn't know quite how to dress the kids in this twilight weather, whether to take their winter jackets or not. If I took them, Liad would inevitably refuse to wear his; but, if I didn't take it, he would surely want it. I grabbed Shai's blue parka and Liad's green fleece, and stuffed them into my backpack, along with a bottle of water and some snacks to be doled out when the kids got bored.

It was 7:30, and we were already late; I had arranged to meet my friend, Michael, and his kids Maya and Daniel, at the corner of Frishman and Ibn Gvirol Streets, at the edge of Malkhei Israel Square. Over the last several months, I had been seeing Michael, a recent widower. He was a wonderful father, whose warmth extended to Liad and Shai. Our growing friendship helped us both in reconstructing our lives in the wreckage after death.

Warnings of a possible terror attack, and of violent counterdemonstrations by Israeli rightwing opposition, had circulated over the last days, and I hesitated at our apartment door, wondering, once again: Should I be taking the kids at all? Michael's presence at the rally was reassuring, but I desperately wished Shuki were here so that we could deal with this dilemma together. To Shai and Liad, this was simply one more activity, a chance to see their friends, like the bicycle parade for bike paths for Tel Aviv. But the simple idea of keeping them close in a crowd of thousands was frightening. What would they *do* at the demonstration, anyway? It was already their bedtime. They were bound to be tired and whiny.

I recalled walking through the streets of downtown Pittsburgh with my mother and father and Seth in a river of thousands of demonstrators in 1968, in mourning and protest of the murder of Martin Luther King, Jr. It had been a beautiful spring day, and I had felt important and grown-up, joining my parents in a show of solidarity with the black community and saying with my 12-year-old body, *We are with you.* I, too, was sad at the death of this wonderful leader, who had galvanized millions to fight discrimination, to cling to a dream. I felt proud that Mom and Dad had brought me; I was a part of their adult lives and beliefs.

Then, as now, the fear of retribution had added a touch of bravery to the march. Then, as now, thousands of citizens had come out to express solidarity in the face of violence, turning the usually busy streets into a platform for public expression. I remembered standing at Point State Park, at the confluence of the Allegheny and Monongahela Rivers, at the concluding rally. We felt warm, despite the chilly air. Tens of thousands of us, black and white, had sung "We Shall Overcome," led by a stately black woman on a far-away stage. Her gospel voice soared over the crowd as we all sang fervently: "Deep in my heart, I do believe that we shall overcome someday!"

Damn it, I cannot not *bring my kids to this rally,* I thought, calling the boys and scooping up my fat JanSport pack.

As we walked down Remez Street toward the Square, I could feel the excitement of the gathering crowd, individuals flowing out of their homes and private lives into the tributaries of a great communal effort. Nearing the Square, we heard strands of popular Israeli music drifting out from powerful amplifiers, and we passed, single-file, through police barricades, set up to monitor everyone who arrived. Liad, his strawberry blond hair shining under the street lights, got tired of walking, so I shifted my pack to my shoulder and hoisted him onto my back. Shai, small and resolute, as usual, walked quietly beside me, his warm palm damp in my cold hand.

Amid the sea of jeans, sneakers, and parkas that closed in tighter and tighter around us as we reached Ibn Gvirol Street, Shai looked up and pointed. An enormous, blue and yellow hot-air balloon floated, tethered, over the Square, proclaiming "Yes to Peace; No to Violence." The recorded voices of popular Israeli singers Ehud Manor and Chava Alberstein lent a festive air to the gathering, and the warm smell of roasted nuts and coffee drifted from all-night stores and cafes. As we crossed the street and entered the Square, the warmth of thousands of bodies took the edge off the night chill, and I smelled the clean scent of aftershave and shampoo. It was, after all, Tel Aviv on a Saturday night, and all the demonstrators knew they would bump into friends and colleagues in this giant social event.

Heading to our meeting place at the southeast corner of the Square, I spotted Michael with his kids, Maya and Daniel, pressed close to him. We decided to stay on the edge of the crowd, far from the podium, which was set atop a flight of stairs leading to City Hall, an oblong eight-story Soviet-style building. As we waited for the rally to begin, I kept Maya and Daniel with me, while Michael ducked into the yellow Magen David bloodmobile, stationed on the sidewalk, to donate blood.

The rally was not only a peace demonstration, but a bonanza for a range of good causes — the blood drive, an animal rights petition, recruitment for Green Action protests against new highway construction, and more. Young communists in red shirts stenciled with Che Guevara's image circulated through the crowd, passing out newsletters documenting the latest conspiracies of capitalism and government. Surveillance helicopters buzzed overhead; police snipers stood on the rooftops surrounding the Square; armed police with night sticks patrolled the perimeter and mingled with the crowd, a presence was both reassuring and unsettling.

As people flowed into the Square, our sense of victory swelled. Over the last months, the streets had belonged to the opponents of the Oslo process. Now, surrounded by hundreds of thousands of Israelis who believed that our future was being built through negotiations with the Palestinians, I was excited. Each of us standing on the Square, stamping our feet to keep the blood circulating, provided a vital lifeline to a government perched on a rickety Knesset coalition.

Finally, the MC took the microphone, and the music gave way to speeches. My back ached from Liad's weight. I wanted to stay to hear Rabin speak, but was haunted by the thought that the most vulnerable moment for a terror attack would be the disarray of the rally's break-up. Shai, rubbing his eyes, pulled on my hand. "Mommy, I want to go home."

As Prime Minister Rabin stepped up to the podium, we said goodbye to Michael and his family and started making our way out of the Square, listening as we walked.

"Permit me to say that I am deeply moved," boomed Rabin's deep, slow voice over the loudspeaker system. "I wish to thank each and every one of you who have come here today to take a stand against violence and for peace. This government, which I am privileged to head, together with my friend Shimon Peres, decided to give peace a chance — a peace that will solve most of Israel's problems."

Great applause and whistling erupted.

"I was a military man for twenty-seven years. I fought as long as there was no chance for peace. I believe that there is now a chance for peace, a great chance. We must take advantage of it for the sake of those standing here, and for those who are not here — and they are many."

Shai, Liad (still on my back) and I wove in and out along the edge of the cheering crowd. My shoulders were cramped and I wished once again for Shuki's help, for his presence at this moment. He was not much of a demonstrator; would he have come? Would he have taken the kids home with him long ago, so I could have stayed until the end of the rally?

"I have always believed that the majority of the people want peace and are ready to take risks for peace. In coming here today, you demonstrate, together with many others who did not come, that the people truly desire peace and oppose violence."

As we reached the corner of King David Street, at the edge of the Square, past the parking lot underneath the steps on which Rabin spoke, we heard his final words echoing from the surrounding buildings: "There are enemies of peace who are trying to hurt us, in order to torpedo the peace process. I want to say bluntly, that we have found a partner for peace among the Palestinians as well: The PLO, which was an enemy, and has ceased to engage in terrorism. Without partners for peace, there can be no peace."

Rabin was nothing if not blunt. His words punctured one of the great myths of the Israeli narrative, that there is no partner for peace. Perhaps that was why Rabin was so hated by the settlers and by the right. He did not duplicitously tell them that he was with them, but confronted them, and told them that their path was an obstacle to peace.

As we passed back through the place where the police barrier had been, we heard the familiar strands of the peace song, "Shir HaShalom," once banned from Israel's Army radio channel, now drifting over the houses: "Let the sun rise/ and the morning bring forth its light . . . Don't say that a day will come/ Bring forth that day/ And in all the city squares/ Shout only peace."

Once out of the crowd, walking the ten minutes home to our apartment, I felt triumphant. Our government was on a healthy track, for which hundreds of thousands of citizens had shown support tonight. It was a track that would help ensure my children's future in this country. By taking part in this rally, Shai and Liad had "voted" for their own future, even if they didn't realize it.

I put the kids to bed, and was just sitting down with a cup of tea, when I became vaguely aware of helicopters buzzing outside our window — odd, since the demonstration had ended some time before. We lived down the street from Ichilov Hospital; perhaps someone had been airlifted in.

The phone rang. It was my brother, Seth, calling from Philadelphia. "Did you hear? Rabin was shot!"

"How could that be?" I was incredulous. "The kids and I just saw him at the demonstration; we heard him speak a few minutes ago."

I snapped on the television to see scenes of the event I had just left. It might as well have been a different place. People were running, sobbing, standing in shocked groups. Over and over, grainy footage showed a scuffle, and Rabin being pushed into his car by his secret service guards. Interlaced with these home video clips, hospital spokesmen conveyed terse reports.

The camera switched to Eytan Haber, Rabin's close aide, who read out, in a flat voice, "The government of Israel announces with astonishment and deep sorrow the death of Prime Minister Yitzhak Rabin, who was murdered by an assassin tonight in Tel Aviv."

I felt empty, numb. This was inconceivable; I had just seen Rabin. He was vibrantly alive, his path vindicated by hundreds of thousands of supporters. Who had killed him? How? What would happen now?

Without thinking, I picked up the phone and dialed the mobile number of Saeb Bamya, Deputy minister for economic cooperation of the Palestinian Authority. Saeb was the Palestinian official who, from the beginning, had been unafraid of the tag of "collaboration" and had encouraged me in building Palestinian-Israeli economic links. Without his backing, these efforts would have withered. As much as anyone, Saeb was my partner.

I reached him in Ramallah. "Saeb," I said. "Did you hear? Rabin was assassinated!"

"Yes, Sarah, I heard." I could hear him inhaling on a cigarette.

Immediately, I felt foolish; of course he knew. He had probably known before me. I realized that I had no idea why I was calling.

"What will happen now?" I asked lamely. "Can we go on meeting?"

"We must go on meeting; there is no other way." As usual, Saeb spoke in clear declaratives. It was comforting to hear his voice, to be told what to do. Perhaps that was why I had called — or to prove to myself that I was not subject to the havoc of an assassin's bullet, that I could maintain human contact across the divide that threatened to remain unbridgeable.

I tiptoed in to the room where Shai and Liad slept, snuggling together like puppies on mattresses on the floor. An hour earlier I had been optimistic about their future in Israel and confident that we were walking a bridge of promise and hope over a deep ravine. Where would our bridge lead now? I imagined my sons as young men in green IDF uniforms, grabbing their duffle-bags, saying goodbye before leaving to fight on the front . . .

Back in the livingroom, I slumped into the old brown armchair. My tea was cold; the TV was on, recycling images: Rabin speaking, the packed Square, Rabin being pushed into his car, Haber announcing his murder, people gathering on the Square with candles in their hands. Finally, I mustered the energy to turn off the TV and stumble into bed, into dreams of bridges collapsing and children falling, and small bands of people scrambling along a ravine, grasping at roots, descending to ford a swollen, rushing river by foot.

I wonder what this day will look like years from now, I wrote in my journal the next day. Was it the turning point toward peace?

The beginning of civil war? Looking back, I think it was both. Rabin's assassination by a national-religious Jew exposed a deepening chasm in Israeli Jewish society between civil and religious authority, between those who believe that ending the occupation and dividing the Land is Israel's vital interest, and those who believe that giving up the Land promised by God is anathema.

We will not reach peace in Israel without determining a winner in this clash of worldviews.

Chapter 12
Wandering

Uri Pinkerfeld, one of the founding members of the Center for Jewish-Arab Economic Development, stomped into the office, holding a thick report alive with maps and pictures: the government's new development plan for the Negev. "It calls for major government funding to bring more Jews to settle the Negev, to improve the demographic balance," he said. "That's fine. Let's develop the Negev; let's bring Jews from the center of the country to the periphery."

As usual, Uri, with his full head of white hair, was wearing simple leather sandals, the kind known as *tanakhi,* biblical. He waved the report with a strong hand, his booming voice belying his sixty-nine years. "But what about the Bedouin? Not one *grush* is invested in a hundred thousand people who already live here!"

Israel's founding father, David Ben Gurion, had envisioned the Negev as the country's last frontier and had moved there to Kibbutz Sde Boker in the final years of his life. He dreamed of the Negev as a thriving area that would draw in the most creative and dynamic of Israel's Jewish youth. In 1996, however, the Zionist dream had yet to be fully realized in the Negev. Less than 10 percent of Israel's population lived in this semi-arid desert that comprises over half of the country's land mass. And of the 432,000 residents of the Negev, about one out of every four was a Bedouin Arab citizen.

Uri, who had known Ben Gurion, represented the Kibbutz Artzi movement on the public board of governors of the Israel

Kibbutz Artzi's Uri Pinkerfeld, a founding member of the Center for Jewish-Arab Economic Development.

Lands Administration (ILA). With both an intimate and encyclopedic knowledge of the geography of Israel, he was perfect for the job. The quintessential *sabra*, Uri has hiked over and through virtually every hill and *wadi* of Israel. As a farmer, he partnered with the land, removing rocks, coaxing it, fertilizing it. As general secretary of Kibbutz Artzi, he helped resolve land disputes between the movement and the government and between *kibbutzim* and neighboring Arab villages. As an autodidact in a range of subjects — from Ottoman, British and Israeli property law to urban planning to turkey breeding — Uri had delved into hundreds of contracts and historical documents and development plans relating to the operations of the ILA and gained an unrivaled knowledge of the use and management of the lands of the state.

The official manager of public lands, which constitute over 90 percent of Israel's territory, the ILA is involved in all Israel's development plans. Most ILA lands were acquired in the early years of the state, expropriated from Arabs as absentee lands, or nationalized in a process of registering unsurveyed or unworked (though possibly claimed) *"mawat,"* "dead" lands like those in the desert.

Over the years, Uri has helped hundreds of individuals and *kibbutzim* solve problems with the ILA. He has made it a point to assist Arab citizens in their struggles with the ILA because "it's only fair," he said. "They live here, they are citizens, and they too need land."

Now Uri invited us to come down to the desert "to meet some people."

As Israel's political situation changed following Rabin's murder, and avenue after avenue of the Center's activity were blocked, we decided to make the Negev our priority. In January 1996, with his coalition government tottering, Prime Minister Shimon Peres called for early elections. He was seeking a public mandate to continue the Oslo process. As election day drew near, Hamas launched a deadly series of bus bombings in the now-familiar cycle of peace talks-terror attacks-retaliation.

On March 4, Ronit, secretary at the Center, received a call, and her face went white. On the other end of the line, her sister was sobbing uncontrollably. She had been on a bus passing Dizengoff Center when a bomb had exploded outside, rocking the bus and shattering glass. Blood, bodies, and body parts were strewn across the street.

Ronit raced to the hospital.

The relentless tide of suicide attacks day after day in Israel's major cities demoralized the public. Fighting heated up in southern Lebanon as well, and Katyusha rockets fell on northern Israel. Were these the fruits of peace?

In May, Likud leader Bibi Netanyahu, who opposed the Oslo accords and had fanned hatred against Rabin, was elected as prime minister. Hope drained from our Center's efforts at cross-border cooperation. Helmi continued travelling to Jordan, but more and more businesspeople confided that they had to be careful not to be seen as advancing *tatbiye*, the derogatory term for the normalization of socio-economic relations in the absence of political progress. We continued training entrepreneurs in Ramallah and Jenin and Gaza, but the Jerusalem headquarters of our Palestinian counterparts, the Palestinian Association for Vocational Training (PAVT), were closed by Israeli authorities in the autumn, and the organization was banned from Jerusalem as a Palestinian institution now deemed illegal in annexed East Jerusalem.

The Negev is not the Lawrence-of-Arabia type desert. It is more like rolling hills of rock that have broken into hard dry earth. As we drove over a rise in Uri's old car, we saw a small herd of camels loping along the hillside, some grazing on the green shoots that had sprouted after the rains. On our right, we passed Rahat, the Negev's only Bedouin city. I quickly counted three minarets poking above grey rows of squat cement homes that housed 23,000 people.

Turning east before Beersheva, we began to see corrugated tin shacks and black goat hair tents dotting the desert bleakness. Jazi Abu Kaf was waiting for us where a dry wadi crossed the road. He got into Uri's car, and began narrating the desert. "These belong to the A-Turi clan," he indicated a random group of shacks on the right. "And this," pointing left, "is our village, Umm Batin."

I peered across the desert, looking for the homes, roads, or schools that would signal a village, even a poor one like Rahat. All I saw was a jumble of tents and shacks with laundry airing in front. A voluminous woman in a shapeless, embroidered, full-length dress was squatting by a fire.

Jazi's hand, as he pointed, was dark, broad, and cracked, a working hand. I thought of my Grandpa Harry, whose hands, even after he had become a lawyer, never lost the power and volume they had gained over years of cutting patterns out of multiple layers of cloth as he worked his way through school.

Jazi, bare-headed, his close-cropped dark hair just beginning to recede, was a high school science teacher in Rahat. The collar of his button down shirt was turned neatly over a dark sweater. Over it he wore an old dark-green quilted polyester jacket that looked like an army *dubon*. Maybe it was; many Bedouin serve in the army.

"Turn here," Jazi directed Uri. I looked for a road and saw none. We bumped off into the desert on path that only a Bedouin tracker could follow, and stopped outside a tent. A square, mustached man, dressed in a flowing white *keffiyeh* and a rumpled suit, limped out to greet us, leaning heavily on a wooden cane.

"Ahalan wasahalan." Abed motioned us into the tent. I ducked to enter the tent and almost banged my head on a stone lintel facing me in the dark. I quickly ducked again. When we were seated on mats on a tiled floor, Abed explained with a grin: "First I put up the tent, then I built the house under it. If I had built the house openly, it would have been torn down by the Green Patrol. My father and grandfather and great grandfather lived on this land, but we are not 'allowed' to be here. The state forbids the electric company and the water company to hook up our houses to the national grids. Only homes with building permits can be hooked up. But because there's no municipality and no town plan, none of us can get a building permit."

Abed's wife appeared at the door in an intricately embroidered Bedouin dress that brushed the floor. Her hair was covered with a white scarf. Abed limped over to retrieve the tray from her; Jazi helped to pass out glasses of tea, heavily sugared and spiced with cinnamon and desert plants, some still floating in the cups.

Abed sat down heavily. "The Ministry of Agriculture is responsible for us, as if we were herds. But the only 'service' it provides is the demolition of 'illegal structures.' In the meantime, they are leaving the tents alone."

Abed followed my glance up to the bare bulb shining from the ceiling. "We all have generators," he explained. "And the water company provides a central water pipe to each village. Each group of families get together and run pirate lines to their homes. One person pays, and we all work out the bill at the end of the month." Abed laughed. "At least we don't pay city taxes."

Wandering, hunting, herding nomadic-type people — whether aborigines in Australia, the Cherokee Nation in the United States, or Bedouin in Israel — are problematic for a modern state. They take up a lot of space; they don't follow Western rules of land ownership; they don't want to settle down.

Before 1948, about 60,000 to 90,000 Bedouin lived in the Negev, leading a semi-nomadic lifestyle of farming and herding. When the War of Independence ended, only 11,000 remained within the borders of the state. Bedouin leaders made an early pact with the new Israeli government: The men would volunteer to serve in Israel's army, mostly as trackers. Despite this understanding, the Bedouin, like other Arabs who suddenly became Israeli citizens, were placed under military administration from 1948 to 1966. In those years, the Bedouin were moved from an area of about 6,000 square kilometers throughout the northern Negev and concentrated in the area of the *siyag* (fence), a 1,000-square-kilometer stretch of land in the least fertile part of the eastern Negev. Like other Arab citizens, they were prohibited from traveling from place to place without permission from the Israeli military governor, and so lost access to their lands outside the *siyag*.

In the 1950s, they lost ownership of their lands altogether, both within the *siyag* and beyond, as a series of laws allowed the state to nationalize over 90 percent of Negev lands. For decades, however, Bedouin families have continued to press their ownership claims, using Ottoman documents. Although an ongoing framework, the Administration for the Advancement of the Bedouin in the Negev, was established to adjudicate or mediate those claims, few have been settled, leaving much of the land of the northern Negev in dispute.

Over the next twenty years, the Bedouin in the *siyag* were neglected. The government built development towns throughout the northern Negev — including Sderot, Dimona, and Yeroham — as well as *moshavim*, semi-collective villages, to bring Jewish population to the Negev and to settle immigrants, mostly *Mizrakhim*, Jewish immigrants from Arab countries, on lands from which the Bedouin were uprooted. In 1965, the area of the *siyag* was deemed to be agricultural, making the construction of cement or stone houses illegal. The Bedouin could only live in tents and shacks.

In the mid-1960s, the government began building towns for the Bedouin, further concentrating them on more limited areas of land. Those who moved into the towns were given modest monetary compensation, in return for relinquishing any possible land claims, and received a plot of land, electricity, running water, schools, and clinics in Tel Sheva and Rahat. In the 1980s, following the peace agreement with Egypt, when the Israeli air force sought land to relocate training bases from the Sinai, five more towns were built in another push to settle the Bedouin and free up additional Negev land. Those who did not move into the towns — about half of the Bedouin population, those with stronger land claims — were deemed "squatters," trespassing on government land, although they had not moved from their own lands. The lack of services, the demolition of homes, the destruction of their crops and herds, became part of a system designed to "encourage" this population of about 65,000 people (in 1996) to leave their lands and move into the towns.

Politics aside, the new towns were unattractive. Those who moved had to give up their traditional ways of life and livelihood, with little in return. The Bedouin were not given the option offered to Jewish immigrants of moving into *moshavim* built in the Negev to enable people to maintain a lifestyle similar to what they had known in their original homes. In contrast to the still-struggling development towns, the Bedouin towns had no industrial areas and no government subsidies to encourage industry to locate there. Former Defense Minister Moshe Arens, who defends the rights of Bedouin soldiers and their families, calls them "urban slums." So perhaps we should not have been surprised when our Center's initial survey of conditions found that per capita income was higher in the unrecognized Bedouin villages than in the government-built towns.

Abed took a brass* finjan *from a bed of coals resting in a metal box on legs against the wall, and poured thick coffee into little cups that had materialized on a tray when I wasn't looking. As we were drinking, I started gathering my things, taking the serving of coffee as a sign that we were about to leave.

"What we need," said Abed, gazing directly at Uri, then at me, "is a town plan."

Uri had recently taken Helmi to a gathering of over a hundred sheikhs from the unrecognized villages, at which they had decided to organize into an NGO that would call itself, and begin to function like, a regional council, the municipal unit that Israel recognized as governing groups of *kibbutzim* or *moshavim*.

"We need to bring in planners, survey the villages, talk to the people, draw maps, and make a town plan," added Jazi. "If the government won't plan for our towns, we will do it and give it to the government. But we don't have the money, and we don't have the planners."

Uri and I glanced at each other. "We can help with that," I said.

When we ducked back outside, the setting sun was softening the hills and spreading a wave of orange across the vast sky. I thought of hiking with a Bedouin man I had met, Jadua, who had adopted and provided for his brother's family after his brother was killed in the line of duty as an army tracker. Emily Silverman, a fellow graduate of Interns for Peace, had first met Jadua while volunteering for a Bedouin rights organization. Her job had been to find girls who were not in school and encourage their families to let them enroll. Education is the one service (other than demolitions) that the Israeli state actually provides to unrecognized villages, which the government calls *hapzurah*, the dispersion, as if they were seeds carelessly scattered across the desert. The schools *are* dispersed through the desert, however, and in order to reach them, girls have to walk miles escorted by their brothers through the lands of other clans to reach bus stop from which they can ride to the often-unheated mobile homes serving as schools. In order to find these scattered girls and talk to them, Emily needed a Bedouin guide — and Jadua, who could not have gone alone to speak to girls, volunteered.

I imagined, now, meeting Jadua with friends at sundown by some telltale rock, baking pita on a piece of metal over a campfire, hearing stories about Joha (the Arab equivalent of Chelm stories), sleeping under the stars, and setting out across the desert at dawn, stopping every now and then to examine near-invisible animal tracks, which Jadua seemed able to identify as made by a male or female hyena. I wondered where in these rocky hills he lived. For years, he had struggled to get the IDF to pay full compensation to his brother's widow and children, who lived in a tent in an unrecognized village in the desert. Finally, he had succeeded, only to see the family forced to relocate.

The Center gathered a group of planning professionals, includ-ing a partner Israeli organization, Bimkom (literally, "in place"), to begin developing a comprehensive municipal framework for the unrecognized villages without forcing the residents to abandon their lands.

Helmi Kittani and Sarah hosted in a Bedouin home
in an unrecognized village in the Negev.

We made a strategic decision to divorce our work from the dispute over land claims. Whether the Bedouin owned the land or the ILA owned the land or they agree to divide ownership, the people living on it were entitled to decent, modern municipal services. Arab planners from northern Israel, as well as Jewish professionals, surveyed the population of the unrecognized villages and began asking people about the towns they envisioned for their children. The model that emerged closely resembled an Israeli *moshav*, a village in which each family owns a home and an agricultural plot, but public spaces as well as certain assets are owned communally, and municipal services are provided for the community as a whole.

The Center's report and proposal galvanized new thinking about how to resolve the issue of the unrecognized villages. It identified forty-five of them, some of which could be recognized individually while smaller ones could be organized into a joint council. We worked with Sheikh al-Hawashla, leader of the largest village, Qasr al-Ser, to start a self-taxed refuse collection service. It was the first municipal service provided under the umbrella of the non-profit Regional Council of Unrecognized Bedouin Villages.

In the years since the Center took on the issue, many Israeli organizations have become involved with Bedouin Rights, including the Coexistence Forum for Negev Equality, the Association for Civil Rights in Israel, and Physicians for Human Rights. In 2003, seven villages were recognized by the government under a new municipal framework called the Abu Basma Regional Council, albeit on a smaller area than the land that was claimed by the residents and with pitifully small development budgets. In 2008, a government commission headed by retired Supreme Court Judge Eliezer Goldberg recommended recognizing most of the still-unrecognized villages, allowing most of the homes to go through a legalization process, and establishing a committee to hear and settle traditional land claims. The commission viewed the issue fundamentally as a conflict between the state and its citizens, not as a nationalist conflict.

Yet the commission's recommendations have still not been implemented. Most of the Bedouin villages remain unrecognized, as do most of the Bedouin's land claims. In 2010, the village of Al Araqib was destroyed scores of times, and the residents, with their ownership claims stuck in Israeli courts, continued to rebuild the shacks that had been demolished on their traditional lands.

The landscape of the desert is stark. In the dry *wadis* and hills of the Negev, the Zionist dream of claiming the Land of Israel for Jews confronts the demands of a democratic society to provide for all its citizens.

Chapter 13
Rules of Engagement

We have described a dynamic web of relations between Jews and Arabs in encounter. The typical pattern can be simplified into five stages. In the initial
stage, the atmosphere is cordial and relaxed . . . In the second stage, the Arab
group begins to feel stronger and act accordingly; this change causes the Jewish group to feel threatened and anxious.

—Rabah Halabi*

Helmi paced the office of the Center for Jewish-Arab Economic
Development, smoking cigarette after cigarette. It was the summer of 1999, and he had been offered the position of Israel's trade
representative to Jordan. It would allow Helmi to use the Ministry
of Industry and Trade to return to the work we had begun pursuing at the Center just a few years before, forging economic ties
between Arab and Jewish Israelis and Jordanian businesspeople.
For Israel, and for the ideas we promoted, I hoped that he would
take the job. Selfishly, however, I didn't want him to leave.

After much consideration, Helmi declined the offer, telling
me, "I couldn't join the diplomatic corps and represent Israel
abroad. Not so much because of Israel's policies, but because of
the need to identify with a Jewish state. If Israel became a state of
all its citizens, I could represent it."

---

* Rabah Halabi, editor, *Israeli and Palestinian Identities in Dialogue: The School for
Peace Approach.* Rutgers University Press, 2004

A "state of all its citizens": Several months earlier, in February, an Israeli philosophy professor and Knesset member had thrown his hat into the ring in the race for prime minister and was campaigning on just that platform, civil equality for all citizens, hardly a radical concept — until you realize that his name was Azmi Bishara.

Bishara's very candidacy opened the previously unimagined possibility that an Arab Israeli, a Palestinian citizen of Israel, could be prime minister of the country. His platform confronted the contradiction inherent in Israel's self-definition as a "Jewish and democratic" state, and put forth the idea that Israel should not be a "Jewish State" but rather "a state of all its citizens." In so doing, he invoked Israel's own Declaration of Independence, which declared that Israel should ensure complete equality, regardless of religion and race:

> The State of Israel . . . will foster the development of the country for the benefit of all its inhabitants; it will be based on freedom, justice and peace . . . it will ensure complete equality of social and political rights to all its inhabitants irrespective of religion, race or sex; it will guarantee freedom of religion, conscience, language, education and culture . . .

Bishara proposed dismantling the network of laws, institutions and practices that favored Jewish citizens. He called for changing the immigration laws, including the Law of Return, which allow Jews from around the world to become citizens in an automatic process while limiting the immigration of non-Jews. In an extensive interview in *Haaretz* (May 29, 1998), Bishara stated that "Israel has to stop being run as if it is the Zionist movement. It is no longer a movement, but a state claiming to be democratic. This means that the special status of the Jewish Agency and the Jewish National Fund must be repealed, and the Law of Return must be rescinded."

For Arab citizens, Bishara's campaign opened a window to fresh air, as he was expressing to the Jewish public notions of equality that previously had been discussed only in private circles. For the vast majority of Jewish citizens, however, he embodied precisely what they feared — losing, through democracy, the young Jewish state so many people had struggled to create out of the ashes of the Holocaust.

I was conflicted. Logically, I could hardly argue against Bishara's call for Israel to be a state of all its citizens. After all, what is a democracy, if not a state of its citizens? Yet on a gut level, I resonated with the Jewish majority. If Israel became a "state of all its citizens," what would keep it from becoming, ultimately, one more Middle East nation, in which, eventually, Arabs and Jews may reach relatively equal numbers? What would preserve the Jewish character of the country — built to assure the safety of Jews and the flourishing of Jewish culture and learning? Indeed, if this were simply one more democratic state in the world, why should I be here?

I asked Helmi what he thought of Azmi Bishara and his platform. "I know Azmi; he is a sharp philosopher and a good politician," Helmi said, running his hand through his thinning hair. "I, myself, have not voted for his party, Balad. But my son, Ehab, who grew up in the post-1967 reality of double identity, double belonging — as an Israeli and a Palestinian — ran on a Balad ticket in his student council. The night before his closing debate, he showed me his speech. It spoke of Palestinian national aspirations, but not about integration. I asked him if those issues are important to him, and he told me yes. So I told him what I have told myself over the years: If you lose votes because your views are less nationalistic than the other person, you have to live with that. But you don't change your views to win votes."

I smiled; I always appreciate Helmi's integrity. I thought of my father, whose Jewishness was part of his autonomic nervous system, and whose integrity was both a value and a stock in trade.

"And what about Israel as a state of all its citizens?" I asked.

"After a process of historic reconciliation between the two national movements — Palestinian and Jewish — I would see Israel as a state where I can live too, and identify," Helmi replied. "We will need to explore ,then, what is Israeli-ness? Now there is no Israeli-ness, just Jewishness. I, as a Muslim, can never join that. But if Israel became a state of all its citizens, I could represent it. Laws would have to be rewritten, and priorities changed, so that there is no difference between a Muslim, a Christian and a Jew. The symbols of the state, such as the flag and the anthem, would have to be reworked so that I, also, can identify with them."

Israel's Declaration of Independence posits both competing

sets of values: for equality, and for Jewish nationalism:

> the right of the Jewish people to national rebirth in its own country . . . to open the gates of the homeland wide to every Jew and confer upon the Jewish people the status of a fully privileged member of the community of nations . . . to assert their right to a life of dignity, freedom and honest toil in their national homeland . . . This right is the natural right of the Jewish people to be masters of their own fate, like all other nations, in their own sovereign State.

Perhaps contradiction is the essence of this country. Or perhaps the founding values draw an ellipse, with two foci, rather than a circle, with one.

Two days before the election, Azmi Bishara withdrew from the race, essentially throwing his votes to Ehud Barak, who was elected by a strong majority on May 17, 1999.

I wanted to believe that we would be picking up where Yitzhak Rabin had left off, as Barak had intimated in his campaign. I craved a return to a path of reconciliation between the Palestinian and Israeli national movements, and to policies aimed at integrating Israeli Arab citizens as full and legitimate partners in Israeli society. In the weeks following the election, however, Barak, who had won a large majority of the popular vote for prime minister but whose party squeaked by with less than a quarter of the Knesset seats, studiously avoided Arab politicians, in an effort to cobble together a coalition resting on a Jewish majority. The resulting hybrid included the ultra-Orthodox Shas and secular-liberal Meretz, but did not include Arab Israelis as ministers or deputy ministers, nor did it count the Arab parties as a part of the government's voting bloc.

Nonetheless, breezes of change rippled through parts of the government administration. Yossi Beilin, one of the main architects of the Oslo peace process, was appointed minister of justice. Swiftly, he began working with the Center's partners in the Regional Council of the Unrecognized Bedouin Villages of the Negev to devise a plan for meeting the development needs of the residents of the unrecognized villages. Ran Cohen, Meretz's *Mizrakhi* activist, was appointed minister of industry and trade. Even though Helmi had turned down Cohen's job offer, the ministry began working with the Center to promote equal opportunity for Arab citizens in economic development.

We now saw the opportunity to realize an old dream: linking Arab citizens to Israel's high-tech sector. High-tech industries in Israel were booming, spurred by a global bull market, and were driving growth in Israel's economy. They comprised about half of Israel's total exports and employed over 70,000 engineers. Despite the hunger for thousands of new engineers, however, less than three hundred were Arab Israelis. The Center started a new program, MATCH (Matching Arabs To Careers in High-Tech), to get qualified candidates into Israeli information-technology companies. We imagined not only Arab engineers, but also Arab entrepreneurs, in Israeli high-tech. Thousands of dot-com start-ups had been established in recent years, and venture capital raised by Israeli companies had reached $1.85 billion in 1999. Over fifty Israeli companies had made initial public offering on NASDAQ and other international stock markets during this period. None was run by an Arab citizen.

One of the major government programs for encouraging high-tech start-ups was the Incubator Program, which provided a physical space, technical assistance, and seed capital from the government. Within our Center, we debated: Should we encourage Arab entrepreneurs to integrate into existing high-tech industries in the Jewish sector, or should we push for a separate technological incubator in an Arab town? One day, I walked into Helmi's office and sat down with my morning coffee.

"Who said that integration means that Arabs travel to high-tech industries in the Jewish towns of Herzliya or Raanana?" I asked, leaning forward. "Why can't Israeli Jews come to work in high tech ventures in an Arab town?"

The Center soon launched a campaign toward a model of integration, based on economic empowerment. Despite Ran Cohen's interest, however, officials in his ministry balked. There was no justification for a new incubator, they said, and our plan ran afoul of the ministry's recent policy of consolidating the two dozen existing incubators rather than building new ones. We would need to raise $2 million in private capital to match the government's investment. And what evidence did we have that qualified Arab technological entrepreneurs existed? Virtually no Arabs had entered the existing incubators, many of which were located in development towns, close to Arab populations. Ministry officials refused to move forward until Arab entrepreneurs began to enter the existing incubators.

A decade had passed since Imad Younis' rejection from the Upper Nazareth incubator in the late 1980s. Despite Imad's success in building his business and accessing other government benefits, the rejection remained fresh and painful in the collective memory of Arab entrepreneurs. How could the Center overturn that image and show that now the government actually wanted Arabs to apply? And if we succeeded in getting Arab entrepreneurs into existing incubators, would we "exhaust the supply," so that no one would be left for the new incubator? We began to work with the ministry of industry to recruit young entrepreneurs for high tech incubators, with the agreement that, if a new incubator were opened in an Arab town, those we recruited could relocate there.

The ministry hired an Arab engineer to begin recruiting. The Center surveyed the pool of Arab students and graduates of the Technion. The Arab Business Club (ABC), an organization of Israeli Arab business leaders established by our Center, offered highly publicized scholarships for young Arab students interested in going into high-tech fields of study. At the same time, we worked behind the scenes to come to a consensus among the Arab mayors as to where the new incubator would be placed, so as to avoid any attempts to sabotage efforts through internal squabbles.

Within months, scores of Arab entrepreneurs applied to the incubators, and many were accepted. The Arab mayors sent a letter to the minister of industry, declaring their support for an incubator in Nazareth. Every day, the Center received requests for information about the incubators, the scholarships, or just plain job openings in high-tech. All that was needed to allow the opening was $2 million of private capital. Whom could we find to invest in the new incubator, when potential Arab investors understood construction but not software and Jewish venture capitalists were reluctant to take risks in an Arab town?

Relations between Arab citizens and the state were shifting in other spheres, as well. In the mid-1990s, Adel Ka'adan and his family from Baqa el Gharbiye had applied to purchase a plot of land and to build a home in Katzir, a new hilltop community adjacent to their town. Their application was rejected because they were Arabs and Katzir was slated to be a Jewish town. The rejection was nothing unusual; many communities in Israel — *kibbutzim, moshavim*, community settlements — have entrance requirements which filter out the people who are "inappropriate" to the character of the community.

What was unusual was that Adel Ka'adan, a long-time nurse at the nearby Hillel Yaffe Hospital, and an Arab Israeli, took the case to court. As he told me: "I spend my nights and days caring for the sick relatives of these families; why shouldn't I live in the same community?"

After five years, during which the judges tried to get the parties to come to an agreement, avoiding the necessity of a court precedent, the High Court ruled that considerations of equality overrode other national considerations. As such, it was illegal to prevent an Israeli citizen from purchasing or leasing state land — even from the Jewish Agency — because of his ethnic or national background. The court ordered the Jewish Agency to allow the Ka'adans to acquire land in Katzir.

Recalling U.S. court decisions in the 1960s rendering housing discrimination illegal, the decision sounded natural to me. In the Israeli context, however, it was revolutionary. Until then, the government itself, directly or through quasi-governmental institutions like the Jewish Agency, had planned and built hundreds of communities for Israel's Jewish population. I thought back to my first year in Tamra, when I toured the new Jewish communities of Misgav being built above Tamra in the program of Judaizing the Galilee.

But the conflict over Israel's state land is even more complicated than how it is zoned and planned and developed. The roots of the conflict over land lie in the founding period of the state. Following Israel's 1948 Declaration of Independence, and the ensuing war, approximately 700,000 Palestinians fled to neighboring Arab countries. When Israel closed the borders to the re-entry of these Palestinians, they became refugees, leaving behind hundreds of thousands of acres of land in critical areas of the Galilee, the Triangle and the Negev, in the cities of Haifa, Acco, Jaffa, Lod and Ramle.

In 1950, the Knesset enacted the Absentee Property Law, nationalizing these lands left behind by the Palestinian refugees and placing them under the authority of the Custodian for Absentee Property. That law allowed the Custodian to seize, without notification or compensation, the property of Palestinian landowners who fled their lands in 1947-49 to take refuge in the Arab countries around Israel, in the Jordanian-occupied West Bank, or "for a place in Israel which was at that time occupied by forces which sought to prevent the establishment of the State of Israel." There was no provision for restoring these lands if the owners returned. The confiscated lands were then transferred or sold to the Development Authority or the Keren Kayemet L'Israel — the Jewish National Fund (JNF) — for development. On these newly declared state lands, *kibbutzim*, *moshavim*, urban neighborhoods, and new development towns were built to house almost a million new Jewish immigrants, many of them refugees themselves.

To make it more complex, thousands of acres of land were taken not from refugees living outside the borders of Israel but also from Arab Israelis who had remained in the country, albeit in villages to which they had fled in the fighting in 1948. Many of their original villages were destroyed, and their lands were declared closed military zones. Until 1966, Arab Israelis were governed by the Military Administration and were required to receive permits in order to travel outside the towns in which they resided. With their movement restricted, these internal refugees were unable to work their lands — and subsequent laws designated that land that had not been worked for a period of years was also absentee property. Vast tracts were seized, as Arab citizens became "present absentees" and saw their lands transformed into Jewish National Fund forests or agricultural land of *kibbutzim*.

This was the situation of the village of Damoun, whose residents had fled to Tamra. The original village lands had become a JNF forest, in which the children of Tamra held their yearly summer camp, where I had worked as a counselor in 1981.

However, the process of Judaizing the land — whether in the Galilee, the Negev, or the so-called mixed cities of Jaffa and Acco — did not stop with the immediate post-state era, as I knew from the development of Misgav in the 1980s and from the current development plans in the Negev. Katzir, where the Ka'adans sought to live, was part of the Seven Stars plan, advanced by then-Housing Minister Arik Sharon in the early 1990s in order to build a strip of Jewish settlement along Israel's pre-1967 borders, the Green Line, that would separate Israeli Arab towns, such as Umm el Fahm, Taibe and Tira, from Palestinian towns in the West Bank, such as Tulkarem and Kalkilye.

Adel Ka'adan and his family did not fit into this plan, and the High Court's decision to prevent the Jewish Agency from discriminating against them in Katzir sent shock waves through the institutions of Jewish settlement — not only the Jewish Agency, but the JNF and the Israel Lands Authority as well. It shook a key pillar of the settlement enterprise within Israel proper, the assumption that using state land only for was a legitimate state function. The Court, fifty years after Israel had nationalized Palestinian-owned lands, was now allowing Arab Israeli citizens equal access to state land. Although the decision was very narrow and related only to the future, not the past, it raised existential fears among Israeli Jews. The rules of engagement were shifting.

In the Center's search for investment for the high-tech incuba-tor, we inadvertently stepped into another zone of discomfort. As I was meeting with an Israeli émigré and high-tech entrepreneur, Davidi Gilo, in his office in the verdant Silicon Valley, hoping to bring him aboard as an investor, the Israeli-Arab-owned investment company Al Manar appealed to the Israeli High Court in protest of the government's seizure of $1 million of the company's assets, which had gone to what the Treasury claimed was a Hamas front organization, Beit el-Mal.

Over the past months, our Center had been negotiating with Al Manar as a possible partner in the Nazareth incubator. When I heard the news, my stomach knotted. Had we been unwittingly aiding and abetting the businesses surrounding Hamas?

I had known some of the Al Manar investors for years, through a variety of development projects in Israeli Arab towns: a shopping mall, a solar energy venture, an Internet company. I knew them to be observant Muslims in the city of Umm el Fahm, center of the more fundamentalist branch of Israel's Islamic Movement, and home to its charismatic leader, Sheikh Raed Salah. It was hard for me to believe, however, that they would support a Hamas organization. Still, the seizure of funds was a serious step. How could I know what went on behind closed doors?

At the fifth annual rally of the Save the Al Aqsa Committee at the Umm el Fahm football stadium, on September 18, 1999, Sheikh Raed Salah — tall, commanding, dressed in white robes — stood before a crowd of 35,000 Israeli Arab believers and called out, "Al Aqsa is in danger!" In his power, his fervor and his separatism, Sheikh Salah recalled Malcom X, advocating Black Power in the volatile 1960s in America. The crowd thundered its response: "In spirit and blood, we shall redeem Al Aqsa!"

Over the prior two years, the Israeli Islamic Movement had become deeply involved with the Muslim Waqf, which adminis-ters the Haram al Sharif/Temple Mount* in Jerusalem's Old City. Considered supremely holy to both Jews and Muslims, it is one of the most incendiary sites in the Middle East. The Islamic Move-ment had raised funds, within Israel and abroad, under the slo-gan "Al Aqsa is in danger," to finance the renovation of Al Aqsa mosque and the building of additional prayer areas under it. In the process of excavating the new foundations, tons of earth had been bulldozed with blatant disregard to the rich Jewish history buried on the historic Temple Mount, where both the First and Second Temple once stood. Israeli archaeologists launched vehe-ment protests.

In addition, the Movement was active throughout Israel prop-er, rehabilitating mosques and Muslim cemeteries in cities such as Tiberias, Safed, Jaffe and Acco, where Arabs had lived before 1948. In this way, the Islamic movement was re-establishing an Arab presence and the memory of Arab history in areas that had become Jewish. I was struck by the similarity of these efforts to those of Jewish organizations restoring Jewish cemeteries and syn-agogues in Europe. The parallel was disturbing.

In the end, we didn't work with Al Manar to establish the high-tech incubator in Nazareth. Instead, our investors included a num-ber of veteran Arab and Jewish businesspeople with established track records. The group included Davidi Gilo, who had sold his

---

* Al Aqsa ("The Farthest") is the mosque in the Old City of Jerusalem, built on the area known by Jews as the Temple Mount and by Muslims as Haram e-Sharif, "the Noble Sanctuary." It is considered to be the third holiest site in Islam.

Israeli start-up venture to Intel for millions of dollars. The Ministry of Industry kept its promise, and New Generations Technology (NGT) opened in a cavernous building amidst the garages and cement block factories in a workshop area of Nazareth.

NGT was not only another Jewish-Arab joint venture in Israel. It marked a new model of relations. "There are many Israeli initiatives that open factories and do different things with Arabs — but basically the Jews are the employers and the Arabs the employees," remarked Davidi Gilo. "NGT is the only project in Israel that is a pure true partnership between Jewish and Arab businessmen in Israel. We're all board members, and we've all invested the same amount of money."

As with all shifts, political and economic, there were losers and winners. Nothing marked this more than NGT's decision to locate in the factory building vacated by Delta Textiles when it moved its production facilities from Arab Israeli towns to Jordan. The Center's efforts, launched with the Weaving Peace Conference in 1994, had assisted this move, which now left thousands of Arab Israeli women unemployed. At the same time, as Delta's CEO, Dov Lautman, noted, the Arab Israeli economy was moving from underwear to software.

Chapter 14
Business on the Brink

The two parties view the economic domain as one of the cornerstones in their mutual relations with a view to enhance their interest in the achievement of a just, lasting and comprehensive peace.

—The Economic Protocols of the Oslo Agreements, 1994

"**I** haven't been in Gaza City since I did reserve duty in 1988, and chased Palestinian kids throwing rocks at us in the Jabalya Refugee Camp," Julio Bocian said, grinning under a chestnut mustache, his brown eyes crinkled at the corners. "It was the *intifada*; I patrolled the alleys, hoping I wouldn't run into one of our subcontractors. Our family business had a lot of Palestinian subcontractors in Gaza."

It was only 9:00 in the morning on a July day in 1999, but already I was glad to be in an air-conditioned bus speeding down the steamy coastal road from Tel Aviv to Gaza. Helmi and I had convinced the Israeli Manufacturers' Association to bring a group of leading Israeli textile manufacturers to Gaza to meet with Palestinian producers and to celebrate the opening of the first businesses in the Gaza Industrial Estate (GIE). For Julio, owner of EMBI Jeans, this was the first time he would see his own factory in the GIE. For most of us, this was our first visit to Gaza since the Palestinian Authority had taken charge there under the Oslo Agreements in 1994.

It was ironic, but perhaps quite natural, that as Israelis and

Palestinians were working out the business of separating into two states, the patterns of movement and contact were becoming more curtailed and choreographed. I could remember traveling to Gaza on a Saturday in the mid-1980s, with a group of peace activists, to talk with Palestinian activists in Jabalya Refugee Camp. It had been easy: We just got into a couple of cars and drove down, had coffee, spoke with dismay of the never-ending occupation, exchanged phone numbers, and went back home. No checkpoints, no borders, just one country running an enlightened occupation with free movement and open labor markets that drew in a young, cheap workforce eager for jobs in the construction sites and restaurants of a dynamic economy. In those years, Palestinian unemployment dipped to 5 percent, and individual levels of income rose, as up to 150,000 Palestinians worked in Israel, helping to fuel our economy's climb from the Third World into the First.

The Bocian family business had been part of that climb. Julio had been active in the Zionist youth movement in Argentina. When his familiy made *aliyah* in 1971, they had set up a textile company, EMBI Jeans, named after Julio's father, Mendel Bocian (M. B., or Em Bi), who had owned a similar business in Buenos Aires.

At first, EMBI manufactured jeans in a factory in Petah Tikva. With fewer and fewer Israelis were ready to work in sewing shops, EMBI had sought out Palestinian subcontractors in Gaza and the West Bank. Among the company's first workers were two brothers from the Hassouneh family, who traveled an hour and a half each way, from the Tel Sultan Refugee Camp in Gaza to the factory. During the week they would sometimes sleep over in Israel, to avoid the long trip.

The Hassouneh brothers had soon started a sewing shop, managed by Zuhir, the eldest brother, and began sewing for Israeli manufacturers, including EMBI. The Israelis supplied the sewing machines, and the cut material. The Palestinians did the sewing and sent the finished jeans back for washing and marketing in Israel.

"Our contractors had four hundred machines sewing for us. I traveled everywhere to supervise the work," Julio recalled. "There were no checkpoints; it didn't occur to me to be afraid. Sometimes, I stayed overnight in a hotel in Gaza and dropped by to visit Zuhir at home."

When the Oslo process began in 1993, Deputy Prime Minister Shimon Peres envisioned a network of industrial estates on the Palestinian side of the borders between Israel and the Palestinian Authority that would generate jobs for Palestinians while drawing on Israeli investment and marketing. The Gaza Industrial Estate (GIE) was the first of these, enabling businesspeople, both Israeli and Palestinian, to capitalize on these opportunities along the seam.

Hassouneh Bros. and EMBI Jeans decided to upgrade their relationship to a joint venture, to rent space in the Gaza Industrial Estate, and to move all manufacturing operations there. "We thought it would be a good idea," recounts Julio. "Israeli know-how and Palestinian skilled labor. We called it Private Label Company. Fifty percent of the shares were owned by EMBI, and fifty percent by Hassouneh."

We arrived at Erez checkpoint at 10:00 a.m. Already, the hot air clung to us as we waited under a corrugated tin roof for our VIP crossing permits. After an hour, we were ushered past lines of Palestinians waiting to enter Israel.

The 1988 intifada *had disrupted the free flow of Palestinians* working in Israel. Workers couldn't always circumvent curfews and closures, and there grew a Palestinian ideology of boycotting Israeli products and workplaces in order to disengage the two economies, which were locked in an exploitative symbiosis. Three years later, during the first Gulf War, when the Palestinian leadership sided with Saddam Hussein, Israeli authorities had instituted a permit system, limiting the number of Palestinians who could get in to work in Israel. Tens of thousands of permits were given, however, and with only a few checkpoints on main roads separating the territories from Israel proper, thousands more snuck into Israel without permits. Israeli construction and agricultural businesses nevertheless clamored for foreign workers to be allowed into Israel to replace missing Palestinian laborers.

In 1994-5, following a rise in terror attacks, Israel had erected a sixty-kilometer electronic border fence around the perimeter of the Gaza Strip, on the old 1949 armistice line, the Green Line, which meant that Gazans and their products could no longer move freely into Israel, but only through Israeli-regulated checkpoints. Although the flow of Palestinian workers into Israel had been regulated to a drizzle, that still left thousands of Palestinians getting up at 4:00 a.m. to make their way to work in Israel every day.

At the head of one line stood an ample middle-aged woman in a long, shapeless, embroidered Palestinian dress, gripping a heavy sack of clothes. She gestured and implored loudly in Arabic. The young soldier checking her was dressed in green fatigues with a helmet, and towered above her. He held a rifle and spoke with authority, in Hebrew: "You can't just bring clothes into Israel; you must go there to register." He pointed to a small room, waiting for her to obey. Instead, the woman, old enough to be his mother, began begging him again, in fervent Arabic. Suddenly, in the midst of the railings and the metal detectors, the border police and the waiting Palestinians, the woman dropped to her knees and began kissing the soldier's boots. Kicking at her in disgust, he yanked her to her feet.

Feeling powerless, I remembered Shuki's military experience in Bethlehem, his shame at making a Palestinian teacher, as his pupils watched, clear a pile of burned tires from blocking a road. Army regulations required Palestinians — not soldiers — to move such obstacles, lest they be booby-trapped.

Rushing to catch up with our group, I glanced back at the line of waiting Palestinians and realized that this incident, as shocking as it was to me, was just one of a thousand such, each day at the Erez Checkpoint.

On the other side of the checkpoint, we boarded a Palestinian bus waiting at the head of a dusty road leading into the heart of the Gaza Strip. Minutes later, we reached the Gaza Industrial Estate (GIE), which had opened to great fanfare just six months earlier. Abdel Malek Jaber, tall and dapper in suit and tie, representing the Palestinian Industrial Estates and Development Company (PIEDCO), the Palestinian management company, gave us a tour of the 123-acre site.

Pre-fab buildings, with white walls as yet untainted by the desert sand, stood in quiet rows, waiting for the dust paths around them to be paved. The water-pumping station and 2.2-megawatt backup generator, built with millions of dollars from the World Bank, the U.S. government, and Palestinian investors, utilized the latest technology to make the estate virtually self-sufficient for the

154

20,000 people who would be working there. Mute cranes towered over the loading area, poised to grasp their first container, which could be checked and sealed here, then loaded onto truck or ship with no further security arrangements. The planned border regime — allowing Palestinians and Israelis each to enter the area from their respective countries, but not to leave to the other's — would create a lock in the canal between Israel's developed economy and the economy that was developing in Gaza.

We entered one of the white pre-fabs, new home of Balal Textiles. Fayed Balal, a short, energetic man with a large mustache, introduced us to representatives of the Gaza Textile Association. We chatted politely above the buzz of sewing machines operated by rows of Palestinian women, who were bent over, eyes fixed on the material they fed in and stitched. In our delegation of textile manufacturers, I was one of only a handful of women.

Over a year earlier, at a meeting of the Center's Business Forum, Balal had met representatives from the Israeli company, Kitan, well-known manufacturer of sheets and towels. The two firms had entered into negotiations to set up a subcontracting arrangement, which they decided to house in a new manufacturing facility in the Gaza Industrial Estate.

With orange and mango juice (so as not to violate the Muslim prohibition on alcohol), we toasted the opening of the new factory and the subcontracting arrangement. As Balal and the Kitan representatives spoke, the seamstresses paused without rising from their machines. They barely noticed the words of optimism — "economic achievement," "Israeli-Palestinian cooperation" — spoken over their heads. At the end of this festive day, each woman would be taking home a pittance.

These silent women constituted the dowry that Palestinian entrepreneurs brought to the Israeli-Palestinian partnership. They were the raw material for joint economic achievement, and only peripherally its beneficiaries. Although individual standards of living in the West Bank and Gaza had leaped up in the 1970s and '80s, Palestinians' annual per capita gross domestic product (GDP) in 1999 hovered around $1,450. While higher than in neighboring Jordan or Egypt, this represented a GDP less than one-tenth the Israeli level — and women were, for the most part, at the bottom of the ladder. As soon as the speeches stopped, the seamstresses resumed their work, distant from the juice and cookies and invisible to the celebrants.

As we walked out of the factory into the withering heat, a jeepload of Palestinian police armed with submachine guns screeched to a halt beside us. I panicked, recalling an incident a few years ago in which an Israeli lawyer had been killed by extremists while visiting his clients in Gaza. After a moment, however, I realized they had come to accompany us during our trip into Gaza City; the Israeli-Palestinian security arrangements called for Palestinian police protection for Israeli groups visiting Gaza. I hoped there would be no need to test their abilities; the eager 20-year-olds looked more like a Middle East version of the Keystone Cops than like bodyguards I could count on in a crisis.

As we drove past Jabalya Refugee Camp, where I had drunk coffee about fifteen years earlier with Palestinian activists, I saw again the thin alleys that trickled between rows of shacks so close together that one could walk through the camp on the rooftops. Even under Egyptian rule, from 1948 to 1967, Gaza had suffered from poverty and overcrowding. One of the most densely populated areas in the world, Gaza had a birthrate comparable to the most underdeveloped areas of Africa: over forty-one births per 1,000 people. Most Gazans lived in families of six children or more, crowded into cramped houses.

Over the years, no government, neither Israeli nor Arab, had invested in building new homes for Gaza. Now, in the distance, sprouted new high-rise housing, built in the last months with international funds, presumably for residents of the refugee camps. Yet unlike Israel in its formative years, when the Ministry of Housing was building thousands of housing units for new immigrants, the Palestinian Authority suffered from cronyism and corruption. Most of the Palestinian tenants moving into these new homes hailed not from the camps, but from the ranks of the favored Palestinian police and civil service.

If any extremists here were interested, they would have no trouble identifying us as a group of Israeli "VIPs." Our vaguely air-conditioned tour bus commandeered the straight and dusty streets on the way toward Gaza City, led by our Palestinian police escort, sirens wailing. Cab drivers and donkeys, a *keffiyeh*-clad gentleman in a worn suit jacket, a stately woman walking with an

156

enormous bundle of kindling on her head, all made way for the "visiting dignitaries." Even when our purpose was discreet cooperation, we were unable pass through Gaza's hot summer streets without being loud and domineering.

In Gaza City, we toured the sewing shops of some of the Palestinian members of the Forum. In large open spaces, often on the ground floor under the homes of the owners, sat rows of olive-skinned young women, most with the *hijab* head covering, operating their sewing machines with quick movements. Fans buzzed, competing with the desert heat, as Israeli and Palestinian manufacturers — all men — walked between the rows, eyeing the quality of the work and judging the speed of the seamstresses.

Lunch was hosted by Palestinian Minister of Industry Saadi el Krunz, at a seaside restaurant. On our drive down Jamal Abdel Nasser Street, we passed the upscale neighborhoods of the Gazan elite, the well-tended grounds of the UN headquarters, and Yasser Arafat's home, protected within a guarded compound. When we reached the beach, I peered north along the Mediterranean shoreline to see if I could catch a glimpse of Ashkelon, but the summer haze hid the Israeli town that lay just ten kilometers north of Gaza City.

Inside the restaurant, I felt instantaneously transported back to Israel. The waiters greeted us in flawless Hebrew, just as they had done in the restaurants of Tel Aviv, where they had worked before the 1991 Gulf War. Like Israelis meeting one another in a foreign country, the Palestinian waiters asked if we had eaten in their former places of employment — "Avazi" or "Tchelet" — clutching at the common threads that bound them to us and to their past lives in a borderless Greater Israel. They were among the fortunate few, of the 100,000 Palestinians no longer working in Israel, who had found jobs back home.

The sea created a gentle background rhythm to the conversations buzzing under canopies. As the waiters brought plate after plate of grilled fish, salads, and roast lamb, the minister and some of his officials sat with an Israeli investor we had invited, discussing the possibilities of joint government-private sector investment in telephone infrastructure and high-tech initiatives. I leaned back, enjoying the salt smells of the sea mingled with the savory aroma of meat, and imagined returning to this hotel restaurant — after a peace agreement — to enjoy the untrammeled white beaches on a holiday with Shai and Liad as young men. In my daydream, sunning himself next to me on the Gaza beach was a new life partner.

At 3:00 in the afternoon, drowsy and sated — with fish and lamb as well as with new options for business — we returned to the Erez checkpoint and bid farewell to our Palestinian police escort. We crossed the checkpoint and, back in our Israeli bus, drove north. In air-conditioned comfort, we rolled past hundreds of Palestinian workers lined up in rows on the Israeli side of the border, separated by metal rails, walking slowly, sweating, waiting to be checked by Israeli soldiers before being let back into Gaza to go home. They looked like convicts, waiting for their daily run in the yard. Or maybe they just looked tired, having started their day at Erez checkpoint at 5:00 a.m. Many carried odd pieces of junk culled from the discards of Israeli homes and fields: broken kids' bicycles, piles of old clothes, sacks of potatoes.

Their weary faces lingered in my mind as we rolled past the neat, green, well-watered fields of three *kibbutzim*, Yad Mordechai, Karmia, and Zikim, built on the sands in the 1940s and '50s. From a world where donkeys carried burdens and barefooted children lived in crowded shacks, we had leaped, as if through a time warp, to a land of computer-controlled drip irrigation, red-roofed houses, and honey made by bees specially bred for pollination.

Business on the brink, like hydro-electric power, is generated through a tumultuous fall between vastly different levels. Not everyone survives the plunge. In contrast to the harmonious vision of the Economic Protocols of the Oslo agreement, the economic dividends of peace were not flowing equally: not to Israelis and Palestinians, nor within each society itself.

In 1999, the Israeli economy was growing. With the cancellation of the Arab boycott against Israel, and a reduction of hostilities in the region, Israel became an ideal place to invest, particularly in research and development. Foreign investment in Israel doubled in a year. As a result of both the budding peace process and the immigration of 700,000 well-educated Jews from the former Soviet Union, the Israeli economy had surged forward, with

158

the high-tech sector leading the advance. Israel's per capita GDP had increased by almost 50 percent over a decade, from $11,000 in 1990 to almost $17,000 in 1999. Prime Minister Barak promised the creation of a whopping 300,000 jobs in the coming years.

Most Palestinians, however, aside from a thin strata of businesspeople and politicians, received only a trickle of the economic benefits of peace. The peace process was accompanied by a surge of terror attacks by Palestinian extremists trying to derail it, and this was met with increased checkpoints and closures by Israeli authorities. Since income from work in Israel still constituted almost a third of Palestinian income, these closures debilitated the Palestinian economy. After the start of the Oslo process, unemployment in the territories rose to 20 percent, and in Gaza alone to 30 percent. In short, contrary to expectations, Palestinians did not reap economic benefits from peace. In fact, from 1992 to 1996, Palestinian real GDP per capita fell by one third.

Every day, thousands of Palestinian workers traveled between these universes, holding the enormous tension of the contradictions in their bodies and souls. Most of them probably ignored the tension as much as they could, but below the surface, the contrasts, the humiliation, the inequality despite political changes, was becoming unbearable. To most Israelis, including me at the time, the vast gaps and the subterranean build-up of tension were largely invisible. We focused on the signs of progress: the growing circles of businesspeople seeking each other out, the final-status negotiations taking place between Israeli and Palestinian officials.

The Oslo Agreements, signed in 1994, had called for the establishment of a Palestinian state next to Israel by September 13, 2000, when the six-year confidence-building period defined by the Agreements would expire. Prime Minister Barak had stated his aim to meet that deadline with a comprehensive agreement. The government's actions on the ground, however, followed another path. In violation of the Agreements, the Israeli government continued to encourage Jewish settlement activity in the West Bank and Gaza, over the constant protest of the Palestinians. In the first year of the Barak administration, funds were allocated for thousands of new housing units throughout the West Bank, creating more settlement activity than under the previous Likud government.

On March 22, 2000, after weeks of stalled negotiations, Israel carried out the redeployment that had been scheduled for December, handing over 6.1 percent more of the territory of the West Bank. The Palestinian Authority now held all major cities in the West Bank and Gaza, including 60 percent of the Palestinian population and almost 40 percent of the land.

Israeli-Palestinian security cooperation continued to foil the efforts of Palestinian extremists bent on derailing the peace process. Palestinian security forces confiscated Hamas explosives discovered in a Gazan elementary school. Such action by the Palestinian Authority against other Palestinian movements was unprecedented. Scores of Israeli and Palestinian border police worked together on joint patrols along the seam line between the two societies.

On July 13, 2000, two months before the designated date for a two-state agreement, final-status talks between Palestinians and Israelis began at Camp David. On the eve of his departure, Barak made the dramatic statement that he proposed a "large Jerusalem" that could be a shared capital of both the Israeli and the Palestinian future state. Until that moment, the subject of sharing or dividing Jerusalem had been taboo for an Israeli politician. I was amazed at the relative ease with which it was accepted.

That night, Orly called. "Sarahleh," she began, in a tone that told me that this was a political discussion, "what is Barak doing? How can he divide Jerusalem?"

"I don't know, but he said 'shared capital.'"

"Shared . . . ?" There was a pause on the line. "Well, if it were shared, we could all stay here . . . but how would that work?

Despite the furor in the press, my sense in talking to people was that they knew, sooner or later, that we would come to this point, that Jerusalem's borders would be redrawn in the context of an agreement. Yet Barak returned to Israel empty-handed, blaming failure of the talks on the Palestinians, and their unwillingness to accept the Israeli offers or to offer counter-proposals of their own. Over the summer months, high-level negotiating teams continued to hammer at the issues, but it was clear that Barak's fragile coalition was falling apart. By September, he could count on only fifty Jewish Knesset votes to ratify a final-status agreement, if one were reached. Even with the ten Arab MKs, the count would still only be half of the 120-member parliament, not a majority.

Egyptian leaders and others began advising the Israelis to consider signing a partial agreement, leaving Jerusalem to be resolved in future negotiations. Israeli defense officials warned that if an agreement were not reached soon, the PA would be unable to control the Palestinian street, and violence would result. When the Palestinian legislative council voted on September 11 to hold off declaring unilateral statehood, Marwan Barghouti, who led a good part of "the Palestinian street," warned that people could hold out perhaps until the end of October, before "taking things into their own hands."

September 13 came and went without an agreement to establish a Palestinian state.

On Thursday, September 28, 2000, in this volatile mix of high stakes and high expectations, MK Ariel Sharon ascended the Temple Mount/Haram al Sharif protected by over 1,000 Israeli police officers, to emphasize what he called Israel's "eternal sovereignty" over the site holy to Jews and Muslims throughout the world. The Hebrew date — 28 Elul — was also the anniversary of the Sabra and Shatilla Massacre of 1982 in Lebanon. For his role in the massacre, Ariel Sharon had been removed from his position of minister of defense, following a governmental commission of inquiry.

His provocative visit violated the decades-old understanding, from the time of Defense Minister Moshe Dayan, that recognized the authority of the Islamic Waqf over the site, even though Israel claimed sovereignty over all of Jerusalem. Years later, a high-ranking Palestinian security officer told me that Palestinian officials were urgently phoning and meeting with Israeli counterparts late into the night before, warning the Israeli government not to allow this unprecedented march to the epicenter of the struggle between Israel and the Palestinians.

On Friday, September 29, Palestinian riots broke out in response to Sharon's act. Following the Friday prayers, Palestinians threw rocks and iron bars from the Temple Mount/Haram al Sharif on Jewish worshippers at the Western Wall below. Police sharpshooters killed two Palestinians. Throughout East Jerusalem, thousands of young Palestinians demonstrated, throwing rocks and Molotov cocktails. Israeli troops killed five more Palestinians and wounded over one hundred in the area of Al Aqsa mosque.

The violence cracked open a major fault line.

III. At Forty-Five: Falling Apart
(2000-2003)

Chapter 15
Days of Awe, October 2000

The month of Tishrei, heading the Jewish year, is wrapped in holiness and soul-searching. The first ten days, between Rosh Ha-Shanah, the New Year, and Yom Kippur, the Day of Atonement, form the Days of Awe. These are the solemn days between the heavenly "signing" of each Jew's fate for the coming year, and the "sealing" of the decree at sundown on Yom Kippur.

On Rosh HaShanah, we recite the ominous prayer, *"Unataneh tokef"*: "We acknowledge the awesome power of this day, its pure sanctity . . . You are judge and prosecutor . . . What is forgotten is remembered and recorded and borne witness to. All deeds are signed and sealed by every human being . . . The great *shofar* is sounded, and a still, small voice is heard . . . The angels are in terror, for judgment is to be decreed against the inhabitants of both heaven and earth."

Our sense of doom grows as we chant: "On Rosh Hashanah it is written and on Yom Kippur it is sealed — who will live and who will die, who will perish by fire and who by water, who by sword, who by hunger and who by earthquake, who will be poor and who will be rich . . . who will be humiliated, and who exalted . . . but Repentance and Prayer and Righteous Acts can transform the severity of the decree."

For years, I misread the prayer as saying that our deeds can transform the evil decree. Only as an adult did I realize that we are given the chance only to transform the extent of the decree, not its basic content.

These days mark a Jew's last chance to influence her fate for the coming year. Observant Jews turn inward and reflect on their deeds of the past year, apologizing to those they have hurt and making restitution — for without restoration of justice on the human level, one cannot ask forgiveness from God on the Holy Day.

On some level, the outbreak of violence in October 2000 constituted a brutal attempt by Palestinians, in Israel and in the territories, to demand justice, which had been long delayed and long denied. But there certainly was no forgiveness on any side, and no restoration.

Throughout northern Israel, violence erupted in waves, starting on the first day of Tishrei, Saturday, September 30. In Umm el Fahm, demonstrators threw stones at police and rioters burned a gas station. In the coming days, Arab youth attacked an Egged bus, and later, a *kibbutznik* driving through Wadi Ara. They forced the drivers from their vehicles, then torched the cars.

On Sunday, October 1, the 2nd of Tishrei, demonstrators in Nazareth threw stones, burned tires, and plundered shops. The police closed one of Israel's main north-south arteries to protect Jewish motorists driving through areas of Arab population. In the course of quelling the violence, police fire killed two demonstrators, igniting riots throughout the Arab sector in Israel.

On October 1-2, in the mixed Arab-Jewish city of Acco, Arab residents hurled Molotov cocktails and shot at police. In Arab Kfar Manda, gangs uprooted street lights and burned tires at the main entrance to the town. Throughout the Galilee, Israeli Arabs set forest fires, in some cases leading to the evacuation of Jewish settlements. In Misgav, hundreds of Arab youth advanced on Kibbutz Lotem before being halted by police. In Upper Nazareth, police stopped a mob of hundreds of Kfar Mashad residents from entering the Jewish neighborhood of Har Yona, but not before they smashed cars and broke windows. In Baqa el Gharbiye and in the Negev Bedouin city of Rahat, residents burned banks and post offices.

As I watched newscasts of masked rioters raging through the main roads of Nazareth, I felt as if I were viewing Hamas cells on the streets of Gaza. Even in Haifa, renowned for its harmonious relations between Arab and Jewish residents, three hundred Arab demonstrators threw stones and burned tires in the Wadi Nisnas neighborhood. When police closed the streets surrounding the neighborhood, Haifa Mayor Amram Mitzna arrived with MK Issam Makhoul and Arab city council members, preventing additional confrontation and restoring calm.

By the end of the fourth day of Tishrei, another three young Israeli Arab men had been killed by police, and cities were ablaze throughout the West Bank and Gaza.

The Palestinian-Israeli joint security arrangements, painstakingly built up over the past two years, collapsed. Yossi Tabaja, an Israeli border guard who operated in joint Palestinian-Israeli security patrols as part of the Oslo peace process, was shot in the head at point blank range by his Palestinian partner, Nayil Suliman, as they were resting after their morning patrol in Kalkilya.

Riots erupted in spontaneous combustion throughout the capital cities of the Arab world — Cairo, Damascus, Amman, Rabat — all calling for Israel's destruction. For the first time since I came to Israel, I felt surrounded by people who hated me and wanted to kill me.

My neighbors in Tel Aviv, survivors of the Holocaust, were traumatized. Mrs. Krelman awoke sweating in the middle of the night, reliving her days in Poland, when friends and neighbors had turned on her and collaborated with the Nazis. Mr. Baranes was thrown back to the War of Independence in 1948; as Egyptian troops had neared Tel Aviv, the Baraneses had feared for their own survival and for that of Israel.

None of us knew exactly what we should fear now. I was disconcerted by the fact that I had spent the last three days in ignorant calm and quiet, praying and enjoying the holidays in the tree-lined heart of Tel Aviv, while Helmi and other colleagues were under siege. That eerie sense of living in a parallel universe only added to my sense of isolation and foreboding.

Hatred of Jews, hatred of Israel, seemed to have crossed every border. The distinctions I had made for years between Palestinians in the West Bank and Palestinian citizens of Israel seemed meaningless. I recalled the recent warnings of the police and of right wing politicians, that the Israeli Arab population had become increasingly and dangerously nationalistic. Were we now seeing a truer picture of the Israeli Arabs' relationship to this country? Was I fooling myself in thinking that dismantling systems of discrimination against Israeli Arabs would open the gate to a more equal society in which all citizens took part? Maybe it would, instead, open the gate to Arabs having more power with which to dismantle the State of Israel as we knew it.

On the other hand, viewing pictures of Israeli police shooting into crowds of young people, I recalled my own experience exactly two years ago in Umm el Fahm. Then it had been clear that police provocation and overreaction had escalated the situation, deepening and prolonging the violence. I had been caught inadvertently in the midst of the conflict. Should I go now, on my own initiative, to the villages to try to broker disengagement, as I had then? I was afraid. I thought of my sons, ages 8 and 9, for whom I was the only living parent, and decided against it.

On October 4, the 5th of Tishrei, my Arab colleagues returned to work, dragging with them the dust, the blood, the broken glass of Nazareth, Taibe, and Arara. When Mohammed Zuabi walked in, he barely met my eyes. An accountant in his early thirties, Mohammed coordinated the Center's efforts to increase Arab employment in high tech companies. Over the past months, he had been visiting high-tech firms throughout the north, convincing Jewish managers, with his ready smile and his folder of resumés, to hire qualified Arab graduates.

I invited him into my office and closed the door. "Tell me what happened."

"My home, Nazareth, became a battlefield. I am a Muslim; Al Aqsa is our holy site. I cannot sit by idly when Muslims are killed on Haram e-Sharif. At the same time, I am an Israeli citizen. The Israeli police are supposed to be my police force, too!" Suddenly, Mohammed began to sob. I waited, feeling as if I had intruded in a place that was not mine. "But they attacked us. They shot at us!"

I sat quietly as Mohammed cried. I had no words of comfort, only my ability to listen.

Kiram Baloum, the elegant and straightforward director of the

166

Center's Women's Unit, hardly spoke. She wanted to know where I stood. What could I tell her, that I didn't know myself whether the police violence was cause or effect? That I suspected extremists in the Arab sector of exploiting the frustrations of the general population to inflame the situation? Was this the right time to speak my thoughts?

I sought out Helmi. For almost a decade, in Cairo, and Amman, and Umm el Fahm, I have turned to him to help make sense of reality. When he describes a situation, I feel that I am there myself, but with his eyes, his history. Like a film director and producer who have worked together for years, we trust one another's editing of events. We share a sense of what is central, and what peripheral. Now Helmi told me of his life over the past days.

"The young people do not have the same fears or the same sensibilities we grew up with. They are unemployed and angry and frustrated — and, at the same time, educated. They do not want to listen to their parents' generation any more, and the leadership is from that generation. We couldn't control them. In Baqa they burned the bank, the post office — any institution connected to the Jews, to the establishment. That never happened before." Helmi looked tired. "One of my friend's sons was killed by police fire, while sitting at a café in Jatt."

Suddenly, his eyes flashed. "But the police are acting on orders from the government, from Barak. He openly gave the green light to use whatever force is necessary to open roads and maintain order. It is part of his strategy with the Palestinians, and it is part of his strategy with us."

I felt a sudden shock of distrust. I could grasp the police using inordinate force, particularly against a population that looks to them like people whom they are told to shoot while in the army. But to call it a strategy? That implied an intention more sinister than I could accept. Still, the question niggled: Had the political leadership given the green light for the police to shoot demonstrators because they wanted forcefully to quell expressions of Palestinian nationalism and show Israeli Arabs "their place"?

My brother-in-law, Moti Komarov, who had been a member of a combat unit in the army, blamed the police. "No matter what was happening, there is no excuse for live fire. Where were the water cannons, the tear gas? The police have methods for crowd control. Why did they shoot live ammunition at civilians?"

At the Center, Jews and Arabs together could relate to the anger and humiliation of our Arab colleagues and to the despair of years of promises unfulfilled. We could relate to their feeling of betrayal as the stark reality of their lives as Arab Israelis had been displayed on the streets: *You may live here, but the state is not your state. The police are not your police. In fact, they are working to protect the Jews from you.*

But could my Arab colleagues relate to my fears? I feared that my children and I are not safe; it could easily have been Shai, Liad and me killed by the Arab hurling a rock on a "Jewish" car passing under the bridge from Jisr e-Zarka. I feared that the very people I had been struggling to include in Israeli society were ready to kill me just because I am Jewish. Arab mobs had tried to enter Jewish communities, prevented only by police action. Vandalism, violence, and hatred had rocked the mixed cities of Jaffo, Acco and Haifa.

My ancient Jewish fear: *They want to kill us.* "They" could be the Nazis in my parents' generation, the Ukrainians in my grandparents' generation, or the Spaniards at the time of the Inquisition. This time, the Cossacks were wearing *keffiyehs.*

My fears seemed to gain proof from the daily news. At the same time, I asked myself, what is the proper place of these fears when "we" are in the majority and setting the political tone and policy of the country vis a vis "them"?

By the end of the fifth of the Days of Awe, ten Israeli Arabs lay dead from police fire; and hundreds were wounded.

By Thursday, October 5, the 6th of Tishrei, the situation began to calm down in northern Israel. In the West Bank and Gaza, however, more and more Palestinians, and some Israeli soldiers, were being killed. From the West Bank town of Beit Jalla, Palestinians shot into homes in the Jerusalem neighborhood of Gilo, on the opposite hill. Tanks were brought to Gilo to protect the neighborhood.

Every day, I thought: *This is a tactic to force the negotiations.* The shooting will end. Arafat will call back his people; the IDF will stop using massive firepower. Then U.S. Secretary of State Madeleine Albright flew to Paris to mediate a ceasefire between

Barak and Arafat. An editorial in the *Jerusalem Post* commented: "Violence does not show that peace is impossible; rather that it is imperative." Yet the shooting and violence in the territories continued, unabated. Within the week of violence, sixty-three people had been killed, and approximately 1,800 wounded.

On Friday, October 6, the 7th of Tishrei — the twenty-seventh anniversary of the 1973 Yom Kippur War — thousands of Jews throughout Israel began to take revenge on their Arab fellow citizens. In Tiberias, Jewish mobs beat up Israeli Arabs on the streets, and the mosque in town, which was about to undergo rehabilitation, was vandalized. Jews and Arabs hurled stones at one another in Upper Nazareth. In Hadera, Jews vandalized and burned Arab-owned stores and offices.

In Tel Aviv's Hatikva neighborhood, three apartments belonging to Arabs were set on fire. Hundreds of the Hatikva residents confronted police while chanting, "Death to the Arabs!" They forced Arab employees of the Avazi restaurant to evacuate the building, then set the restaurant on fire. In Jaffa, Bat Yam, Karmiel, and Petah Tikva, Jewish mobs rampaged, beating Arabs on the streets and vandalizing property.

On October 8, the 9th of Tishrei, the eve of Yom Kippur, as Jews all over the world prepared for the fast that marked the holiest day of the Jewish year, hundreds of Israeli Jews advanced on the eastern neighborhoods of Arab Nazareth. When police arrived to form a buffer between Arabs and Jews, both sides stoned them. In the subsequent confrontations, the police controlled the Jewish crowd without firearms, while two Israeli Arabs were shot and killed, either by police fire or by shooting from the Jewish crowd.

During Yom Kippur, I recited the prayers I had said for forty years. Most years I read the words quickly, experiencing very little of the liturgy as relevant to me. This year, however, it seemed particularly poignant that the prayers are written in the first-person plural: "We have become guilty; we have betrayed . . ." In the Talmud, it is written: "Every Jew is responsible one for the other." We are part of a community. On Yom Kippur, therefore, we pray not only for forgiveness for our own personal sins, we ask forgiveness for the sins of the people of which we are part. If we did not prevent other Jews from sinning, we must hold part of the responsibility.

This year the words resounded like a recitation of the daily news:" . . . we have stolen, we have spoken slander. We have caused perversion, we have caused wickedness, we have sinned willfully, we have been violent; we have falsely accused."

The litany continued: "For the sin that we have sinned against You under duress, or willingly, for the sin that we have sinned against You unknowingly, for the sin that we have sinned against You by exercising power, for the sin that we have sinned against You through haughtiness, for the sin that we have sinned against You through baseless hatred. For them all, O God of forgiveness, forgive us, pardon us, atone for us."

Usually, after a day of fasting, reflection and praying, I feel lighter, cleansed, ready to start afresh. Now I dreaded the end of the Holy Day, the resumption of "normal" life. I dreaded hearing what had happened over the past twenty-four hours. All the fasting and praying would not atone for the events occurring in my name.

As the first stars came out and we broke the fast on Monday evening, word passed around the synagogue that a demonstration was to take place next to the memorial for Yitzhak Rabin, to protest the retributive violence of thousands of Israeli Jews and the behavior of the Israeli police, who had used crowd control techniques with Jews and live ammunition with Arabs. The demonstration comprised less than a hundred people, more of a gathering of colleagues mourning the passing of the path of reconciliation that had been trod by the man killed on this spot not even five years ago.

The ten Days of Awe ended with almost a hundred people dead and close to 2,000 wounded. The dead included twelve Israeli Arab citizens, one Israeli Jewish citizen, and five Israeli soldiers and border police. The rest were Palestinians from the West Bank and Gaza.

*As the days dragged on, I began hearing of isolated but numer*ous incidents of individual human courage in the face of mob violence. In Jaffa, where a mob of Jewish vandals had been about to break into an Arab-owned shop, a Jewish neighbor, a cameraman at a local television station, had stepped out of the shadows holding a stick. "If you touch that shop, I'll break your hands,"

170

he growled. The gang moved on. Later, the cameraman explained, "We've lived in the same building for years. His daughter and my daughter take vacations together. I couldn't let them vandalize his shop."

Such heroism made me feel a bit ashamed that I had done nothing personally to halt the violence of the past weeks. I had been frightened and caught up in the prevailing air of suspicion and defensiveness. I had made no statements, taken no public action. In fact, I still felt ambivalent and confused about what to say or do. I do not tend to see things in black and white, but now, in the face of the infinite shades of dark grey surrounding me, I felt overwhelmed, pulled in many directions by my fears and my beliefs.

I believed that the violence of Israeli Arabs stemmed primarily from years of discrimination, exclusion and humiliation. I believed that at its core, a Jewish state must rest on a firm commitment to justice and assure that no minority in our midst be treated as Jews have been treated through the centuries. Still, I could not shake the realization that, beneath the anger of a discriminated minority, lurked a layer of hatred and a desire to see the destruction of Israel as a Jewish state. I could not declare, even to myself, who was right and who was wrong — the right and the wrong seemed to stain every side.

I did know, however, that our Center's work always thrived in the times between crises, when what was required was not personal courage in the face of imminent danger but patient and unswerving efforts to promote equality of economic opportunity and fair allocation of public resources. I was a stubborn enough leader, moreover, not to allow myself to be swallowed up in this multi-layered crisis. That realization released me from my paralysis and my cowardice, and I began assessing our situation in a less emotional, more strategic way. At the Center, we held a series of discussions among Jewish and Arab colleagues about what they had experienced and how they had felt over the past days. People began to come out of their trauma and reconnect, like hedgehogs unrolling and beginning to move.

Israeli political leaders, interested in achieving calm, implored the public to restore coexistence and refrain from further damaging what one announcement called the "fragile fabric of life between us."

Nevertheless, the events of the past days had opened wounds that had long been festering in Israeli society. This was not the time to return hummus-eating, coffee-drinking "good relations" of the past. It was a time, rather, to examine the infection that had been exposed and to cleanse the wounds. It was a time to conduct deep discussions about the place of Arab citizens in the Jewish State. It was a time to delve into the tension between maintaining democratic equality for all citizens and maintaining the Jewish nature of the state.

At an emergency meeting at Neve Shalom on October 11, the 12th of Tishrei, hundreds of veterans of Jewish-Arab groups did not mourn the death of the former "coexistence," but celebrated it. We began planning a series of public actions aimed at exposing systematic inequality, and pointing the way to a more equal civic partnership based, not on living together as owner and guest in a "Jewish state," but on a different model of statehood and shared citizenship.

We felt it was important to create a significant joint Jewish-Arab presence on the streets, allowing both Arab and Jewish leadership to condemn the mob violence, on the one hand, and to expose the police brutality and Israeli policies that were fueling massive violence in the territories, on the other hand. Peace Now decided to join in and, perhaps for the first time, organize a demonstration together with Israeli Arabs on matters of internal policy rather than on issues of external peace. The veteran peace organization, however, while expert at turning out *kibbutzniks* and liberal *Ashkenazim*, had few contacts in the Israeli Arab sector.

I contacted Abed Anabtawi, secretary general of the Association of Arab Mayors, and asked if they would be ready to be partners in planning and organizing such a demonstration. After consulting with the Arab leadership, he came back with the answer that if we could all agree on the purposes, messages and speakers, the Mayors' Association would participate.

In the ensuing discussions, Peace Now activists, who had met with Palestinian counterparts for over a decade, found that they did not understand the sensitivities of their fellow citizens. For years, Peace Now had cultivated its image as a Jewish, rather than a civic, organization, emphasizing its origins as a movement of

172

army reservists wishing to use the territories won in the 1967 Six-Day War as bargaining chips to reach peace. Peace Now had always seen a two-state solution as helping to preserve the Jewish majority and the Jewish character of Israel. After peace, Israel would continue to be the Jewish state, and Palestine would be the state for Palestinians. In this equation, the Israeli Arabs — or Palestinian citizens of Israel — had no place. Planning a joint demonstration became an exercise in renegotiating civic partnership.

On October 12, the 13th of Tishrei, two IDF reservists lost their way driving to their base in the West Bank and stumbled into Ramallah. They were taken in by the Palestinian police, but a mob of Palestinians broke into the cell in which they were held and murdered them with their bare hands, in cold blood. Over and over again, I watched Israeli news broadcasts of the perpetrators holding up their bloody hands in triumph at the window of the police station. I felt sickened by the look on their faces, sickened by the abased sense of glory in the killing of another human being. My horror was magnified when I realized that only a month earlier, I had been a few blocks away from that police station in Ramallah, in consultations with the Palestinian Information Technology Association. This was not a far-away land, it was where I had been doing business — fifty miles from Tel Aviv.

During Sukkot, an eight-day holiday from the 15th to the 23rd of Tishre, my kids and I usually traveled to the Galilee to visit our friends in Tivon. Now I hesitated: Was it safe to drive the roads? It had been almost five days since the last reported incident of violence in northern Israel. In America, five days is a short period of time, but the Israeli body politic has a very rapid metabolism: tragedy and joy are devoured, broken down, and made part of the tissue almost instantaneously. Five days can mark a new era. In five days, a war can be won or lost, a peace agreement concluded, a son lost forever.

I decided I could not live in fear of what might happen. After all, my friends continued to live in the Galilee and to travel the roads to work. I packed the kids in the car and started on the ninety-minute trip north.

We passed under the bridge from which the Jisr e-Zerka resident had thrown the fatal rock. We passed the Fureidis Junction, where, only days ago, stones were thrown at Jewish motorists. We passed the charred remains of streetlights lying mangled at the entrances of Arab villages. I could imagine the mobs ripping them from the ground. Few motorists were on the roads. All was quiet; as in the aftermath of an attack by some great beast, who, for the moment, is mollified.

In Tivon, Shlomo and Tami took me for a walk around town to show me the houses whose windows had been broken by stones thrown from the Bedouin town, Bosmat Tivon, which borders on Jewish Tivon. Then we drove with all our kids to the Bedouin town of Zarzir, where a "peace tent" had been put up by residents of all the neighboring towns.

The atmosphere was festive. In a black Bedouin tent hastily erected on an empty lot at the edge of the community, kids (mostly Jewish) were painting and doing origami. In the shade of a nearby tree, rugs had been spread on the ground, and some of the local leaders reclined against pillows, drinking coffee, talking with a group of young Jewish adults about how they saw the disturbances of the past two weeks.

At first, I ridiculed the event as one more superficial "coexistence" effort. But when I recalled the grisly aftermath of the violence on the roads, the broken windows, the mob scenes, I realized that just reconnecting, just having Jews come to an Arab village, was important, even if those visiting were the already-converted.

Over the past two weeks, almost no Jews had entered Arab villages. The restaurants and markets of Arab villages, which used to teem with Jewish Israelis on holidays, were quiet and subdued. Most Jews stayed away because they were frightened. However, some community leaders — in Misgav and Ma'alot — had begun calling for a boycott of Arab goods and services, in punishment for the riots and destruction of the last weeks.

Similarly, few Arabs were setting foot in Jewish towns. Women, in particular, noticeable in their traditional head-coverings, feared that they would be insulted or beaten on their way to the health clinic or the National Insurance office. And since many social services were available only in the Jewish towns, many families went without. Arab families discontinued their jaunts to the discount supermarkets in shopping malls, and returned to the neighborhood markets, as they had done decades ago. People withdrew to their own tribes, drawing the wagons close. The absence of normal human contact fertilized the suspicion and distrust aroused by the riots.

The next day, my friend Tami and I went with a local Jewish peace activist to the village of Arrabe, to pay a condolence call to the family of Assil Asaleh. Assil, 17 years old, had been active in Seeds of Peace, the youth organization set up after the signing of the Oslo agreements to get Israeli, Palestinian and Jordanian young people together. His young mother, stately in her black mourning dress, was a high school teacher in town, herself involved in community organizations. She thanked the scores of mourners for coming. She described, without emotion, the family's efforts to assure an accurate autopsy, which showed that Assil had been shot at close range in the neck. Friends said that he was shot by a police officer in the olive grove between Arrabe and Lotem while trying to get away from the demonstration. I wondered what had brought him to the olive grove. Had he been participating in violence, or running from it?

As Im Assil spoke, I could see myself in her place. She had done what she could to raise a good boy, with self-confidence and political awareness. He had gone out to take part in a demonstration, and now he was dead. I thought of Helmi's worry for his sons in Baqa. I thought of my own sons, still young, and tears sprang into my eyes.

On our way back to Tivon, I called my old friend, Kassem Abu Raia, strategic planner for the Sakhin municipality. He immediately invited us to stop by.

Kassem and I had met in the 1980s while he was studying at Hebrew University. Over the years, we had often worked together to remove government obstacles to the economic development of Sakhnin. Kassem's professional reputation and personal integrity had allowed him to remain in his position under two opposing mayors. I wanted to hear his sense of what had happened between Sakhnin and Misgav and the police.

We turned off the main two-lane road, which was lined with restaurants and cement block factories, into a network of dirt roads snaking between imposing stone villas. The city hadn't keep up with the pace of private building, so private affluence sat amidst public poverty. Kassem, a solidly built man in his early forties, met us at the door with a smile. His wife welcomed us in to their spacious living room, which would not have looked out of place in an upscale neighborhood of Tel Aviv.

Drinking cold juice, we talked about the difficulty the Jewish-Arab school, Yad B'Yad ("Hand in Hand"), was having in recruiting Jewish families. Kassem's daughter, going into 3rd grade there, enjoyed the school; she spoke with us in flawless Hebrew. Many Arab families, seeking a high-quality, open school, had signed up for Yad B'Yad. But Jewish parents, with more options and more fears, were reluctant.

Our talk turned to the events of the past weeks. Kassem described the situation in Sakhnin. After the Palestinians had been killed on the Temple Mount on Saturday, September 30, there had been a non-violent protest in Sakhnin, with thousands of people marching through the town. The police had stayed away, and local leaders had ensured quiet. Only the next day, when news came of the police killing demonstrators in Umm el Fahm, did trouble begin. The second demonstration, on October 2, was unruly, and the police entered the town. Kassem had witnessed the clashes in the western part of the town, near the Tradion Junction and Misgav's Industrial Area.

"The mayor, Mustafa Abu Raia, and I were in constant contact with the police," he said. "We tried to get the police to leave so things would settle down. Mustafa tried to calm the crowd, but the police used sniper fire. You know, this is a very small town; we know all the people in the police station. We know one of the snipers, too; he is a Druze man from the neighboring village."

Yet another irony of this situation: One of the police officers himself was an Arab, albeit Druze. In 1948, at the founding of the State, the Druze elders, remembering their own persecution at the hands of Muslim authorities in Greater Syria, had agreed that their young men would serve in the Israeli army. Despite that fact, they continue to suffer the same discrimination — the same underdevelopment and neglect — as the Muslim Arabs of Sakhnin.

I asked about what I had read, that angry crowds had advanced on Misgav's Tradion Industrial area and on the Jewish community of Lotem, with violent intent. Kassem could not speak personally about Lotem, but he was adamant that no mob from Sakhnin attempted to enter the Tradion Industrial Area to destroy factories.

The Or Commission, a government commission of inquiry established to look into such confrontations between the security forces and Israeli citizens, later corroborated Kassem's view of the events. Regarding the incidents at the Tradion Junction, the Commission reported: "The events [stone throwing and clashes with police] continued for hours, during which attempts were made to open talks between the commanding officers and local leaders. At the end of the day, these contacts led to the calming of the situation."

Tami and I left Sakhnin by the road to Tamra, which had by now been widened to match the new road to Carmiel. I remembered walking these hills twenty years earlier with Aziz from Tamra, before there had been an industrial area, or Kibbutz Lotem. I wondered what would have happened had the Misgav settlements been built in the context of a regional development plan, for the benefit of both the Arab and the Jewish population of the area — that is, if government policy had been designed to close socio-economic gaps between the communities of Misgav and Sakhnin rather than widen them? If the experience of the past twenty years had been one of cooperative advancement, rather than aggressive Jewish development to limit Arab urban growth, would the lives of Assil and the five others who were killed in this area have been saved?

In economic development circles, a constant debate rages: Can development preclude political unrest? I maintain that underdevelopment and discriminatory development can exacerbate unrest, but that even-handed development cannot necessarily prevent it. It is a necessary but not sufficient condition for a healthy, equitable society. Certainly, if economic development is viewed as a substitute for political legitimacy, participation, and self-determination, it is doomed to failure.

Here, in the Galilee, however, the Israeli government had not even attempted to buy off the Arab population through economic development. Instead, the policies of the 1970s of Judaizing the Galilee and developing the expanses of land between Arab towns for Jews only continued into the 21st century. The notion that government policy could be a tool for increasing the participation and identification of Arab citizens in the state was foreign to Israeli government thinking.

On October 21, the 22nd of Tishrei, the joint demonstration of the Arab Mayors' Committee, Peace Now, the Israeli Communist Party, and others took place in Haifa. The speakers list was unusual in its Jewish-Arab parity. For the first time, Peace Now called on a Labor government — not the Likud — to halt its massive use of firepower in the West Bank and to return to negotiations. As in all Peace Now demonstrations, the Israeli flag was flown. Unlike at other Peace Now rallies, the Palestinian flag was also unfurled.

The significance of the rally lay not in its size but in the very fact of its existence, putting Palestinian and Jewish citizens back on the street, together. It provided one of the first public platforms since the start of the Al Aqsa *intifada* for Arab mayors. They had suffered more and had more practical concerns than the Arab Knesset members, whose nationalist rhetoric had dominated the public sphere before October. It was the Arab mayors who had been in the streets trying to calm their citizens and broker agreements to prevent more police violence. It was Arab mayors who now had to convince the technicians (all Jewish) of the Electric Company to enter Arab towns to restore electric poles and street lights ripped down in the weeks of violence. It was the Arab mayors who still depended on government allocations for the vast majority of their municipal budgets. And it was the Arab mayors who had to console family members and get social services going again for their electorate.

The "match" that began the violence in Arab society in Israel had been religious and national. Certainly, the response of the police in northern Israel had not reduced the violence but escalated it. It is notable that in the Negev, there were major violent demonstrations by Bedouin — in Rahat, Tel Sheva and other towns, with banks and other institutions attacked and burned — yet no one had been killed. Instead, the Southern District police commander had worked with the local leadership of the towns to calm the demonstrators and restore order.

The "fuel" that fed the explosions of violence was socio-economic. Infant mortality in the Arab sector was nearly double that among Jews. Since 1975, the government had built 337,000 residential housing units in the Jewish sector and 1,000 in the Arab sector. The area under jurisdiction of Arab municipalities covered-about 2.5 percent of the state's territory. It had barely increased,

178

despite the fact that the Arab population has grown from about 150,000 in 1948 to almost 1 million.

As the dust settled at the end of October, the Arab mayors and the Arab population returned to this same reality. The high hopes of the previous months had collapsed. Virtually no one now was seeking reconciliation, only the safety of their own people and their old concepts. In September, Arabs and Jews had sought opportunities for economic partnership; in October, they were afraid to enter each other's towns. The narrow mountain path leading to a two-state solution, winding thinly along a steep cliff, had emptied into a deep ravine.

Why had this violence erupted just as the possibility for a final, comprehensive peace accord seemed imminent? I believe it was precisely because we were so close to reaching a peace agreement with the Palestinians. Many of the Palestinian refugees from Ramle, Lod, and villages in Israel that no longer exist would have had to abandon the hopes of ever returning to the lands and the homes of their birth. The Palestinian leadership would have had to sell this to their people and begin to be judged not by their militancy toward Israel but by their ability to forge a viable society for the Palestinian population.

Israel, meanwhile, had been on the verge of giving up the historic lands of the West Bank — the Biblical lands of Abraham, Isaac and Jacob — in order to allow establishment of a Palestinian state. We were poised to go back to the uneasy borders of 1967, with a neighboring state run by the PLO, which had been dedicated to destroying Israel. That is terrifying to many Israeli Jews, and anathema to some.

For Israeli Arabs, the possibility of a Palestinian state provoked deep questions of identity and national belonging. Arabs living within Israel felt deeply torn between national sentiments and feelings of solidarity with Palestinians in the Palestinian Authority on the one hand, and the reality of their lives as Israeli citizens on the other. After the establishment of a Palestinian State, what would be their place in the Jewish one?

Once the unrest started, the fact that violence spread from the Palestinian Authority across the Green Line into Israel fueled Jewish fears that, after giving back land and recognizing a Palestinian state, Israel would face a situation in which its own Palestinian citizens would stage a revolution from within, either through violent conflict — as we saw in Jaffa and in the Gush Segev area of the Galilee — or through whittling away the Jewish character and symbols of the state, as Azmi Bishara had proposed. The legitimate political questions he had raised played into the deepest fears of Jewish Israelis.

In short, the confrontations of October 2000 exacerbated everyone's worst fears: for Jews, that Israeli Arabs are a fifth column and must always be contained; for Arabs, that they have no legitimate place in the Jewish state.

On October 28, Tishrei ended. The autumn rains began to wash away the summer's dust and the traces of tires burned at village entrances. Throughout Arab towns in Israel, damaged buildings and streetlights were cleaned up and rebuilt. The human fabric of the country, however, remained charred and twisted. The conflagrations of October 2000 had struck like a neutron bomb, leaving the outer shell of our lives intact while killing off the human element within.

Thinking back to my prayers of Rosh HaShanah, I wondered what fate had been signed and sealed for us this year. At the beginning of November, I began to find out.

Chapter 16
Cancer

Anyone who visits the sick takes one-sixtieth of his illness.
—Rabbi Aha bar Hanina in Baba Metzia 30b, Talmud

Dr. Katz, my physician at the Kupat Holim health clinic, asked me to come to her office. "I received the results of your mammogram," she told me, "and there is a shadow here I don't like. I want you to do a higher-resolution test at the hospital."

"I have two little kids," I said, my mind immediately jumping to the diagnosis I feared. My own mother had been diagnosed with breast cancer at age 45; I was in college when her lump was found. With a jolt, I realized that I was about to turn 45 in three months.

"I know," said Dr. Katz, looking into my reddening eyes. "Let's see what it is first; then we'll know what to do."

In the evening, I watched Liad and Shai, 9 and 10, lying side by side on their stomachs on the livingroom floor, building a Lego battleship. They looked so secure, so oblivious to any impending danger. My throat tightened. *I'm too young to die,* I thought in silent protest. *I can't leave the kids now. What would they do without me? Oh God, please keep me alive, if not for me, for them!*

Tears coursed down my cheeks, and I quickly slipped into my bedroom so that Shai and Liad wouldn't hear me sobbing.

Two weeks later, after more mammograms and a biopsy, I sat with my sister-in-law, Yael, in the doctor's waiting room, fum-

181

bling with memories and fears.

I had been in my late twenties when my mother's breast cancer metastasized to her lungs. After the doctors had stopped offering treatment, Mom told me, 'Well, I won't die a young woman. I can look back over a wonderful relationship with your father, and be very proud of how I've raised you and your brother." She was 54 years old when she died.

Now, as a 44-year-old widow, I could say none of these things. I still felt like a young woman; I could look back over only six years of a meaningful relationship, which had been sometimes wonderful and often problematic. The results were not yet in on my child-rearing. And everything I had worked for, professionally, was disintegrating. I felt small, helpless, and stuck in a web, waiting for a giant spider I could not yet see.

The doctor called us in. After a few awkward pleasantries, he got to the point. "The results of the needle biopsy show that you have a small cancerous tumor growing in your right breast. We want to schedule surgery as soon as possible."

I had dreaded and expected this answer. Immediately, my mind detached from my feelings, and I began a quest for information. The doctor, pleased to be talking about disease-related facts with a rational woman, obliged with details about the size of the tumor, its affinity for estrogen, and the likely course of treatment — six months of chemotherapy and radiation.

Just before rising to leave, I voiced the meaningless question, niggling in my mind: "How long has this been growing?" I was expecting an answer of a few months to a year, thinking I could go over the year and discern some critical event that might have stirred up the malign activity.

"It probably started growing years ago," he said, "But the growth could be slow at first, and it wouldn't evidence itself for a long period."

I left the office with a diagnosis of cancer and no one to blame. I could seek no dramatic cause for my situation, just DNA, environmental triggers, and God or karma or chance.

In my obsessive quest not to deal with my feelings, it occurred to me that the long-term processes that had broken out inside me mirrored the sickness infiltrating the tissues of our society. In Israel, too, cancer had been growing for years, felt on some level as a vague discomfort, sometimes an unexplained pain, but not given attention as a major disease that could endanger the general health of the society. Now the social illness was exposed, but the "doctors" were divided as to the treatment.

Actually, they disagreed about the nature of the disease itself. Some experts saw it as the rising tides of nationalism among the Arab citizens of Israel; others, as structural discrimination and injustice in Israeli society; still others, as the racism of the police, and the hyper-vigilance of the Israeli government, which saw all unrest in the Arab sector as sprouts of national uprising. I suspected that all of the above were symptoms, or side-effects, of an underlying illness: Israel's basic design as an "ethnic democracy," still trying to define and consolidate itself by excluding its Arab citizens.

Over the past twenty years,I had seen the clash between Arab and Jewish citizens as a civil conflict. I had viewed myself as part of a struggle to broaden the spectrum of civic participation of Israeli Arabs, to level the playing field, to help empower the least well-off, and to create a society based on equal opportunities and equal rights. Now, with the clashes of October 2000, I was coming to see that the discrimination in Israeli society arises not just from ingrained prejudice, but is built into the basic design of the country. The conflict between Arabs and Jews in Israel is not only a civil conflict, but a national one. The problem is not just the participation of an excluded ethnic minority in the systems of society, but the existential clash between the two national movements, locked into what appears to be a zero-sum game.

I had not been blind to the national conflict, of course. Rather, I had cordoned it off to the arena of Israeli-Palestinian peacemaking. I had assumed that historic resolution between the two national movements would come in the form of a two-state solution, Israel for the Jews and Palestine for the Palestinians. But even if we separate and coalesce into two states, the Israeli state would not be entirely Jewish. It would continue to include a significant Palestinian minority, the Arab citizens of Israel. In the context of historic reconciliation, what should be the official status of the Palestinian citizens of Israel (as Arab Israelis began calling themselves), and what the official definition of the State of Israel?

For twenty years, I had put off dealing with the issue: What

183

sort of state do we ultimately want? I hadn't given much weight to the existential questions, and had left aside the questions regarding the legitimacy of the Law of Return, the national anthem, and the flag — all of which exclude Arab citizens, actually or symbolically.

I had closed my eyes to the fact that my long-term partners and I may be working for the same things in the short run, but very different things in the long run. Although we rarely spoke of our visions for the state, Helmi certainly was not looking to strengthen Israel as a Jewish state, but rather, as a state of all its citizens.

What sort of state was I working for — Jewish or democratic? Would I have to choose? If Israel were to be a state of all its citizens, where would that leave me? I came here because Israel is defined as "Jewish." What justification do I have for staying, if I do not believe that it should be so? On the other hand, how can I not advocate for a society that regards all its citizens as being essentially and fundamentally equal?

The disease I had begun to discern in the body politic was not a deficiency, curable through a program of improved nutrition. It was a cancer, the unbounded growth of a potent dream gone awry. But how many people saw this illness? And who knew how to treat it?

My own course of cancer treatment was clear. Surgery was scheduled within two weeks of diagnosis. One night, as I was putting Liad to bed, he turned to me and said in his sweet little voice, "Mom, maybe the lump is cancer!" Then he started explaining excitedly how cancer cells overflow their boundaries like a cup overflowing. I was flabbergasted; how did he know this? And what did it mean to him?

"Well, maybe it is," I told him, thinking fast. "We'll have to wait until they take it out. And if it is, breast cancer is one of the kinds the doctors know how to take care of." As I reassured Liad, I tried desperately to believe my own words.

The surgery went well. By the end of the week I was attending Liad's class' ceremony for receiving the Torah. I wore a floppy shirt that concealed a plastic tube leading from the area of my excised lymph nodes into the bottle of the medical drain tucked quietly into my pants pocket. I felt proud watching representatives of the class standing in a solemn line while their parents carefully passed the Book of the Torah down the row, from generation to generation, illustrating the Hebrew meaning of the word tradition — *masoret* — which derives from the root "m-s-r," to "convey." It was my Book that was being passed down, as well, and my son was about to receive it and enter this ancient Peoplehood of the Book.

Out of the corner of my eye I saw the mother of Liad's Christian Arab classmate, Souad, shifting in her chair. I thought of myself at Sterrett School in Pittsburgh, sinking into my seat as I watched Mitchell Livingston and Susie Kirschenbaum playing Joseph and Mary in the school's Christmas play. I remembered how happy I was in 2nd grade when I heard that the school play that year would be "Frosty the Snowman." Following the 1962 Supreme Court ruling that banned prayer in the schools, the principal had done away with the crèche play, and I'd felt an undefined, 7-year-old's sense triumph that I was no longer excluded from the school ceremony because it was Christian and I was Jewish.

Yet, here I was in Israel, hypocritically kvelling over my son receiving the Torah in the public Science and Nature School.

When I went to consult about the next phase of my treatment, I saw that in death, as in life, Jewish and Arab worldviews diverge. Walking into the doctor's office, I found myself face to face with Dr. Inbar, the beefy oncologist who had treated Shuki in his final phases of cancer. Recognizing me, he blurted out, "Most people wouldn't come back after an initial experience like yours."

"But you didn't kill Shuki; there was nothing you could have done at that point."

"Ah, that is a very Arab attitude," said Dr. Inbar. "You know, if one of my Jewish patients dies, the family blames the doctor. If, on the other hand, he recovers, they thank God. For the Arabs, if someone dies, it is from Allah. But, if he recovers, they thank the doctors."

Despite (or perhaps because of) the fact that I was being asked to choose between a chemotherapy regimen that would make me violently ill four times, and one that would make me less ill six times, I burst out laughing.

Leaving the hospital, I was thankful that I lived in Israel, which, despite globalization, still clung to the last of its socialist roots. Throughout the months of surgery, hospitalization, chemotherapy, radiotherapy, and consultation with doctors, social workers, and physiotherapists, I would pay nothing (beyond reasonable monthly HMO payments) for excellent care at the Ichilov public hospital.

My life now entered a rhythm dictated by the death and renewal of my white blood cells. Mustering one last element of control, before the first treatment, I shaved my head, in order to beat the chemotherapy to the punch. On chemo day, my friend Linda would come with me to the hospital, read me jokes from *The Big Book of Jewish Humor,* and talk to me to keep my mind off the poison dripping into my veins.

For three days following the treatment I lay in bed, dozing, feeling nauseous, and eating ice chips. Our *kibbutz* relatives and friends came to stay with us. I felt comfortable knowing that their taking days off from work had no financial implications for them. *Kibbutzim* had been built to provide community in hard times. Now, the last vestiges of that collectivism enveloped me in Tel Aviv.

On the fourth day, Emily took me to a sumptuous lunch by the sea. Initially, as I glanced at the food on the plates around me, I was overcome by a wave of nausea, but after forcing myself to take a mouthful, I felt ravenous. I was dazzled by the bright blues and deep greens of the sea, by the dancing white caps of the waves. The warmth of the sun, the tang of fish, the fragrance of fresh bread infused me with energy. I felt like Rip Van Winkle awakening from a hundred-year sleep.

I would have three weeks to resume a "normal life" before repeating the whole procedure again.

Behind the wonderful network of friends who helped out constantly stood Havurat Tel Aviv, the small congregation that the kids and I had belonged to since moving to Tel Aviv. The *havurah* organized people to cook for my family after each treatment. Members invited Shai and Liad over to play. Every Friday, I knew I could go to pray — and just to be — with people who cared about us and about our well-being. They cared both as friends and out of a shared commitment to *bikkur kholim*, the *mitzvah* of visiting the sick. *Bikkur kholim* is one of the nine acts of *gemilut khasadim*, lovingkindness, and ranks in importance with providing hospitality, honoring one's parents, bringing arguing friends back together, taking care of animals, comforting the bereaved, and enabling the bride and groom to rejoice. All are acts of compassion, for which there is no maximum measure, and no expectation of being repaid.

They could not keep me from throwing up, from feeling tired and overwhelmed, from worrying whether I would die from the cancer that had been found, or from despairing about the future of our society. But throughout that winter of 2000-01, the members of Havurat Tel Aviv kept me from feeling alone, and so took away many sixtieths of my personal anguish.

Yet as I was undergoing chemotherapy and radiation, the Al Aqsa *intifada* was eating away, like a cancer, at the connecting tissues between Arabs and Jews — and at the hopes and dreams that had fueled my work of twenty years.

Chapter 17
"Death as a Way of Life"*

Shai, my 10-year-old, proudly presented me with a cartoon he'd drawn. In the first frame, Israelis relaxed and swam at a beach. The second frame showed them running from a suspicious object on the shore, seeking refuge at a lifeguard stand. In the final frame, arms and legs flew in all directions, as a suicide bomber blew them all up at the guard stand. Shai's innocent, round face turned toward me, expectantly awaiting my laugh and praise.

I stared at the drawing, frozen between pride at his ability, shared by Jews throughout the ages, to deflect our precarious situation into humor — and anguish that my optimistic son, who had, at 3, instinctively assumed that the doctors would learn how to save his father from cancer, was now learning to become inured to random murder. I wrapped my arms around Shai, as if I could actually protect him, then pulled him close, so he wouldn't see my tears.

The new high-tech park under construction near Tulkarem, touted in the Center's meeting of high-tech entrepreneurs in September 2000, was caught in crossfire between Palestinian gunmen and Israeli tanks. The Ramada Renaissance Hotel, opened with great fanfare in the Arab town of Nazareth in early 2000 as a joint venture between Arab and Jewish investors, with unprecedented

---

* Taken from the title of David Grossman's book, published 2003 by Bloomsbury Publishing PL.

government assistance, was shuttered. The flow of pilgrims and tourists expected to visit the Holy Land drizzled to a halt.

Every week brought scores of Palestinian deaths in clashes with Israeli troops. Every week, ordinary Israelis were blown up in ordinary places — in Jerusalem's Mahane Yehuda market, on the #16 bus, on a Hadera street. One Palestinian, dressed in the *shtreimel* and long black coat of the ultra-Orthodox, detonated himself in the midst of a *bar mitzvah* celebration, killing eleven Israeli Jews and injuring fifty.

On February 14, 2001, a veteran bus driver from Gaza rammed his Egged bus into the crowd of soldiers and civilians waiting at the Azor junction, killing eight Israelis and maiming twenty-five. The attack also destroyed the plan to expand the Center's Building Business Bridges (BBB) program to young Palestinians, whose permits to enter Israel were cancelled. The program, conceived in the mid-1990s to foster the emergence of a young Palestinian-Israeli-Jordanian business leadership for the burgeoning matrix of the New Middle East, shrank to a local initiative for Israeli Arabs and Jews.

On March 7, 2001, Ariel Sharon — who had been forced to resign in disgrace as minister of defense for his role in the 1982 Sabra and Shatilla massacre in Lebanon, and who had sparked the current *intifada* with his arrogant visit to the Temple Mount in September 2000 — was elected prime minister of Israel. Palestinian terrorists stepped up the pace of bombings in Israel. Sharon picked up the pace of assassinations, or "targeted killings," of Palestinian leaders.

On the streets of Tel Aviv, between sessions of chemotherapy, I lived a giant game of Russian roulette. When I entered a café, I wondered: Would this café, at this time, be the one that a suicide bomber would enter, blowing me to bits just as the doctors are working to beat my cancer? I censored my movements with personal magical rules: Don't ride buses, but department stores are okay; meet friends at a forgotten neighborhood café, but not at the crowded one on Dizengoff Street.

On Friday evening, June 1, students from the Shevah Moffet High School went out to celebrate the end of the school year at Tel Aviv's Dolphinarium disco club, not far from the music center where Shai studied violin. As they waited excitedly to enter, a suicide bomber detonated his explosive belt in the midst of the crowd, killing twenty-one teenagers and wounding 120, most of them immigrants from the former Soviet Union.

The terror thus penetrated some previously respected boundary. It was not only the targeting of high school students that dragged me into dread, it was the intimacy of the bomber's knowledge of the patterns of my society's life. A Palestinian strapped with explosives knew that on Friday nights, hundreds of young people gathered at this popular, dilapidated building on the Tel Aviv beach to drink and dance. Had he worked at the Dolphinarium, washing glasses? Or even gone dancing there himself, returning now for one last deadly tango?

I was being violated in my own home. In late summer, I finished my radiation therapy, and was now free to resume my life as before — but what life was I resuming? In the words of Israeli author David Grossman, death had become a way of life.

Always looking, perhaps obsessively, for what could be built, I struggled to find a new foundation for hope. I met with Yossi Rein, a global strategic consultant, in his sparse, white, minimalist Tel Aviv office to discuss the possibility for strategic action on the part of business leaders to jump-start negotiations with the Palestinians. Leaning back in his cleanly designed chair, he said, "There is nothing you can do." He ran his fingers through his hair, and said in a tired voice, "What we need now is a paradigm shift. To achieve a paradigm shift, you must be in crisis. Our situation now is painful; but it is not a crisis. Only after 3,000 Israelis die will our society be able to make a paradigm shift."

I stared at Yossi, paralyzed by his cold statistics of doom. Our death toll had reached less than two hundred. Would I be alive when we reached 3,000 dead? Would Shai, Liad? What should we do in the meantime, wait helplessly for the rising tide of death?

Just months earlier, our two peoples had been within reach of a final status peace deal. Palestinian and Israeli businesspeople had sought each other out, with the Center for Jewish-Arab Economic Development as a key connector, working to build a linked future. Now, Jewish leaders throughout the Galilee were urging Jews to boycott the garages and restaurants of neighboring Arab villages, and Arab Israelis thought twice about venturing into the neighboring Jewish cities; those who didn't absolutely need to,

190

stayed home. Like a tired swimmer, I felt myself being sucked out to sea in a thirsty undertow, and I was weakening as I watched the shore recede.

Despite Yossi's warnings, however, Helmi and I managed to scrape together a handful of Israeli and Palestinian businesspeople, who traveled hours to meet in the high-ceilinged colonial elegance of the American Colony Hotel in Jerusalem. Leaders of industry who had been colleagues just months ago in information technology, in construction, in textiles, could now barely reach one another across the thicket of checkpoints that had spawned in response to the *intifada*. One young Palestinian man, who had given up a job in Silicon Valley to resettle in Ramallah when the Palestinian Authority was established in 1993, described with quiet equanimity each checkpoint on his three-hour trip from Ramallah to Jerusalem — a journey that used to take thirty minutes. I imagined him in California, driving freely from Stanford University to San Francisco without a thought, then saw him transposed to a checkpoint where a frightened 18-year-old Israeli soldier (who would love to live in California) pointed a gun at him and demanded his ID card. I was overwhelmed with the sadness and the absurdity.

Samir Huleileh, who had been director general of the Palestinian Ministry of Economics and Trade, stated quietly, "We cannot now think of doing business across these divides. But we must remember that, someday, we will come back to trade and work with one another. That is the basis of both peoples' lives in this region."

My eyes filled with tears. At the door, Israeli and Palestinian men parted — some with handshakes, some with hugs. None of us knew if and when we would meet again.

In September 2001, my niece, Frances, came to live with us for her gap year, to polish her Hebrew and volunteer in Israel before going to Columbia University. My brother and sister-in-law, her father and mother, anguished: Should they allow her to come to Tel Aviv, where young people were being blown up in cafes? Should they try to curb her love for Israel, her interest in being here, in learning, in joining the Jewish people in this time of distress — because of their fear for her safety? What was the right message for liberal Jewish parents to give to their 18-year-old, spreading her wings? I was moved that, despite their anxiety, they stood behind their daughter's choice.

Days later, as Frances, Shai, Liad and I sat in our Tel Aviv living room, watching television images of the Twin Towers collapsing in the terror attack of 9/11, I was struck by the absurdity of our choices. If Frances had stayed in the U.S., she would have been in New York at the time.

Her optimistic presence in the midst of the *intifada* was like a life-buoy for me. Tall, with wavy blond hair, Frances, like her mother, has prodigious energy, and, like her father, a keen analysis of society and an encyclopedic curiosity. She takes life as it comes, lighting up a room with her smile, and finding something helpful to do in almost any situation.

Every day, as I returned from work, discouraged and impotent, Frances helped me cook, and cheerfully told us stories from her *ulpan* of new phrases and new friends. In many ways, she reminded me of an improved model of myself at her age: intrepid, idealistic. Twenty years before, I had arrived in Israel at about her age, excited to be part of this society, to learn, to hike, to engage, to help make the country more just, because it is Jewish.

Both Israel and I have grown more sober over the years. When I arrived in 1980, Israel was more adolescent — still socialist and collective, still building itself, still colored by the Eastern European founding generation. Now, Israel was more middle-aged — bourgeois, with greater social gaps, some uneasy peace agreements, and internal contradictions blowing up in our streets. After two decades of founding and running a social-change organization, raising two sons alone, battling cancer, and now fearing for my children's (and my niece's) lives on the streets, as well as their souls, I was confused and depleted.

In March 2002, my brother, Seth, his wife, Nancy, and their daughter, Rena, came to celebrate Passover with us. Although I desperately wanted to arrange a feast at which my family would met my friends, I was too tired and depressed to do it. The one family I managed to invite cancelled two days before the seder. Nancy valiantly injected her boundless energy to salvage the event, rushing around the apartment arranging pillows, cooking, setting the table, leading the service.

Reclining on the floor of our Tel Aviv apartment, I sank into the seder's tone of oppression: "They persecuted us; they put task masters over Israel to conscript their labor . . . We cried out to the Lord, the God of our fathers; God heard our voice, he saw our persecution, our toil, and our oppression."

Who was hearing our pain now? Who was trying to maintain any sense of vision in the growing atmosphere of retribution?

No one, perhaps, except Hani al Hassan. The day before, I had received a lone fax at my office. It had arrived without a phone call, without a context, from a man I'd never met. I read out to my family the strange and moving greetings from Fatah that had arrived mysteriously:

The Palestine Liberation Movement
Fatah Foreign Relations Department
20/3/2002

Dear Mrs. Kreimer,
    On the occasion of the Pessah Holiday, I wish you: 'Hag Pessah Kashair V'sameh.' May God bless all the region's peoples with peace.
    Hani Al-Hassan Head of Fatah Foreign Relations Dept. President of Sons of Avraham — Palestine
    By celebrating Pessah don't deny the right of Palestine's Sons of Avra-ham to have their own Pessah and to win their freedom and independence. Remember: Israelis and Palestinians will inevitably coexist together on this land. Therefore, bloodshed and hatred spreading are worthless and helpless.

I tried to imagine how Hani had learned the traditional bless-ing one Jew gives to another: for a Happy and Kosher Holiday. Had he heard his Israeli jailers wish it to one another? Or had his customers in the Tel Aviv restaurant told him, when he was a young waiter? In the midst of sending out his holiday messages to sympathetic Israelis, had Hani gone on coffee breaks with the guys down the hall, who were planning the next terror attack?

Whoever he was, Hani Al Hassan had thought enough about my festival of freedom to ask me to infuse the ancient story with meaning for today — to urge me to see that, as we relive the age-old story of our oppression, and as Jewish children are being blown up in the bars of Tel Aviv, Israel now plays the role not of oppressed but of oppressor. In his note, he asked that out of this awareness we do something to change the situation. I felt grateful to this anonymous Palestinian, who penetrated the clouds of my depression and brought me back the original meaning of our festival of liberation, as stated in Exodus 23:9: "You shall not oppress a stranger: for you know the heart of a stranger, seeing you were strangers in the Land of Egypt."

As we were speaking of ancient liberation, 130 miles up the Mediterranean coast, in Beirut, the members of the Council of the Arab League debated a peace proposal brought by the Saudi Crown Prince Abdullah. It laid out a four-point plan for achieving peace: Israel's withdrawal to the pre-1967 borders; creation of a Palestinian state on the lands of the West Bank and Gaza; Jerusalem as capital of Palestine; an agreed-upon and just solution for the refugees, including their compensation and relocation, not necessarily in Israel, but also in Palestine and other states. In exchange, all the Arab states would recognize Israel and its right to exist, and would open normal relations.

The meeting was not well attended. Nevertheless, the Saudi Initiative was approved, representing a key landmark in the Arab states' approach to Israel. Diametrically opposed to the decision of the Arab Summit Conference in Khartoum in 1967 — no peace with Israel, no recognition of Israel, no negotiations with Israel — this decision represented the first Arab plan for historic reconciliation of the Israeli-Arab conflict.

As they debated, the delegates to the Arab League were oblivious to the festivities about to begin 116 miles south of them, in Israel's coastal town of Netanya. There, hundreds of people were sitting down to enjoy a huge seder at the Park Hotel. As they raised their glasses with the words, "Here I am, ready to perform the *mitzvah* of the first cup of wine, and to dedicate this evening to telling the story of miracles and wonders that were performed for our ancestors in Egypt on the night of the fifteenth of Nisan more than 3200 years ago," a Palestinian from Tulkarem strode into the dining room and detonated a suitcase full of explosives. The bombing shattered bodies and wine cups, killing twenty-eight people and wounding 140. The dead included six married couples — the eldest among them, Alter and Frieda Britvich, 88 and 86.

When I learned of the attack the next day, I felt as if the air had suddenly been removed from the room and I was suffocating — as if something had gone terribly wrong in our ancient story, and instead of our passing between the walls of water on our exodus from Egypt, the Sea of Suf was crashing in on us, burying us under tons of water.

Or perhaps we were becoming Pharaoh's soldiers.

Arik Sharon's response was to ignore the Saudi Initiative and to resume his catechism: There is no partner for peace, we have no option other than military action. The Israeli government began Operation Defensive Shield on March 29, 2000, calling up 20,000 reserve soldiers and sending tanks to reoccupy Ramallah, Nablus, Tulkarem, and Bethlehem in the largest military operation in the West Bank since 1967. As a member of an elite fighting unit, my nephew, Sagi, from Kibbutz Kinneret, took part in Defensive Shield, guarding the outskirts of a West Bank town, to allow the security services and regular troops to search for people and information.

Before Defensive Shield, I felt powerless, afraid to go to a café or take a bus. Now the fear was accompanied by deep shame about how we were using our state power. I felt anger about the power we were choosing *not* to use: the power to negotiate, to seek a political resolution.

As Defensive Shield wore on, the Israeli businesspeople from the small group that had met in the American Colony sent food and basic supplies from their business' warehouses to the Palestinian populations under curfew. Although they provided the items wholeheartedly, none wanted their business' names used, for fear of Israeli consumer retaliation against their companies. Using their private names, without the company association, they placed an advertisement in the Israeli press, calling on our government to respond not only to the terrorism of the Park Hotel, but also to the Saudi initiative. To them, as businesspeople who constantly monitor their environment looking for opportunities and dangers, ignoring this diplomatic initiative made no sense. But their voices were lost in the roar of Israeli tanks and Palestinian suicide bombers.

As the IDF continued its West Bank military operation, the Israel Lands Authority (ILA) began to crack down on Israeli Bedouin who were trying to use desert lands in the Negev that they saw as their own. Throughout the spring, the ILA, which administers the lands nationalized by the government, had been dusting the disputed fields with herbicides, killing thousands of dunams of young crops planted by Bedouin families. The Israeli Arab leadership decided to highlight this policy on Land Day, March 30, which since 1976 had been marked by protests of the expropriation of land from the Israeli Arab population for the purposes of Jewish settlement.

I had not attended a Land Day event for years, feeling that it was a day for the Arab citizens of Israel to speak in their own voice. This year, however, because of the Center's involvement with the unrecognized Bedouin villages, I knew many of the families whose crops had been destroyed in the Negev. Frances, who had been living and volunteering there in the Bedouin town of Laqiya, wanted to express solidarity with her friends and neighbors. We decided to join the demonstration.

Frances and I arrived early and were waved to a provisional parking area on a hillock in the middle of the desert. Young Bedouin men stationed around the grounds smiled and welcomed us, showing us to a huge black tent set up on the rise, surrounded by acres of dusty earth. Collapsed sprouts lay withering in the desert sun, the latest casualties in the fight to expropriate the lands of Israel exclusively for the Jewish people.

Flags waved gaily in the warm breeze. Although I had not expected to see Israeli flags in this commemoration of the Palestinians' struggle to maintain their lands and their identities, I was not prepared for my own visceral reaction at being surrounded by a sea of Palestinian flags. With whom was I identifying by being here, while Palestinian suicide bombers were attacking the cities of Israel and my nephew Sagi was serving his reserve duty?

Looking west across the desert, I saw the hazy buildings of the Israeli port town of Ashkelon in the distance, to the north. In 1948, this had been the Palestinian town of Al Majdal, home to almost 12,000 Palestinians, including a boy named Ahmed Yassin, then 12. Most of Yassin's neighbors had fled Al Majdal south along the coast during the war in 1948. Yassin was one of 1,500 people who stayed behind. In 1950, using the new Absentee Property Law, Israel had confiscated the lands of the Al Majdal residents and deported the remaining 1,500 to the Gaza Strip, which was then under Egyptian control. Yassin went on to become a revered Islamic leader and the spiritual father of the Hamas — which was now sending young men to blow themselves up in Tel Aviv, Lod and Ashkelon.

We were all living our lives on the remains of Sheikh Munis, Lydda and Al Majdal.

What was I doing here? Who were the people around me, and what did they want? Were they flying the Palestinian flag as a matter of identity, as Palestinian citizens of Israel, protesting their government's efforts to confiscate their historic lands and push them into urban slums? Or did they share Hamas' vision of re-claiming Palestine, desiring that the green-black-red Palestinian flag, which flew here in the winds of the Negev, would be the flag of their country? When a group of young people came marching through the grounds, carrying huge photographs of Hassan Nasrallah, and chanting in rhythmic Arabic, "Hassan, Hassan, a friend indeed; send missiles on Tel Aviv," I stifled a scream of rage. Who were these arrogant children gleefully calling for Hezballah in Lebanon to launch missiles to kill my children in Tel Aviv? Did they understand that in no other nation of the Middle East — not in Palestine, not in Lebanon, not in Egypt — could they stage such a demonstration calling for an outside power to launch attacks on their own country?

I had come here in solidarity with the plight of the Bedouin whose lands are being unjustly taken from them by our government. Now I was being told that my children were nothing but cannon fodder. How many people sitting here agreed with this cheerful band? Despite the many people in the audience whom I knew, and who assured me that the group was marginal, I felt isolated, afraid, and offended.

Days later, I discovered that my co-director Helmi's son, Ehab, a lawyer in Beersheva, was representing these friends of Hassan Nas-rallah, who had been arrested by the Israeli authorities. Apparently, not only my sensibilities had been offended — though apparently, my partner's son's sensibilities were much different than my own.

On a much deeper level than I ever imagined, many Palestinians living in, and citizens of, Israel have never recognized the legitimacy of Jewish claims to the Land. They see the Jews' arrival as that of European colonialists, desiring to make their home in the Levant, on lands of the native Palestinians. They do not recognize deep ties of the Jewish people to this Land, abandoned two millennia ago, and they are skeptical of claims that the Jews needed a land because of thousands of years of persecution, most recently, the Holocaust. Why should they, in the Middle East, pay with their lands for the sins of Europe?

In the Israeli Bedouin town of Laqiye, as Holocaust Day (Yom HaShoah), April 9, approached, Frances devoted a meeting of her high-school English club to the subject of the Holocaust. The kids, 15 to 16, all grew up as Israeli citizens, albeit in a poor and neglected town in the Negev desert, and had gone through at least ten years of Israeli schooling. All had televisions at home, and were up to date with the latest sports, fashions and video games.

"I don't really think there was a Holocaust," said one boy. "Not the way the Israelis tell."

"It is probably exaggerated," said another, "just like all the other Israeli propaganda."

"I don't believe it was six million. Maybe tens of thousands, but not six million."

Despite all my years in Jewish-Arab relations, I was shocked to hear about this. I knew that Israeli Arabs dismiss the Israeli pathos around the Holocaust, much of which is manipulatively directed toward "proving" that because the Jewish people were massacred and are still hated throughout the world, there was no alternative to a Jewish State in 1948. But to dismiss the fact of the Holocaust altogether — to see it as a Zionist gimmick?

Both Palestinians and Israelis were playing a zero-sum-game of legitimacy-through-victimhood. In such a game, recognizing your legitimate place in this land — achieved by being a greater victim — amounts to annihilating my legitimate claim. So we wee caught in a race to appear the greater victim, and to sabotage the others' claims, the others' history.

In such a game, I could not win. If my making *aliyah* to Israel, and being accepted immediately as a citizen, a "member of the club," meant that my colleagues' place here was less legitimate, then I was unwittingly buying into a game in which I did not believe. Perhaps, in such a country, I — and my optimistic sons — had no place.

Chapter 18
No Return to Old Dreams

Shattered dreams are a hallmark of our mortal life.

—Martin Luther King, Jr.

Morning after morning, I snapped awake at 5:00 a.m., heart pounding, not knowing why I'd woken up but unable to return to sleep. Cold and alone, I stared at the ceiling. Would I live to see my children grown? In what kind of hateful society would they become adults? I'd throw off the covers and pace the living room like a caged animal. Nothing meant anything any more. What had I accomplished all these years? What could I point to? What was left?

I felt breathless, caught in a whirlpool that was pulling me deeper and deeper into waters I couldn't escape. Apparently — with the doctors' skilled help — I had successfully survived cancer. But I no longer knew what I am living for.

At work, I watched Helmi taking direction of the Center. Kiram, Mohammed, Ronit entered his office for supervision and advice. I sat alone in front of my computer, correcting texts that were adequate to begin with, spending tremendous energy on tiny details. No focus, no point. Things happened without my involvement or my input. Helmi consulted with me as a formality.

I could no longer muster the energy, the belief, the hope needed to continue. Depleted, I decided to leave the Center. This time, when I told Helmi of my decision, he did not argue and threaten to quit if I left, as he had eight years earlier, when I was caring for Shuki in his final months.

At home, in my despair and impotence, I would lose patience with Shai and Liad. "When I start yelling at you for no real reason," I offered, "tell me: Mom, you are a human being." They looked at me and nodded carefully.

In the world outside, suicide bombings continued in Israel's cities; the IDF reoccupied the West Bank; the government decided to build a barrier wall to separate Palestinians from Israelis.

In June 2002, Helmi and I made one last public appearance together, in the halls of the Knesset, to accept the Speaker of the Knesset's Award for Contributing to the Quality of Life in the Field of Tolerance. Helmi spoke of the universal values that guided him as a Muslim in leading the Center, quoting the Muslim *hadith:* "You will not gain entrance to Paradise until you believe; and you cannot believe until you love your fellow-man. The way to love is to spread peace among God's creatures." I quoted *Pirkei Avoth:* "The sword comes into the world because of justice delayed and justice denied." I spoke of what the Center had done to bring justice in the past. I could say little about how to bring it now.

I looked at the kids, sitting attentively in the polished seats of the Knesset. Intense, curly-haired Shai was 11, and Liad, blond and elfish, was 9. It was for them and their future in this country that I had labored all these years. What, now, was I giving them?

I could not say, in the halls of the Knesset, what I was beginning to believe: that the vision of Israel as a Jewish, democratic state is flawed at its core; that the systemic neglect of economic development in Arab towns, and the hyper-development of Jewish ones, is not just the result of the discrimination of a majority against a minority — that can be eased by greater understanding, capacity building, and more equitable legislation, as the Center has aimed to bring about — but is part of the continuing struggle of the Israeli national movement against the Palestinian national movement to control land and resources and the character of society. This struggle grinds on, not only in the occupied West Bank, but in the Galilee and the Negev as well.

I had started my journey in Israeli society a generation after Israel's traumatic birth, in 1980, when the Israeli government was building Misgav, a network of Jewish hilltop settlements, to claim

200

the lands of the Galilee. I had created the Center in 1988, when the Ministry of Industry was establishing the massive Tsippori Industrial Zone — not in order to stimulate the economic development of the three poor Arab towns whose lands were taken for this project, but in order to strengthen the Jewish city of Upper Nazareth, miles away. I had worked with the Bedouin of the Negev over the last years to help them eke out decent, recognized communities in the desert, while the Ministry of Agriculture had poisoned their crops — and, when the anger of the young people of these communities erupted, the police had fired on them with live ammunition.

For years, I had not concerned myself with an ultimate vision for Israel. At the Center, I had created a kind of home that purposely provided a "shortsighted" vision, a vision for now. Whatever we all desired for Israel "at the end of days," we could all agree that it was our shared country and that we want to share it more equitably. Now, in the aftershocks of the second *intifada*, most Israelis didn't want to share anything. Instead, there was a desire to vanquish, separate, and build walls.

The Center was my life's work, my dream, my home. My best creative energy had flowed into envisioning it, drawing others into the vision, designing it, building, working, revising, re-building. Now I was leaving that home, watching the Center float away — a small, battered boat upon a dreadful ocean — without me.

*I was tired of being alone, and tired of fighting. I wanted some-*one else to share the burden of my decisions, someone else to love and parent Liad and Shai. But there was no one else. I wanted someone to hold me at night while I cried, and kiss me and tell me I was okay and that we would figure it out together. I dreamed of returning to the veteran expatriate community I had been part of in my twenties in Jerusalem, centered around the Reform synagogue of Kol HaNeshama and a progressive community of human rights organizations.

What would such a move do to the kids? They were happy, in a good school with good friends. And in Jerusalem, more than in Tel Aviv, suicide bombers were blowing themselves up in cafés and buses. Jerusalemites were moving to Tel Aviv, not the opposite. Jerusalem was ground zero of this conflict. What if we moved to Jerusalem and my kids got blown to pieces on a bus?

If we went, I might hurt my children or worse. If I stayed, I would continue dying slowly from within, caught in a bubble of Tel Aviv high-tech "lightness of being" that ignored the vicious conflict around us. I was withering away in loneliness, lacking vision, lacking a sense of how to get out of the deadly spiral we were in — and I was in.

When I was accepted to a mid-career training program in Jerusalem, I took it as a sign, and we made preparations to move. The kids said goodbye to the friends with whom they had grown up. Havurat Tel Aviv gave us a beautiful send-off, complete with t-shirts and speeches and clever *gematria* on our names. Tova, my *sabra* friend and mother of Liad's best buddy, in whose home Liad feels totally accepted, was hurt that I was breaking up friendships that had grown to be like family, between her son and mine and between the two of us. "The kids will always remember this choice," she said in her matter-of-fact way. "You are doing what you need to do. But don't be surprised if they are angry and choose to abandon you when they are older."

"I am taking that chance," I answered in a hollow voice.

Days before we left, in the chaos of boxes and the minutiae of decisions — what to take, what to discard — I released a frustrated tirade upon the kids. Cringing, Shai mumbled, "Mom, you're a human being." I dropped down onto one of the boxes and drew him near.

Broken and unsure, I left the home in Tel Aviv where Liad and Shai had grown up, where Shuki had died, where I had vomited my guts out during chemotherapy. I mustered my energy to set up a new home in Jerusalem, hoping to recover a community I'd once had, and to escape my loneliness. I was hoping to find a partner with whom I could recreate the kind of home and family that I had always dreamed about and assumed would be mine. I was hoping to refind the Israeli-ness that had drawn me to this country decades ago, and to confront some of the fundamental, existential questions about the country that I had adopted, and that had adopted me.

People dressed differently in Jerusalem than they did in Tel
Aviv. There were fewer tank tops, longer skirts, more black coats,

more *kippot*. In stores, people still smoked, even though the anti-smoking law had long been enforced and internalized in Tel Aviv. Shopkeepers still tried to sell the goods they had rather than the ones customers wanted, just as they did in 1980 when I first came to Israel. The sea — the openness to the globalized world — seemed far away. Landlocked in the desert hills, I felt the power of the ancient, the traditional, in people's lives.

I was surprised to hear English spoken everywhere in the public space, on the streets, in parks, in museums, in offices. Apparently, tourists and *yeshiva-bokhers* from New York were drawn to Jerusalem, while Tel Aviv remained a Hebrew city, with thriving Hebrew theater, Israeli art, and dance.

Shai and Liad hated Jerusalem. They hated leaving their friends; they hated leaving the openness of Tel Aviv. They hated the small-town clannishness of atomized communities, each of which seemed to have its own school. Shai went to the elite academic high school, with many schoolmates whose parents taught at Hebrew University or had attended this same high school a generation ago. Liad attended a school connected to the Reform movement, where, despite attempts toward *gibush* (Israeli-style social cohesion), an atmosphere of American-style competition seeped into the classroom from immigrant homes.

As the kids continued to feel estranged, I realized that by moving to Jerusalem I had not only returned to the roots of the Palestinian-Israeli conflict, but that the wrenching loss of friends, and their helplessness in the face of upheaval, had thrown Shai and Liad back to the core conflict in their lives: the loss of their father. Unlike that loss, for which they could blame no one, the loss of Tel Aviv had an address: me. While I found some healing in Jerusalem — new work, the comforting bubble of the American-Israeli community, the rhythm of the week as streets quieted on Shabbat, reconnecting to the friends of my early years in Israel — for my sons, old wounds opened. They were wounds that took years for me to recognize, wounds that I could not redress.

In short, the equilibrium I gained in Jerusalem came at great cost to my family. Years after moving there, I found myself living in a truncated and incomplete home. The dream I'd had of community and a loving partner remained a dream, and Liad and Shai could not enter that dream, for their community had been in Tel

Aviv. Even for me, coming back to the community as a widowed mother and cancer survivor at mid-life did not hold the same allure as entering that community as a single woman on the brink of her career. Perhaps I, like Israel, had disengaged from some fundamental part of myself and didn't even know it. And perhaps there is no going back, no return possible to lost dreams or old visions — there is only the creation and pursuit of new ones.

IV. At Fifty: Offering Counsel
(2004-2010)

Chapter 19
You Can Use the Facilities, But You Can't be a Member

In the third stage [of Jewish-Arab encounter] the Jewish group attempts to return to the status quo ante (before the Arab group became stronger); its doing so engenders an acute conflict, and the atmosphere turns bitter, sometimes intolerably so. In the fourth stage, when the Arab group refuses to retreat, the atmosphere becomes one of impasse.

—Rabah Halabi*

In the dry summer heat, Liad, Shai and I were creating a home in Jerusalem. We painted old furniture, set up the stereo, found the right nooks for favorite books and toys. Our 20-year-old cat, Pushkin, went into hiding, emerging two days later to survey her new domain. Friends, and my niece Frances, indefatigable in her generous assistance on her visit over the summer, unpacked boxes, bought plants for the balcony, invited us to dinner. We were swept up in the energy of our new place.

Then came the first day of school, when Liad balked on the threshold of his new classroom, trepidation and sadness in his eyes. Instead of being greeted by old friends, he stood on the outside of cliques of strangers — kids who all felt at home with each

---

* Rabah Halabi, editor, *Israeli and Palestinian Identities in Dialogue: The School for Peace Approach*, Rutgers University Press, 2004.

207

other, whom he had not chosen and to whom he did not belong. My heart ached at his sense of homelessness.

At 11:20 p.m. on September 9, 2003, I had just turned out my lights and settled into bed when I heard the explosion. *Maybe it's a truck backfiring,* I thought lamely. Then I heard sirens and automatically switched on the radio. The late-night easy-listening program was interrupted: ". . . a bomb has ripped through the popular Café Hillel on Emek Refaim Street in the German Colony of Jerusalem. Crews of Magen David Adom are evacuating scores of wounded to Shaare Zedek Hospital. There are unconfirmed reports of fatalities. Extensive damage is reported to the premises . . ."

My cellphone began to ring. Again and again I reassured friends and family that we were okay. I made a mental list of friends I thought might have been in the area, and began calling, dialing multiple times before getting a free line in the overload of calls. All were safe, thank God.

Finally, with no more obsessive rituals of helplessness left to carry out, I dropped off to sleep. When I awoke the next morning, I was exhausted. Sixteen people had been killed in this and another bombing, and over eighty wounded.

Among the victims were Dr. David Appelbaum, 51, and his daughter, Nava, 20, who was to have been married that day. Dr. Applebaum had headed the emergency room at Shaare Zedek. He was known for his acute attention to detail and for his immense personal dedication. More than once, he had rushed to the scene of a terror attack to treat the wounded himself. Appelbaum had returned that afternoon from the U.S., where, on the second anniversary of 9-11, he had delivered a lecture on the organization of emergency care in terror attacks. He had met his daughter, Nava, for a father-daughter talk at Café Hillel on the eve of her wedding. The Hamas terrorist had detonated his explosive belt just inside the entrance to the café.

I stood at the door to my sons' room as they breathed deeply in early morning sleep. I tried to imagine Shai as a young man, beaming, in a crisp new suit, about to marry the woman he loves and launch a new home. As tears stung my eyes, I envisioned David Applebaum speaking with his daughter. I saw him taking her hand and wishing her joy in her new life. I imagined her hair, freshly coiffed, and her nervous excitement. It must have been hard for her to carve out a quiet moment for her father the night before she was to be married. But she had, and now she was dead. Murdered.

I choked on my tears and my rage. I ran to the bathroom and retched. I wanted to scream, run into the street, grab passersby and shake them, wake them from their stupor. What had I done, bringing my sons to Jerusalem, to the heart of the conflict and violence?

My sister-in-law Yael phoned from Kibbutz Kinneret. "Sarah, how are you, how are the boys? That Café is near your home, no?" She had been baffled by my choice to move the family to Jerusalem, and undoubtedly opposed it. But she was not the type to not second-guess others' decisions, and generously supported us however she could. Yael spoke with uncharacteristic bitterness — "We are creating enemies who will hate us for generations"— and told of the experience of her son, Sagi, in Ramallah. A strapping 28-year-old, he had been studying in a college preparatory program and had served in an elite infantry unit in the army, carrying out missions we would never hear about. As a reservist, he had been called up for Operation Defensive Shield and entered the cities of the West Bank, doing house-to-house searches, commandeering private homes as guard posts. Later he told me, "It's something intimate, entering a Palestinian family's home, smelling the food in the kitchen, seeing their beds. To do the work of a soldier, you have to disconnect from yourself. At some point, I began to ask myself, what reality am I living in; what reality am I choosing in my life?"

As a mother, I, too began to wonder. What are we doing to our young people, who learn to accept unacceptable situations? What are we doing to Palestinian young people, who are awakened in the middle of the night by Israeli soldiers in their bedroom? What are Palestinians doing to their own young people, who are increasingly ready to blow themselves up and kill ours? How do I raise Shai and Liad, who may be called to missions similar to Sagi's to defend me in the future?

I joined a training program for Jewish and Arab mediators, with the idea of forming a joint "SWAT" team that could step in to defuse tension in times of conflict. Part of our training included connecting to our own traumas and fears in relation to the Jewish-Arab conflict.

One Jewish participant, Chassia, the daughter of a Holocaust survivor, described how her fears in the recent violence had been amplified by the ever-present, inherited trauma of her mother's experience in Poland. Chassia's mother, an extraordinarily beautiful woman, had been taken with other young Jewish beauties from the Warsaw ghetto to serve as prostitutes for Nazi soldiers. Having already lost her family, she had decided that she would rather die and stepped out of the marching lines, expecting to be shot. Surprisingly, no one stopped her. Half-starved and with no possessions, she managed to survive in the Polish forests and remote villages, pretending to be a Polish-Christian refugee.

"In October 2000," Chassia told us, "as a crowd of Palestinian Israelis marched toward the hilltop community where I live in the Galilee, I felt that my family and I were about to be slaughtered in a pogrom."

I recalled the partial evacuation of Kibbutz Lotem in the Misgav area in first days of the second *intifada*.

"Of course, the police protected us, but the fear remains here," Chassia stated, placing her hand on her stomach. "I will not let that fear rule my life." As Chassia spoke, I could see her mother's beauty and determination echoed in her own face.

Surprisingly, many Arab colleagues told of incidents not from the current *intifada*, and not from 1967, but from 1948. The stories all followed a common theme of dispossession.

Younis, a tall, soft-spoken engineer in a major Israeli company, related his memories with straightforward simplicity. "Before the war my town, Tarshiha, was a major Arab village in the Galilee, with over 5,000 people, some of whom were quite wealthy. I remember some of the beautiful old stone houses that still stood when I was a child. I was born in 1958, so I didn't see the events I want to tell you about. But I have heard them told scores of times — by my grandmother and grandfather, by uncles and aunts, by the elders in our village — as if they happened yesterday. And so they are a part of me.

"In 1948 Israeli planes bombed our village. After the first day, some people moved into the mosque, assuming that there they would be safe. The next day, the mosque was bombed and many were killed. By the way, Abie Nathan [later a renowned and cavalier peace activist who flew to Egypt in 1966 to deliver a petition for peace to President Gamal Abdel Nasser] was one of the pilots. Years later he came to our village and visited a woman who had been paralyzed from her waist down in the bombing. He brought her an electric wheelchair, which she accepted as a symbol of reparation."

Younis took a sip of water, adjusted his glasses, and looked at Chassia. "After the war," he continued, "only about 500 of Tarshiha's original inhabitants remained. Most had fled to Lebanon. The abandoned homes were taken over by the army, including my grandparents' home, although my grandparents never left the Galilee.

"In 1949 to '50, Jewish refugees were settled in the abandoned homes, and these strangers became our neighbors — instead of our own relatives. Most of the newcomers were from Romania. We developed good relations with them. In the evenings I remember sitting outside as the adults drank coffee together.

"During the day, my grandmother would sometimes begin crying over her brothers and their families, who used to live next door and now were gone. I couldn't understand how my grandmother could be crying by day and in the evening could sit drinking coffee and eating cookies with these strangers who were living in her brothers' homes."

Younis looked around to see how we were reacting. We waited in breathless silence for him to continue.

"My grandmother herself was not living in her own house. When the army left the village, their home, which had been commandeered as an army post, was turned over to the Jewish Agency, and converted into a kindergarten for the children of the Jewish families. I grew up living with my grandparents next to the mosque, in a house owned by the Waqf.

"My grandfather never gave up trying to recover the family home. Many times, the authorities offered to let him move into one of the abandoned properties, but he refused. Only in 1965, after bitter court battles, did my grandfather recover our old home.

"In 1957, [the Jewish development town] Maalot was built next to Tarshiha, and in 1963, the two were joined into one municipality. We thought the merger would improve services for our town. Housing was built in Maalot for the Jewish immigrants, and they left Tarshiha. Then the government decided to destroy the old houses of Arab families who had fled. I remember one elegant, two-story stone house. You know, it is unusual to build a two-story house of stone. It wasn't easy to demolish it. I remember my grandmother cursing the Jews as the bulldozers pulled it down."

Younis wiped his forehead with a napkin. Chassia poured him another cup of water.

"Israeli society erases Arab culture. It is a strategy of the government to keep Arabs on the margins; then it is easier to wipe them out. My fear is that I, too, will be thrown out of the country, that there will be a 'final solution' for Arabs here."

The muscles below my left shoulder were tightening into a knot. I pictured Yaakov, whom I'd met in Safed in my first year in Israel, jumping out a window to escape being murdered by Palestinian terrorists in Maalot in 1974. Where had Younis been at that moment, and what had he thought when he learned of the massacre?

In surprise, I caught myself slipping seamlessly into the Palestinian-Israeli trauma competition. The "winner" could defend his people's behavior by claiming greater victimization, greater legitimate right to a homeland, greater justification for using whatever means necessary necessary to maintain it. The competition is skewed from the start, for we Jews can trump any trauma with the Holocaust. In the end, however, whether winners or losers, we all remain traumatized victims.

With his fair skin, light brown hair and impeccable Hebrew, Younis could easily "pass" as an Ashkenazi Jew in Israeli society. Perhaps, for many years, he had. Now, looking around at all of us to make sure we were with him, he told us how different he was. His voice was calm. "My son used to play soccer in the Maalot club. He practiced with them, went to all the games. Sometimes there would be comments, but he was accepted." Younis' left hand rubbed his right forearm. "One day, after October 2000, coming back from a game, an argument broke out on the bus. His teammates called him a 'dirty Arab.' After that, my son didn't want to play with the Maalot club; he joined the team in Tarshiha.

"Now Arab society is becoming more violent. The Israeli government doesn't feel like our representative; and doesn't seem to care what's going on. So there is no sense of belonging.

"You want to understand the experience of being an Arab in the 'Jewish State'?" Younis caught my gaze. "It is like being a woman in an all-male club. You can use the facilities, but you can't be a member."

I thought of Liad, standing at the door of his new classroom, gazing in to a group of kids who all grew up together and of whom he was not a part. But Liad was the newcomer and Younis was the veteran, prevented from joining the club that was built around him on land that used to belong to his grandfather.

Amiram, one of the Jewish participants, pointed out that in 2080, excluding the high birthrate of the ultra-Orthodox Jews, current demographic trends within Israel proper (without the West Bank or Gaza) would result in half the citizens of the state being Palestinians. That would mean that even if we jettisoned the West Bank and Gaza tomorrow, if the Jewish nature of the state were based on maintaining a Jewish majority, we would have about three generations left as a "Jewish State." Only the ultra-Orthodox Jews, whose birthrate is higher than the Arab birthrate, would "save us" from this fate, or at least buy us more time.

Of course, this future could be staved off by "getting rid" of a significant portion of the current Palestinian population of Israel — through border changes, population transfers, or creating pressure for "voluntary" emigration. Israeli Arabs are keenly aware that all these methods were used in the past by the Zionist enterprise, primarily in the midst and the aftermath of the 1948 and 1967 wars. Therefore, current-day speeches by Israeli leaders about the "demographic threat" posed by Arab Israelis, or proposals to "swap" major Arab population areas (such as Umm el Fahm and Wadi Ara) for Israeli settlement blocs in the West Bank in a Palestinian-Israeli final-status deal, activate the worst fears of Arab citizens.

Through this lens of trauma, I saw *kibbutz galuyot* (the ingathering of the exiles) not only as an effort to save endangered Jewish communities, but also as a strategy to change the demographic balance in the fledgling Jewish state. Suddenly I understood the suspicion expressed by many Arabs that Mossad agents had been involved in terrorist acts against the Jewish communities of Arab countries in the 1950s, in order to cause almost a million Jews from Iraq, North Africa, Yemen, Egypt and Syria to come to Israel.

If demography defines the Jewishness of the state, we are existentially bound to see our fellow Arab citizens as a threat and to take increasingly discriminatory measures in order to "win" the demographic war. This vision contradicts every democratic value with which I was raised — as a Jew growing up in America.

Yet this is a part of the country I have adopted. The numbers games, the preferential treatment of Jews over Arabs, the competition for the role of victim, the Law of Return that allows Jews — even those who hardly see themselves as Jews — to become immediate citizens with more rights than those who have lived here all their lives, the continued efforts to Judaize the Galilee and the Negev: All are an existential part of the State of Israel.

What then, was I doing here?

I went back to Israel's foundations, to look again at the past.
Reading the account by Israeli "new" historian Benny Morris of the events surrounding Israel's founding in 1948, I realized that it was not just the radical fringe, the Irgun and Etsel militias, that had committed atrocities and expulsions of Palestinians in the pre-state era. Rather, the mainstream Haganah, and later the Israel Defense Forces, also systematically intimidated and expelled the Palestinian population in the period of the War of Independence.

I wondered what my position would have been had I lived in this land on the eve of Israel's Declaration of Independence, when Palestine included about 850,000 Arabs and 750,000 Jews. Would I have accepted as necessary the policies designed to rid the new state of its native Palestinian population?

After the Palestinians were expelled or fled — encouraged also by Arab leaders — Ben Gurion, the revered and practical father of the state, decided to close the borders of Israel in 1949. This kept the approximately 700,000 Palestinian refugees from returning to their homes, and ensured a Jewish majority in the new country. The Israeli Knesset, led by the mainstream Labor Party, passed the draconian Law of Absentee Property in 1950, declaring lands owned by those living during the period of the war in enemy nations — or lands not worked during the period of the war and its aftermath — to be absentee lands. These properties then "reverted" to state ownership, virtually without due process. In the 1950s, 1960s and '70s, thousands of acres of land were thus expropriated and transferred from Arab ownership and use to Jewish use.

On this land were built *kibbutzim, moshavim* and devolopment towns: Carmiel, Upper Nazareth and Misgav in the Galilee, as well as Omer and Dimona in the Negev. Some of these new towns were established on lands taken from so-called "present absentees," Arab Israelis who never left the borders of Israel but were prevented from reaching their lands by the military administration under which they lived until 1966. I remembered the "internal refugees" living in Tamra, who watched their village of Damoun become a forest of the Jewish National Fund, where they later sent their kids to summer camp.

Even more disturbing was the realization that we have not given up that tradition of "Judaizing" the public space. In the 1980s and '90s, and currently, Israel has continued its policy of concentrating Israeli Arabs on as little land as possible. In the Negev, poor, naked towns were built to contain tens of thousands of Bedouin, enabling the confiscation of their former lands for Jewish settlement.

In confusion, I decided to go see my friend and colleague, Uri Pinkerfeld, one of the founders of Israel, who had first brought the Center for Jewish-Arab Economic Development to work with the Bedouin in the Negev. Born in Jerusalem in 1928, Uri represents the Israel I loved, the Israel I thought I was joining when I came in 1980.

It took me a few weeks to catch up with him. "He's in Greece," his wife Geula said when I called. "He took his rucksack and went."

"Still trekking?" I remarked with admiration.

Geula snorted. "If you're an adventurer, it doesn't matter how old you are. The only difference is that this time, he put wheels on his pack."

It was a hot day in May when I sat down with Uri in his simple home in Kibbutz Revadim. He greeted me with his broad grin, and offered me homemade cakes left over from his 75th birthday party, celebrated with his four children and their spouses, eight grandchildren, and one great-grandchild. (When my kids came to visit the Center, Uri would always take them out to buy ice cream and talk to them about what they were up to.) Geula set a pitcher of fresh-squeezed lemonade on the table.

Uri had grown up with the fervor of ideological debates about the likes of Kropotkin and Ahad Ha'am. He had found his ideological home in the HaShomer HaTsa'ir, the Young Guard, which spawned the Mapam party and Kibbutz Artzi movement, of which he became secretary general in the 1970s. Uri hiked the length and breadth of Eretz Israel with a canvas rucksack and army-issue canteens. He had helped found Kibbutz Revadim, located originally in Gush Etzion, and became a farmer, learning about drip irrigation and turkey breeding.

In 1948, Uri had fought in the War of Independence and watched Gush Etzion fall into the hands of the Jordanians. His father had been killed by a sniper's bullet in the battle for Jerusalem. For sixty years, Uri and his wife Geula have lived in Kibbutz Revadim, relocated on the road to Ramle. He had served for over two decades as a public representative on the Board of Directors of the Israel Lands Authority, and knew more about the regulation of land than anyone I'd met. In the 1980s, he established a Jewish-Arab movement, connected to Mapam, to improve the situation of Arab citizens in Israel's periphery. He thought it was good for Mapam — and the right thing to do.

I asked Uri about his vision for Israel. Sitting at the pine table with his strong, bowed legs sticking out of blue work shorts, he looked sad and suddenly old.

"I have a very strong connection to Eretz Israel. I feel myself a citizen of the land, but I am ashamed to be a citizen of the state. The racism. The social gaps. The cynicism and corruption."

I felt the cloud of despair closing in on me. The airy little room felt hot.

"It's not just the current government," he continued. "It's most of the public that allows this. That the people can choose Arik Sharon as prime minister, after all that he has done in his life? I see a small and shrinking group that still holds humanistic values, universal values. Why is this group contracting? Because despair is growing; and there is a turning inward."

Uri sighed, bending his slightly oversized head to look at his hands, broad, powerful and sun-spotted. "I am no less a patriot than anyone else. The Zionist enterprise is an historic achievement. I love the land, the place, its past. Not the distant past, but the one I experienced as a youth: the landscape, the people, the spirit of creation." Suddenly he laughed, his full head of white hair shaking. "I love this land, but I hate the state!" The surprising words gave him release, like saying for the first time in therapy: *I hate my mother.* "Yes, definitely, I hate this state!"

He refilled his glass from a pitcher of cold lemonade that Geula had made, and topped off mine. "A critical transformation must take place in the Jewish people, so that it can look at itself," he said. "From now on, Israel should be a place of refuge for Jews. There's a problem with anti-Semitism a need for a place of refuge? Yes. But not every Jew needs to come to Israel. We should not see it as a catastrophe that less than half of the Jewish people live in Israel. It is not the numbers that count; I want this to be a spiritual center.

"We already have a territorial center, and this must remain. God forbid it should not. Now Judaism and Zionism, little by little, need to build the content of the society. I think that Zionism has many values that are more cultural, spiritual, from a certain understanding of Judaism. We, the Jewish public, we need now to differentiate between Eretz Israel as the homeland of the Jews, and the political solution. People thought that the conquest of 1967 was a completion of the War of Independence. But it was not; the intervening years created a different reality. It was not the crisis of 1948; in 1967, we had a state. There was no justification for keeping the lands won in 1967 — not political, and certainly not humanitarian.

"I don't accept the claims, that if we give them back the West Bank, they'll want Yaffo and Ramle. If they want, they want. I, too, want all sorts of things. I want Eretz Israel to the Golan, and to the Gilad. So what? At the end of the War of Independence, from the military aspect, it would have been possible to conquer the whole land, with the military capability of the IDF at the time. And there were plans to carry that out. But Ben Gurion didn't authorize the action."

Uri leaned toward me and told of standing on a hilltop with other soldiers in 1948, poised to attack Jordanian troops below, to take back the evacuated Kibbutz Revadim. Hour after hour, day after day, they waited for the order that never came. Gush Etzion, including his *kibbutz*, was lost.

Uri tipped back in his chair. "It was not an accident. Ben Gurion didn't want the Arab population of the West Bank. With them, it would have been impossible to make a Jewish state with a Jewish majority."

I was surprised; I had always thought of Israel's 1948 borders as a fallback position, imposed by harsh reality, not as an astute political choice. Perhaps, in the midst of war, it was a combination of the two.

I looked around the neat *kibbutz* room, with its simple cushioned wood couch and little kitchenette. Geula, who had been a teacher all her life, had recently taken up painting. Two of her pictures hung on the walls. their flowing rainbow colors contrasting with the tans and browns of the upholstery. Their home reminded me of the home of the Snitzes, my adopted family on Kibbutz Barkai, whom I would visit in the afternoons during my training period with Interns for Peace in 1980. The same simplicity, the same sense that what they had was good, and there was no need for more. *Dayenu* — it is enough for us.

I had worked in the banana groves in early dawn and come back to the dining hall with my fellow laborers for a breakfast of fresh cucumbers, white cheese and halva. My *kibbutz* "siblings" slept in communal children's houses and were active in the HaShomer HaTsa'ir youth movement. Following the Sabra and Shatilla massacres in 1982, the *kibbutzim*, the youth movements, and the popular consciousness of the IDF as an army of defense, quickly mobilized 400,000 people to protest Israel's — Arik Sharon's — involvement. Today, twenty years later, Israel's communal systems have deteriorated. My own children refuse to be in youth movements. People stay at home in silent and isolated despair.

Unwilling to wallow in the past, Uri continued, speaking of the future, in words that flowed with vigor. "So if there were an expert in political science who was brought in from the moon, or from Australia, and he were to come in and learn the problems of the Palestinian-Israeli conflict, from its roots, I have no doubt he would get to the conclusion that there must be some kind of federative, confederative solution in all of Eretz Israel together. No other solution will end the conflict. No other solution will withstand the osmotic pressure that you have today, when in Israel you have a per capita income of $15,000, and in Palestine, barely $700. It's clear that is not sustainable. I think," he added, "we will come back to the political outlook of HaShomer HaTsa'ir in its youth."

I realized that I had no idea what HaShomer HaTsa'ir had envisioned in its early years, before World War II. Uri summed it up with the words on the masthead of the Mapam newspaper, *Al HaMishmar:* 'For Revolutionary Socialism, for Greater Zionism, and for the Brotherhood of Peoples.' The words sounded so inspiring, so visionary, and so anachronistic. I thought of the vibrant 90-year-old Bundist woman I had interviewed for my senior thesis at Yale. Her eyes had danced as she recalled her youth, running messages for the revolutionary underground in 1917, telling the workers: "The sun belongs to everyone." That was revolutionary socialism.

I sighed, and asked Uri about Greater Zionism.

"For HaShomer HaTsa'ir, in the 1930s it was concentration of the majority of the Jewish People — at that time, before the Holocaust, 16 million — in Eretz Israel and her surroundings. And her surroundings! Greater Eretz Israel is very broad, including both banks of the Jordan River, Gilad, Bashan, maybe the Golan, which has a rich Jewish past. In my thinking, Eretz Israel is definitely the Greater Land of Israel from a Jewish viewpoint.

"How does this connect to Brotherhood of Peoples? Eretz Israel is a joint homeland to the Jewish People, which is returning to it, and to the Arab people, which is residing in it. This is the theory of HaShomer HaTsa'ir, on one foot.

"And what is Brotherhood of Peoples? A binational state. On the eve of the UN Partition Plan, there were 600,000 Jews and 1,300,000 Arabs in the land between the Jordan River and the Mediterranean Sea. In September, 1947, the partition map was published. The international committee of the UN finished its work. It was clear what was being recommended, and they were waiting for the General Assembly to decide: yes or no.

"On that map, thirty-some Jewish settlements were included in the Arab state. Kiryat Anavim and Ma'ale HaHamisha were included in the area of Jerusalem, which was to be international, and our *kibbutz*, Revadim, was to be in the Arab state, as was all Gush Etzion. Out of forty *kibbutzim* of HaShomer HaTsa'ir, eight or nine were within the Arab state.

"What did we think: to evacuate, to move to within the Jewish state? No! There would be Jewish settlements in the Arab state, just as there would be tens, if not hundreds, of Arab settlements within the borders of the Jewish state. There were 600,000 Jews within the borders of the planned Jewish state, and almost 400,000 Arabs. So what? We didn't see this as a problem.

"We weren't happy about the fact that a Jewish state was to be established and we'd be in the Arab state – but it's Eretz Israel! If there were real peace in this whole region, then what would be so bad about being in the Arab state, if they were able to agree to it? We were acquainted with the Arabs. We had lived through the riots of 1929 and 1936 — and we didn't know what it was to have a state.

"After the Holocaust, the great catastrophe, it was possible to unite Mapam around the idea that there was no alternative to a Jewish state. But not as a worldview.

"Today, you could say that this is some kind of a dream," he concluded. "I agree — the solution is not on the horizon. Getting there must be a process. Perhaps there should be two states, or, with Jordan, three states. But for vision, we must seek the solution beyond the horizon. And that will have ramifications for the current situation. I really don't have answers. It is enough that a possible direction is charted, even if it is academic, theoretical. We need, somewhere, to create some kind of hope. Otherwise, you run into so many fears, from insecurity."

I left Uri's home, walking along the lush, well-tended gardens of Kibbutz Revadim and waffling between hope and despair. On the one hand, Uri rejected the demographic numbers game, posing instead the ultimate Kantian challenge: What kind of society could we create in the next three generations that would ensure that Jewish values and culture be intact, respectable, and respected, if we share this country in relative demographic parity with our Palestinian fellow-citizens? What laws, character and values did we have to we propagate *now*, so that our great-great grandchildren could live in safety and harmony with their fellow Palestinian citizens when the tables turned and Jews were in the minority here? In this scenario, what was the "Jewish" nature of Israeli society that we might strive to preserve and strengthen?

On the other hand, in order to create a country in which everyone felt "at home," we needed to delve into the roots of the conflict. The relationship of Arab citizens to the State of Israel, and the character of our joint state, would not be resolved without a resolution to the Palestinian-Israeli conflict. That brought another tough realization: that a true peace required not only ending the occupation of lands won in the 1967 war, and facilitating the birth of a Palestinian state next to Israel, but accounting for the fundamental tragedies of Israel's birth and existence for the Palestinian people. It meant providing some sort of restitution to the people of Tarshiha and Jaffo and Sakhnin for the wrongs of 1948: the Nakba, the catastrophe, the misery and dispossession that accompanied our independence. It meant not only telling the world that Palestinians don't recognize the legitimacy of the Jewish state, but recognizing that we Jews don't really recognize the legitimacy of the Palestinians sharing that state with us, as full citizens. Maybe it also meant returning to the old dreams of some of Israel's founders, which had been rejected because of our traumas.

I wanted to be involved in conducting that kind of social "root canal" surgery.

I thought of the five stages of dialogue I had learned years ago from the group facilitators of Neve Shalom. Stage one: cordial, exploratory overtures. Stage two: the Arab minority becomes stronger. Stage three: the Jewish majority feels threatened and tries to restore the relations before the Arab group becomes more dominant. The atmosphere gets harsh. Stage four: the Arab group refuses to retreat, leading to impasse. As a society, we were stuck in that impasse. Could we reach stage five: a breakthrough, when relations become more reciprocal and egalitarian?

We in Israeli society seemed to be on the verge of historic resolution with the Palestinians, but we couldn't go that final step of facing the realities and the choices that Uri had described so simply. Neither could the Palestinians. So we were reverting to an earlier insularity. In the midst of suicide bombings and a reoccupation of the West Bank, who was ready to deal with the basic issues, and redefine the rules of the club? Instead, all around us, walls were cementing the boundaries of our national home, and we were rigidifying the entrance requirements.

Chapter 20
Good Fences Make Good Neighbors?

Before I built a wall I'd ask to know
What I was walling in or walling out,
And to whom I was like to give offense.
Something there is that doesn't love a wall.

—Robert Frost, "Mending Wall"

July 2004: We stand in the dusty urban heat of the Jerusalem neighborhood of Abu Dis, in the middle of what used to be the main road from Jerusalem to Jericho. A city bus rumbles by, grinding its gears and spraying exhaust as it turns, skirting our little group, to climb the steep grade up to the Mount of Olives. No longer can the bus continue straight along the Jericho Road, for behind me, to the east, tower grey concrete slabs, twenty-five feet high, truncating this major artery. To my left, only a neighborhood grocery and a gas station remain from a once-bustling commercial thoroughfare.

On the other side of this concrete wall, I know — although I cannot now see it — the road winds down into the Jordan Valley, past the five-story white-stone apartment buildings and the garages and houseware stores lining the main street of the town of Al Azzariye, then out to the Judean desert and the Allenby Bridge, which crosses to Jordan.

In front of me, a scruffy collection of Israeli police cadets eye the phalanx of concrete. I remind them of the Israeli cabinet's

222

decision in 2002 to put up a Separation Barrier designed to keep suicide bombers from crossing into Israel and to divide between Israel proper and the West Bank. "But where do you place such a barrier in Jerusalem," I pose to them, watching a swarthy cadet spit casually on the street, "when the policies of the last thirty-seven years, since 1967, have built new Israeli neighborhoods around the old Palestinian areas of East Jerusalem, in order to prevent a division of the city?"

Silence.

"You talk about the Security Fence as if it's a problem," says an older man, a veteran policemen, using the Hebrew word for "fence," although the barrier is a concrete wall, "but it's keeping out terrorists."

"Our government has a duty to protect us," I reply. "But let's look at the whole picture — the route of the Barrier," that's the word I use, "and its effects, which may not be to protect us." I tell them of Brigadier General Ilan Paz's comment as head of the Civil Administration for the West Bank, when he established the Qalandiya checkpoint, causing thousands of Palestinians to undergo long and humiliating checks by Israeli soldiers, day in and day out, on their way from home to work in Jerusalem" "I knew that I had to put up that checkpoint to stop the suicide bombers today. And, at the same time, I knew I was creating the suicide bombers of tomorrow."

A short, muscular cadet calls out: "I could climb that wall. I just jam my feet into the seams between the slabs, cling onto the crack with my hands, and shimmy up."

I turn around and crane my neck up to imagine this young policeman clinging like a monkey in the cracks of the Separation Barrier, high above my head. In fact, Palestinian young men do exactly what this cadet described, in order to get into Jerusalem to work, while hoping they will not be caught.

How can I describe this surrealistic picture to those who live in normal cities, where roads link one neighborhood to another, so you might get in a car on a Sunday to drive from Center City, Philadelphia to Manayunk, or from Brooklyn to White Plains, or from Palo Alto to San Jose? Imagine that suddenly, on a noisy commercial thoroughfare with a strip mall and a Dairy Queen, you can no longer proceed because a concrete wall blocks your way. Not a tollbooth, like an entrance to a highway, that regulates entry — this is a grey wall into which you would smash your car if you continued driving, a wall that you can't see around or go around. Now, in order to finish your journey, you have to turn aside and wind forty-five minutes through back streets to get to a tollbooth along a different road where there is entry for those with the right permits. But at this tollbooth they don't ask you to pay your $1.50 and go on your way, they ask for your passport to check to see if you have permission to go on to White Plains, even if White Plains is where you have lived all your life.

Imagine, further, that sovereignty over New York City is disputed. Brooklyn and the Bronx are claimed by the United States, while Queens and Staten Island are claimed by Canada. And both sides maintain historic claims to Manhattan. Roughly speaking, that is the situation in Jerusalem.

In September 2004 I joined the start-up team of Ir Amim, the "City of Nations/Peoples." My search for civic equality between Arab and Jewish citizens had led me to the roots of the Palestinian-Israeli conflict, and I wanted to be involved in tackling the core issues. None was more central or symbolic than Jerusalem, which was claimed as the religious, historic and national capital of both nations.

Ir Amim, a new non-profit organization, aimed to ease the path for the two peoples to reach agreements on how to share and divide Jerusalem, its borders and holy places. Who belongs to the city, and to whom does it belong? Who has power or sovereignty over the Temple Mount/Haram al-Sharif, the site of the First and Second Temples, which Jews believe housed the Holy of Holies where God's presence dwelled, and of the Al Aqsa Mosque, the site where Muslims believe Mohammed ascended to heaven? Who can pray and visit? And how do three quarters of a million Palestinians and Israelis live together in the meantime, under a municipality whose authority is disputed, and which needs to provide schools, building permits, and garbage pick-up?

Part of my job was to guide groups of Israelis — police cadets, high school principals, youth movement leaders and Knesset members — along the seam between East and West Jerusalem, to see and feel and discuss our own capital city.

Jerusalem, with its religious centrality to the three monotheistic faiths, has long been a political bone of contention, claimed by Israelis and Palestinians as a capital. Deemed holy also to the Christian world as the city of Jesus' crucifixion and burial, Jerusalem under the 1947 UN Partition Plan was designated to be under neither Israeli nor Palestinian sovereignty, but under international control. For this reason, the international community, including the United States, has never recognized any border for Jerusalem, and does not recognize Jerusalem as Israel's capital — not even the seemingly undisputed "West Jerusalem," home of the Knesset, the Supreme Court, and the prime minister's residence.

In the 1948 War of Independence, the historic heart of Jerusalem — the Old City, with the Church of the Holy Sepulchre, the Temple Mount, and al Aqsa Mosque — was taken by Jordan. For nineteen years, the city was divided by an earlier separation wall, which has long since been taken down, and Israelis could only gaze at the outside of the Old City stone walls. In the 1967 war, Israel took over not only the Old City of Jerusalem, but the entire West Bank. Israeli Jews, and indeed, Jews throughout the world, were ecstatic to see the city reunited. Two weeks after the war, Israel declared new borders for Jerusalem, including not only the historic areas of Jerusalem but almost seventy square kilometers of surrounding West Bank land as well. This area, although it extends to the north and south as well, is called East Jerusalem, and its inclusion within Israel is not recognized by the international community. For this reason, when the government decided in the 1970s to build Israeli neighborhoods on this land, even Israel's best friends such as Britain and the United States objected, seeing this construction outside of Israel's internationally recognized border as being no different, legally, than building West Bank settlements.

The 70,000 Palestinians living in the annexed areas saw themselves living under occupation, as were their relatives in the West Bank and Gaza. They were given the status not of citizens, which they did not want, but of "permanent residents."

This is the city I now aimed to highlight to my fellow citizens. Our Ir Amim tours drove through the Israeli neighborhoods, with white apartment buildings and schools and post offices and community centers built on the land unilaterally added to Jerusalem's borders after the 1967 war. We wound along the narrow streets of the existing Palestinian neighborhoods, with their potholes and open sewage, with no sidewalks or playgrounds, with a 50 percent high school drop-out rate, and with elementary schools operating in two shifts because of the lack of classroom space. We aimed to help people understand, on the ground, the ramifications of Israeli policies. The most recent and dramatic of these was constructing a Separation Barrier in and around the city, defining a robust Jewish Greater Jerusalem, dissecting Palestinian Jerusalem from its natural metropolitan area, and walling in a quarter million Palestinian Jerusalemites — to a polity in which they cannot get building permits for new homes nor vote for the Knesset. Our goal in the tours, indeed in all Ir Amim's work, was not only to understand, but to examine possible ways forward from here.

I envied the tour guides I met on the Talpiot Promenade overlooking the Old City. They showed Israelis and tourists the beauty of Jerusalem — the rich history, the scenic stone walls built by Suleiman the Magnificent, bathed in gold at sunset. I looked at the same scenes, and pointed out Jerusalem's blemishes — the social gaps, the discrimination, the political pitfalls.

My work with Ir Amim, fascinating and crucial, also brought me immense sadness. I had returned to Jerusalem, uprooted Shai and Liad to come here, because I loved the city. But I could no longer naively enjoy shopping on Jaffa Street, touring the church-

Sarah, at right, showing Israel's Separation Barrier on an Ir Amim tour.

es along the Mount of Olives, or basking in the insular American expatriate community congregated around Kol HaNeshama synagogue. Instead, I would walk the city streets thinking of the poverty, the disenfranchisement, the sense of occupation experienced by my fellow Jerusalemites, the Palestinians, living a fifteen-minute drive away. I could understand why many Israelis, and many Jews from England, France, or the U.S., didn't want to take our tours and puncture the comfortable myths with which we all grew up.

Guiding one tour to view Kafr Aqab, the northernmost Jerusalem neighborhood stranded on the Palestinian side of Qalandiya checkpoint, I drove with a group of curious Israelis, retirees who don't hesitate to ask questions, as well as students and mothers , along the once-bustling main road to Ramallah. Just four years earlier, in September 2000, I had traveled this same road with a group of Israeli high-tech managers on our way to a business conference designed to facilitate joint ventures with Palestinian entrepreneurs from the Palestinian Information Technology Association in Ramallah's Grand Hotel. The road, a four-lane jumble of bakeries, banks and health clinics, joined the two societies whose leaders were trying to hammer out a peace agreement.

U.S. President Bill Clinton had proposed a simple set of parameters for reaching agreement on new borders for a Jerusalem that could serve as both Palestinian and Israeli capitals: What is Jewish is Israeli, what is Arab is Palestinian. The proposal recognized the Israeli neighborhoods built after 1967 as part of Israel's capital, and recognized the Arab neighborhoods of Jerusalem as part of a new Palestinian capital, with a ragged but possible borderline between them. Under Clinton's plan, the tiny historic Old City, ground zero of the Palestinian-Israeli conflict, would be subdivided as well (albeit without walls), with the Jewish and Armenian quarters under Israeli sovereignty, and Muslim and Christian quarters under Palestinian jurisdiction. The Temple Mount/Haram al-Sharif would be divided vertically, with a Palestinian top and an Israeli base.

Israeli Prime Minister Barak had looked favorably at the proposal, and the Israeli public, surprisingly, seemed to accept it with sobriety. Palestinian leadership had examined the proposal as well. Instead of entering into an agreement, however, our two societies had been pulled into the vortex of the second *intifada*. Now the main artery joining the cities was split down the middle by a cement wall. Our group drove in the abandoned western lanes, with the wall on our right. An unseen Palestinian making a parallel trip could drive on the other side, the wall on her left. But the unseen Palestinian was now forbidden to cross into Jerusalem, and I was forbidden from visiting Ramallah. Clinton's parameters for resolving the conflict were forgotten.

*Outside Jerusalem, in contradiction to Israel's thirty-seven-*year policy of more or less seamless connection between Israel and the West Bank, the Barrier was redefining our physical, national sense of self. In many ways, the Barrier was the physical expression of a political mitosis, begun with the Oslo process and entailing both costs and benefits. Indeed, discrete pieces of the Barrier were erected in the 1990's, under direction of Prime Minister Yitzhak Rabin, following the murder of an Israeli girl in Jerusalem. At that time, Rabin said, "We have to decide on separation as a philosophy. There has to be a clear border. Without demarcating the lines, whoever wants to swallow 1.8 million Arabs will just bring greater support for Hamas . . . We want to reach a separation between us and them. We do not want a majority of the Jewish residents of the state of Israel, 98 percent of whom live within the borders of sovereign Israel, including a united Jerusalem, to be subject to terrorism."

Now, the Separation Barrier winds throughout the West Bank, marking out a mile boundary between Israel proper and the territories. My family, colleagues and I live on the "good" side of the wall; despite the suicide bombings, ours is the side with a decent economy, elected representatives, a High Court, freedom of movement, beaches on the Mediterranean, and an airport. On the other side, there are targeted assassinations and nightly searches, villages blocked off from their city centers, men sitting at home, cut off from the restaurants and garages and construction sites where they used to work, women no longer able to access the hospitals of East Jerusalem for births and treatments.

This redefinition of territory is opposed both by Palestinians and by Israeli settlers. Settlers oppose the Barrier because it slashes their vision of one uninterrupted Greater Israel and places many of them on the Palestinian side. Palestinians oppose the Barrier because it facilitates a de facto Israeli annexation of about 9 percent of the West Bank. Much of the Barrier's route does not run along the internationally recognized 1949 armistice line or the Green Line (as does the barrier erected around Gaza in the 1990s, with little international opposition). Rather, it dips deep into the West Bank, placing huge stretches of Palestinian land on the "Israeli" side and severing many Palestinian families from their olive groves and fields.

In building a Separation Barrier in the Jerusalem area, no Israeli policymaker had begun to consider using the old Green Line that had painfully separated Jews from the Western Wall, the Temple Mount, and the historic Mount of Olives cemetery during the nineteen years of Jordanian rule. Instead, the Barrier snakes along a circuitous route that includes most of the land annexed in 1967, except certain densely populated Palestinian neighborhoods of Jerusalem that were left on the Palestinian side, and adds 164 square kilometers of additional West Bank land. The Barrier encircles three major settlement blocs around Jerusalem, attached by a system of tunnel roads: Gush Etzion in the south, Maale Adumim in the east, and Givat Zeev in the north. Concrete slabs amputate the main roads to the Palestinian towns of Jericho, Bethlehem and Ramallah.

Gone are the days when I could drive fifteen minutes on a Saturday from my Jerusalem home into Bethlehem for a hummus lunch. In place of a flimsy checkpoint, a grey cement wall towers twenty-five feet in the air, sealing Bethlehem off-limits. According to a standing Israeli Army order, Israelis are not permitted to enter Area A, the cities of the West Bank under Palestinian Authority control, including Ramallah, Nablus, Bethlehem — presumably, because the army cannot be responsible for our safety there. The Israeli government maintains to the international community,that the Barrier is "temporary" and can be moved. Yet there is something final about a wall.

Asi lives in Har Homa, the most recent Israeli community built in the southernmost part of the area that was annexed to Jerusalem in 1967. He is my hairdresser, and my barometer of the feeling of Israelis who grew up in the 1970s and '80s and went into the army out of conviction, believing in "the purity of arms," that our intentions were to make peace, and that Israel was basically good and doing the best it could against many enemies.

Asi moved to Har Homa because there he could afford a flat for his wife and family-to-be. He knows that it's over the Green Line, and that it is particularly controversial because it was built after the start of the Oslo peace process. "That's not my problem," he says. "If the politicians change the borders of Jerusalem and give Har Homa to the Palestinians, I'll move. Until then, it's not a bad place to raise a family."

When Israel unilaterally annexed East Jerusalem, about one-third of it was expropriated by the Israeli government, in order to build new "neighborhoods" (seen as settlements by the international community) to be populated by Israeli Jews. Since 1967, Israel has built eight such Jewish communities on the hilltops around Palestinian East Jerusalem, from Gilo in the south to French Hill in the East to Ramot in the north. These have altered the physical and mental map of the city by creating a giant ring around the old borders and preventing any future arrangement that would again leave Jerusalem's Old City outside of Israeli sovereignty. Today, almost 200,000 Israelis live in East Jerusalem, in areas such as Ramot, Gilo and Har Homa, although when they speak of "East Jerusalem" they mean the areas where Arabs live in the city; for them and indeed for the rest of the Israelis, these neighborhoods have become a cognitive part of West Jerusalem, that is, where Jews live. Be that as it may, the Separation Barrier encloses these areas on the Israeli side, physically cementing Jerusalem's disputed boundaries.

In his hair salon — beneath a blaring video of voluptuous singers with flowing locks — Asi tells me of his Jerusalem. "I wouldn't live anywhere else," he says, lifting up a chunk of my graying hair and snipping away. "Jerusalem has depth. There's a spirituality in the air. Even for me, who's modern, there is something you absorb in the stones. My parents used to take me to the Old City; I still go myself to the Western Wall sometimes."

A pair of dark-haired, olive-skinned guys in their thirties saunter loudly into the salon. They greet Asi as "Bro'," and offer him a cigarette. Seamlessly, he breaks off his *Ashkenazi* theoretical-style discussion to give each of them a slap on the back and a bear hug. "What's happenin', how's Hezi? Hey, man, I'm in the middle here;

you want coffee? Come back around in half an hour."

Asi's mother is *Ashkenazi*, his father *Mizrachi*. Thin, dark, and quick in his movements and with his smile, Asi is an amphibian, at home in both cultures. "In the army, everyone can tell the Jerusalemites. We're *laff-laffim* — square." He grins, then tells me why, after four years in America, he left and returned to Jerusalem: "I had everything I wanted in Los Angeles: good job, car, apartment. I studied with the big names; I styled the hair of the extras and the stars before they went on set in Hollywood. My flat looked out over the Pacific Ocean at sunset, just like in those Marlboro commercials we saw growing up. It was what I dreamed of." Asi pauses and studies my hair in mid-snip. "But for ten minutes every day, I felt like a foreigner. And for those ten minutes, the rest wasn't worth it.

"When I got my first car on lease, I was proud. I wanted to show my parents, my friends — the *chevre* — and to enjoy it with them. But they weren't there; they were far away in Israel. Even if I was successful, I was alone.

"This is where I belong. My friends in LA used to complain that life was hard. I'd tell them what they told us in the army: hard is for bread crusts; here we keep going. What's happening now in Israel, in Jerusalem, is hard: the terror attacks, the fence going up around the city, the fear. It's hard for Palestinians too. I see them when they walk down the street and they won't look me in the eye. Everyone's afraid." Asi stopped to look at his handiwork. He took out another scissor — the kind with the holes — and snipped. "I love the land, but I don't like the country."

I turned my head abruptly to look at Asi's face. Why was he saying precisely what Uri Pinkerfeld had told me not long ago? What is happening in Israel that leads people of different ages, different backgrounds, different politics to the same sentiment? Some vital Israeliness is being lost. Some basic decency, some sense that we are on the right track, struggling in good faith for the right things.

Jerusalem's secrets emerge in the midst of heat, like the coded messages we used to write as kids using toothpicks and lemon juice. When you received a secret missive, you held the paper over a flame, and, if you were careful (and didn't light the whole paper on fire), the lemon juice would darken, and you could read the invisible words.

On Thursday, November 11, 2004, Yasser Arafat died of an unidentified disorder in a French military hospital in Paris. Arafat's family had wanted him buried in Jerusalem, but the Israeli government forbade it. "Jerusalem is the city where Jewish kings are buried, not Arab terrorists," stated Israeli Justice Minister Tommy Lapid (father of Israel's current media-personality-turned-politician, Yair Lapid). Instead, Arafat was given a military funeral in Cairo on Friday, and then his body was flown by helicopter to Ramallah for burial outside the Muqata, the government compound where he had been virtually imprisoned over the last two years. Palestinian negotiator Saeb Erakat vowed that the grave in Ramallah would be temporary. "One day, we will have our own independent state with east Jerusalem as its capital," he said.

For almost half a century, Yasser Arafat, who masterminded gruesome murders of innocent Israelis, had been the embodiment of the Palestinian dream of a state. His death marked the end of an era. Fearing spontaneous combustion, the Israeli army placed the West Bank and Gaza under military closure. Like that lemon-juice writing appearing on the heated page, the boundaries between Palestinians and Israelis became perfectly clear. In Jerusalem, police checkpoints cut roads leading from Palestinian to Israeli neighborhoods. If anyone were to ask them, the Jerusalem police could draw the lines of the Clinton parameters (what's Jewish is Israeli, what's Arab is Palestinian) with intimate precision.

As Yasser Arafat's body was making its last journey to Ramallah, I stood in the warm, early-winter sun on the Haas Promenade near my home, looking out over the southern walls of the Old City at the Jewish Quarter and Al Aqsa Mosque. The landscape was eerily quiet: Jerusalemites, like snails, withdraw into their homes when sensing danger. Then the low reedy tones of the Muslim call to prayer floated up from the Kidron Valley: *"Allahu akbar!"* Other chants wove in from Sur Baher, from Silwan, from Jabel Mukaber, winding around the trees in Oriental quarter-tones.

The Promenade, on the seam between Palestinian Jabel Mukaber and Israeli Talpiyot, bristled with border police. Above me stood an unlikely couple — an old stubble-bearded Arab and a young *yeshiva bokher* with a black *kippa*. At first I thought they were plainclothesmen, until I overheard their conversation — in Hebrew, mixed with Arabic slang.

"*Wallah*, we are all human beings — Arab, Jew," drawled the Palestinian, adjusting his *keffiyeh*. "What is this — all Arabs are bad? There are good ones and bad ones, just like you Jews! How can a man can be walking down the street with his wife, his children, his friend, and get blown up? I'm against it."

"Really?" the *yeshiva bokher*'s eyes widened, not sure whether to believe what he heard. "You're against the terror attacks?"

The Palestinian leaned on his cane. "Why can't we solve our problems by talking: we'll take this part, you take that?"

I wondered, now that Arafat is gone, would it be possible for Palestinian and Israeli leadership to talk, as this old man had so simply proposed?

Three days later, on Sunday, November 14, 2004, the Palestinian leadership announced that elections would be held in sixty days to choose Arafat's successor — a new president of the Palestinian Authority (PA). This was only the second time in history that Palestinians had voted for their leaders. Would the elections be conducted fairly and freely? Would Palestinian Jerusalemites, who are residents of Israel, but not citizens, be allowed to vote in these elections?

Palestinians live in Jerusalem precariously. If they are absent from Israel for seven years, or if the "center of life" is not Jerusalem, they can lose their residency rights — their freedom of movement, their social security benefits and the right to live legally in their own homes. On the one hand, as Israeli residents, Palestinian Jerusalemites pay Israeli taxes and have the right to receive social entitlements, like social security, public education, etc. Yet as non-citizens, Palestinian Jerusalemites are not allowed to vote in national elections for the Israeli Knesset.

And if this were not convoluted enough, the Israeli government forbids the Palestinian Authority from operating in Jerusalem. So even if allowed to vote for the Palestinian parliament or presidency, Palestinian Jerusalemites would receive no benefit or services from those they might help to elect. In other words, they are not allowed to vote for the national government that has actual authority over their lives, but might be allowed to vote for leaders who are prevented from serving them.

Under international pressure, the Israeli government agreed to honor agreements made in the first PA elections in 1996, and Jerusalemite Palestinians were to be allowed to vote. However, a potential voting population of almost 100,000 was provided only five polling places, at cramped post offices, as if they were expatriates voting by absentee ballot for a distant authority. In addition, people feared that if they were seen voting in PA elections, they would lose their Israeli residency status. Ir Amim worked with a Palestinian organization to explain voting rights and procedures and to dispel the fear that voting might endanger Jerusalem residency status.

Meanwhile, Jerusalem remained tensely quiet. The roadblocks disappeared, and Jerusalemites emerged from their homes to continue maintaining the semblance of normal life in this united/divided/shared city.

At 8:00 on a cold December night, I strode with my colleagues through the massive stone Damascus Gate into the silent alleys of the Old City's Muslim Quarter. Until then, I had only visited the Quarter as a tourist in a cacophonous market, where anonymous shopkeepers hawked their wares and the flayed hindquarters of sheep hung on nasty meat hooks. I had never thought of it as a place where people live, but now, with its shops shuttered, the Old City shed the mantle of a bazaar, revealing a dark, litter-strewn neighborhood of 25,000 people, where layers of life thrummed, unseen, in crowded courtyards walled off from the street. At the entrance to the Youth Association where we were to speak, a grey-coated gentleman, wrapped in a *keffiyeh* and leaning on a cane, warned that plainclothes Israeli Shabak agents (Israel's internal security service, like the FBI) were waiting inside.

In the cavernous, drafty hall, crowded with men and smoke, the speeches began. I sat amidst a smattering of women, beneath the poorly plastered, ancient arched ceiling, and peered around to see if I could identify the undercover agents. I could not. I pulled my coat tighter around me, trying to warm myself from the damp chill seeping into my bones. The feeble electric space heaters stationed around the hall stood no chance against the moldy cold. As Ir Amim's legal advisor assured the audience that no harm would come to them because of voting, our Palestinian

234

colleague leaned over and pointed out a nondescript man by the door. "He is *mukhabarat*," he whispered, using the Arabic word for security services.

I remembered people in Tamra telling about life in the Galilee in the 1950s and '60s and '70s, when informers were a constant presence in the community and teachers were hired only with approval of the Shabak. To this day, the Shabak is involved on some level in the appointment of the principals of Arab Israeli schools. I felt as if I were in a time warp, experiencing how Israel's military administration had been used to subdue the rural Israeli Arab population in the early years of the state — but now it was fifty years later, and I was in the heart of the city most deeply claimed and most deeply disputed in the conflict.

It felt eerie to be on the side of those being watched. In the dim light of naked light bulbs, I felt subversive. The "watchers" were Israeli, like me. Yet the "watched," Palestinians, had come to find out about their rights to vote in a democratic process sanctioned by Israel. If I, too, was being watched, was I now working against my own country? Asi's words came back to me: "I love the land, but I don't like the country."

I thought of the American Jews who went down to the South to register black voters and encourage them to vote. Although also seen as subversive, they were all working to be part of the same country and to make that country fair and decent. In Jerusalem, I was working to facilitate Palestinians' participation in someone else's state, a state-in-construction that sometimes acted violently against my country. Yet neither Israel nor the Palestinians themselves wanted a quarter-million Palestinian Jerusalemites to be full participants in the Israeli polity instead of in their own state.

As the countdown to Election Day began, the lemon juice was turning brown, revealing the realities of Israel's "eternal United Capital."

The next day, the director of the Youth Association that hosted the event was called to the Kishleh police station in the Old City for questioning. Why had he held the event; who were the organizers; who attended? Ir Amim and our Palestinian partners continued to hold additional voter information evenings in Palestinian neighborhoods of Jerusalem. We guided study tours for the scores of international observers who came to supervise the voting procedures, so they could understand the geo-political terrain of East Jerusalem. On Election Day, January 9, 2005, we ran a hotline for inquiries and troubleshooting.

Despite our best efforts, voter turnout remained abysmally low: Only about 6,000 Palestinians out of a voting-age population of about 100,000 cast their ballots in the post offices of Jerusalem and in sites just outside the municipal boundaries. Most Palestinian Jerusalemites just stayed home, and didn't bother voting for a Palestinian president who could not bring them health or welfare services, or even set foot in the city of Jerusalem.

Not only in voting are Palestinian Jerusalemites "absentees." In the winter of 2004-05, Ir Amim began receiving complaints from Palestinian landowners living just outside the Separation Barrier in the Bethlehem area. They owned olive groves inside Jerusalem, and had applied to the Civil Administration to be allowed to cross the Barrier to work their lands. One after the other, they had received the answer that access was denied because the groves no longer were registered in their names. Putting the pieces together, we realized that Israeli authorities had begun using the 1950 Absentee Property Law in East Jerusalem to claim these groves.

I knew of the Absentee Property Law from my time in Tamra, where I had met a number of "present absentees:" people who had temporarily fled their lands at the time of the War of Independence — to a neighboring town in Israel — and had been denied the chance to return to those lands. After the war, these residents of now-destroyed villages had settled in Tamra.

But I had thought that the Absentee Property Law, which had been used in the 1950s to nationalize hundreds of thousands of dunams of land in the Galilee and Negev, in Jaffa, Lod and West Jerusalem, was consigned to Israel's difficult past. I was stunned to learn that the law had been revived in 2005 to confiscate lands in East Jerusalem that became defined as part of Israel. The landowners affected were not dwelling in distant enemy lands, but merely hundreds of yards away, in towns and villages of the West Bank that were under Israeli authority.

Since 1967, moreover, Israel's attorneys general had insisted that the Absentee Property Law was not meant to be applied to East Jerusalem. As we investigated, however, we discovered that, on June 22, 2004, a ministerial committee — including the Soviet Jewish freedom fighter and Israeli Minister without Portfolio Natan Sharansky (who today chairs the Jewish Agency) — had secretly authorized the use of the law. When investigative reporters and Ir Amim exposed this, an international outcry ensued, echoed by opposition within Israel's legal community. In a swift and dramatic decision, Attorney General Menachem Mazuz ruled the secret decision illegal and called a halt to the confiscations. Within two weeks, this furtive and massive appropriation of land was stopped.

I was succeeding beyond my wildest imaginings in delving into the roots of the Israeli-Palestinian conflict: I was watching, in East Jerusalem, a replay of the establishment of the state, featuring some of the same the techniques used with Israel's Arab citizens in the 1950s and 1960s to establish state control, dispossess Palestinians of their lands, and change the character of the public space.

One dry day in early summer, Dror Etkes, square-jawed leader of Peace Now's Settlement Watch, drove with a group of us from Ir Amim out of Jerusalem into the Judean desert, to visit the E-1 area between Maale Adumim and Jerusalem. We cruised up a half-built road, got out on a parched hilltop in the Judean Desert, and looked out across bald hills: brown sand, brown haze, brown plants that dried and turned to thorn waiting for water.

In front of us, to the south, the red rooftops of Maale Adumim spilled down the ridge. Other small settlements dotted some of the distant hilltops. Over our shoulders, in the distance to the west, the communications tower on Mount Scopus poked the horizon. Bare-headed in the scorching sun, Dror, a once-Orthodox *sabra* who drives his jeep into the heart of the most virulent settlements, counting every new mobile home and the pouring of every new foundation, swept his arm across the landscape. "In the 1970s, all this land was designated as part of Maale Adumim's municipal area — fifty-three square kilometers, an area larger than Tel Aviv. Now, the Israeli government is advancing plans to build a huge new settlement in the E-1 area — to create an urban connection between Maale Adumim and the Israeli areas of East Jerusalem, and to split the continuum of Palestinian towns that are Jerusalem's Arab suburbs."

I thought back to my hike with Im and Abu Anan above Tamra,

twenty-five years earlier, when the hilltop communities of Misgav were being built. I recalled how the Regional Council of Misgav was established in the 1980s on a vast amoeba of land carved out of areas that had previously belonged to the Arab villages of Sakhnin, Deir Hanna and Arrabe; how this area of the Galilee was designated for Jewish settlement; how the middle-class communities of Manof, Shoreshim, Mitzpe Aviv had gradually filled the wind-blown hilltops, breaking up the blocs of Israeli Arab villages so that they would not become contiguous.

Now, in 2005, I saw the same successful strategy advancing below me in the Judean desert, in a continuing colonizing of the West Bank the land that is due someday, theoretically, to constitute a Palestinian state next to Israel.

"I have an old map that Arik Sharon drew in the early 1970's," Dror said, grinning conspiratorially. "It lays out his plan for settling the West Bank: eighty percent of the territory is Israeli, and the Palestinian population is contained in cantons on the remaining bits. When I drive the West Bank today, I see that Israel already controls sixty percent of the territory, and Israel's settlements are following the routes of Sharon's map."

In exasperation, I asked, "How do you keep from being totally depressed about all this?"

Dror looked puzzled. "Because I know how it's going to end." He rubbed his hand across his short-cropped hair. "We can't sustain this situation. Either we will have two states, or we will have one democratic one. I can live with either; although I don't think most Jews or Palestinians are ready to live in one state. There's too much hatred." With a certainty I could not fathom, Dror concluded: "The apartheid we have now is unacceptable, and it won't last."

Standing in the desert, with the fine sand of E-1 clinging to my hair, my shirt, irritating my eyes, I wanted to scream in frustration. How might I, Ir Amim, or any of the other Israeli organizations or leaders bring home to the Israeli public the recognition of the crisis we are bringing on ourselves, how we are closing off our own future options?

One of the most consistent Jewish Israeli conveyors of this message, journalist Amira Hass, was with us on the visit to E-1. Physically small but unshakeable, Amira, the daughter of Holocaust survivors, lived for years in Gaza and reported on daily life.

Now she lives in Ramallah.

She squinted into the late-afternoon sun. She spoke simply, in a flat voice. "Eventually people believe, just years too late. At the beginning of the *intifada*, when I wrote that Israeli soldiers were shooting in all directions and killing kids who were in no way endangering their lives, the newspaper wouldn't print it. Finally, they printed it, but on page ten. When I wrote that soldiers were bullying civilians at checkpoints, and that one had put a gun to a boy's head, no one believed me. Now, soldiers tell me that they can trust what I write, because each case is corroborated. The news media are a product of the society."

On the way back to Jerusalem, she talked of her inability to rejoin Israeli society as a Jew, to sit in cafés with friends in Tel Aviv, and pretend to live a normal life, when just a few miles away, Palestinians have to clamber over boulders placed at the entrance of their village in order to travel to hospital.

"I don't know more than anyone else, I just put myself in places where I see things that others don't see." Amira shakes her unruly black hair. "That's why I never believed the euphoria of the left during the Oslo years. I was living in Gaza then. As our leaders were talking peace, settlements were being expanded, and bypass roads were being built. During the Rabin years, the tunnel road was built connecting Gush Etsion to Jerusalem, and Maale Adumim got its big push forward. Arafat agreed to the bypass roads; he didn't really 'get' the plan.

"I ask myself: Was Oslo a 'plot,' or is this kind of thinking just 'in our genes,' deeply ingrained in our experience of facts-on-the-ground state-building by settling 'one more goat, and one more dunam' — from the pre-state era? I think it is in our genes: We are constantly trying to take more and more land under Israeli control. And the Palestinians are not organized; they easily fall into clan loyalties and lose the overarching picture. People in the West Bank don't care about Gaza, and vice versa. Now that Israel has cut up the West Bank with bypass roads, the Wall, the checkpoints, and barriers at the entrances of villages, the clan sensibilities are exacerbated."

In the heat of August 2005, after a year of intense Knesset and Cabinet debate and public protest, Israel took another step in redefinition. The disengagement from Gaza and from four settlements in the West Bank was carried out by thousands of Israeli troops and police, who dismantled army bases and removed Israeli settlements from this narrow strip of land, which had been seized in the 1967 War.

Many of the approximately 9,000 settlers left their twenty-five communities voluntarily, after the Knesset narrowly approved the disengagement plan and a compensation package for the settlers. Soldiers and Israeli volunteers helped them pack up the homes and businesses they had built, and cart off the remains of the lives they had lived for over a generation. However, hundreds of settlers remained in their homes, refusing to leave.

The Israeli public was deeply divided about the disengagement, and protests continued under the motto, "A Jew does not expel a Jew." In the weeks leading up to the start of the disengagement, massive protests were held, with settlers blocking major traffic intersections in Jerusalem. Five days before the planned disengagement, tens of thousands of settlers and national-religious rabbis prayed at the Western Wall for Divine intervention to halt the disengagement.

After weeks of training, tens of thousands of IDF soldiers and the Israeli police, some with tears in their eyes, evacuated settlement by settlement. Even those settlers who barricaded themselves into their homes, climbed to their roofs, and threatened soldiers with their guns, eventually succumbed with relatively little violence. Finally, in September, Israeli forces blew up the houses, factories and army bases that had constituted Israel's thirty-eight-year presence in the Gaza Strip.

Only the synagogues and greenhouses remained after the disengagement. The Israeli government refused to demolish the synagogues, and the greenhouses were bought for the Palestinian Authority for $14 million — money provided by the organization founded by the Jewish Israeli Yossi Beilin, the Economic Cooperation Foundation, which had spearheaded the Geneva Initiative. The day after the disengagement was completed, however, Palestinian rioters defaced the synagogues and ripped apart the greenhouses, which would have provided productive agro-tech employment for Gazans.

As I watched daily television broadcasts of the evacuation —

the prayers, the tears, the young men and women in uniform carrying out their duties despite their own personal opinions — I felt a mixture of trepidation and tentative hope. Israel was disengaging not only from the Gaza Strip, but from old myths and dreams. No longer was the religious settlement movement seen as the symbol of modern Zionist fulfillment. In an amazing step, Arik Sharon, one of the main engineers of the settlement project, had convinced the Knesset and the public that withdrawing from part of the Land of Israel would strengthen our future as a Jewish state. I was torn between my distrust of Arik Sharon and my belief that, regardless of the intention behind the policy, withdrawing from Gaza and dismantling settlements would create a positive dynamic of its own and help redefine Israel for a more successful future.

By carrying out the disengagement unilaterally, however, not in the context of an agreement with the Palestinian Authority and its newly chosen leader, Mahmous Abbas, it strengthened the hand of the Palestinian unilateralists — Hamas. It also provided a smokescreen for a redoubling of settlement efforts in the West Bank.

I recalled an interview published the year before in *Haaretz* with Dov Weisglass, Sharon's chief of staff: "The significance of the disengagement plan is the freezing of the peace process," he said. "When you freeze that process, you prevent the establishment of a Palestinian state and you prevent a discussion on the refugees, the borders and Jerusalem. Disengagement supplies the amount of formaldehyde necessary so there will not be a political process with the Palestinians."

None of us knew what would happen next. Apparently it takes more than good fences to make good neighbors.

Chapter 21
Seamless in Silwan

On November 5, 2008, I awoke to a more hopeful world. In a dazzling election victory, Barack Hussein Obama had become President-elect of the United States of America. One generation after African-Americans had been denied entry to schools and voting booths in America's South, and just decades after the last segregationist state had done away with laws against "miscegenation," America elected a biracial man as president. He was a community organizer with black sisters in Kenya and white grandparents who had raised him; he was a man who had experienced racial discrimination and benefitted from the finest academic institutions in the world. Obama's victory was the victory of the America I love. It was the victory of a worldview that cherishes the power of every person to change a room, to change a state, to change the world. Obama's victory rekindled my sense that justice is achievable and the pursuit of it is not only worthy but feasible.

Infused with this glow of hope, I entered the Ir Amim office. Ahmad Sublaban, our Palestinian Jerusalemite field worker — a slight, black-haired, young father, with an open demeanor and an intimate knowledge of the Jerusalem street — was talking on two phones at once. His face, usually calm in the most harried situations, was tense. Ahmad, who had been a journalist, and a "fixer" for international news outlets, asked terse questions: *The house next to the empty lot at the bottom of the valley? Where are the bulldozers now? How many policemen?* Loud voices spewed from the other end of the line.

From snatches of overheard conversation and Ahmad's quick explanations between calls, I pieced together the picture: Border patrol troops were flooding Silwan, the dense Palestinian neighborhood crowded below the southern walls of the Old City, hundreds of meters from Al Aqsa Mosque and the Temple Mount. The troops were securing the area for an impending home demolition in the Bustan Valley. My hopeful glow flickered out.

In Palestinian neighborhoods of East Jerusalem, home demolitions are a relatively common occurrence. About eighty homes are demolished each year throughout the city, most in a relatively random way. Since 1967, Israeli urban planning and zoning has been used to bolster the Israeli Jewish population and to limit the growth of the Palestinian population, reflecting a constant Jewish concern over the demographic balance of the city. Over a third of the land annexed to form East Jerusalem was expropriated by the government to build 50,000 housing units for the Jewish population in new neighborhoods or settlements for Israelis over the years. At the same time, fewer than six hundred homes were built by the government for Palestinians. Even though the Palestinian population has quadrupled over the years to almost 300,000 people, only a handful of building permits are granted for private construction each year; in 2008, only 125 were granted.

Permit requests are denied for a variety of reasons: an inability to prove land ownership (since no official land survey has been conducted for most of the Palestinian neighborhoods); no approved town plans, or old town plans that don't allow for development and growth; land located in "park areas" (about one-fifth of East Jerusalem is zoned in this way, although no actual parks are planned, and garbage fills the unpermitted spaces). That means that over 20,000 homes in East Jerusalem have been built without permit, and demolition orders hover over the heads and homes of thousands of Palestinian Jerusalemites.

Within this general picture, Silwan is a special case. Abutting the Old City walls, just meters from ground-zero of the Israeli-Palestinian conflict, the Temple Mount/Haram al Sharif area, Silwan has become a focus for Israeli settlement activity. Populated for almost 4,000 years, Silwan, once known as Siloam or Shiloah, was the site of Hebrew government at least from the 8th century

BCE, when King Hezekiah built an underground tunnel to channel water into the city in time of siege. According to Samuel 2 in the Bible, the site dates from the time of King David.

In the late 19th century, archaeological missions began to dig in the area while Arab families and a Yeminite Jewish community settled the slopes. After the Arab riots of 1936, Jewish families fled the area, and it became a Palestinian neighborhood, which greatly expanded after 1967 — almost entirely with construction that lacked permits.

Until the 1980s, Israeli government policy followed the policy of Teddy Kollek, Jerusalem's mythic mayor, who built the reunited/annexed/occupied city from 1967 until 1993 and was opposed to Jewish settlement inside Palestinian neighborhoods.Indeed, Kollek's strategic construction of the Israeli neighborhoods in East Jerusalem on hilltops around the Green Line allowed for the logic of the Clinton Parameters. But from the 1980s, and especially since the Oslo Accords in 1993, a competing vision for Jerusalem had taken hold, led by Minister of Planning and Construction Ariel Sharon.

This vision included changing the character of East Jerusalem's Palestinian neighborhoods by "restoring" pre-1948 Jewish properties and communities and otherwise acquiring land to advance Jewish presence in and around the Old City — to thwart any possibility of reaching an agreement for a division of sovereignty over East Jerusalem. Of course, efforts to honor pre-1948 Jewish land claims in East Jerusalem were not accompanied by parallel efforts to honor Palestinian claims to properties in West Jerusalem, in neighborhoods such as Talbiyeh, Baka and Ein Karem.

Silwan, with its rich history and strategic location, became a focus for this settlement effort — through application (legal and illegal) of the absentee property law, declaration of large areas of Silwan as the City of David National Park, granting the management of the park to the El-Ad settlement organization, and now, building the Kings' Valley Park through the Bustan neighborhood at the foot of Silwan, requiring the demolition of eighty-eight Palestinian homes.

We jumped into Ahmad's four-wheel drive and arrived in minutes at the Spring of Shiloah, at the foot of Silwan. I glanced up and saw the sandstone homes of the Jewish Quarter beyond the Old City walls up the road above us. We scrambled down to the Bustan Valley through a tangle of fig trees and onto the narrow mud paths of this shantytown neighborhood, trying to reach the endangered home. At every turn we encountered YAMAM Special Forces police in grey uniforms and helmets, armed with M-16 rifles, blocking our way and ordering us to get out. Finally, we admitted defeat and climbed back up the hill to the street by the spring to watch helplessly as a yellow bulldozer rambled slowly toward a one-room shack in the Bustan Valley below us.

Outside the shack, the innards of a family's life were vomited into the dirt yard: a metal bed, boxes, pots, a gas burner. Fahri, the head of the neighborhood committee, shuttled between the border guards and the door of the house. "The old woman is still inside," a shop owner remarked. The bulldozer (which he said was actually a hydraulic jackhammer) idled on the street behind the house.

A tall thin man in a dark suit and red tie strode over to the guards and began talking. Unlike the others, he didn't gesture with his hands. He spoke politely and listened, then stepped back to the street and placed a call on his cell phone. I recognized him as an American diplomat, and could only imagine the conversation he might be having with the surprised officer on duty at the State Department in Washington the day after Obama's election.

Skinny teenage boys, grouped by a house down the street, sullenly watching the drama below us.

The shop owner smoked a cigarette at the door of his grocery, his bald head gleaming in the winter sun. Robust Silwan women stood in headscarves on their porches, watching. Journalists from around the world, armed with cameras and cellphones, mingled with diplomats. All had rushed here from their offices in Jerusalem and Ramallah. Probably no city in the world has better international representation than Jerusalem, which is both livable and a hub for covering the conflicts of the Middle East.

I thought back to the summer of 1970, when I was 15 — like the boys down the street — here in Silwan with a summer program of the National Federation of Temple Youth (NFTY). I was in my bathing suit, walking through thigh-deep water in the dark of Hezekiah's Tunnel. An unknown Silwan boy slipped into the tunnel behind me, and slid his hand into the bottom of my two-piece bathing suit. I never saw his face; when I yelled at him, he melted back into the dark and disappeared. It was my first encounter with an Arab.

I glanced at the shop owner next to me; I could smell his sweat in the warmth of midday. He was about my age, and lived next to that same spring. Could he have been the boy that had molested me thirty-eight years ago? He and his friends might have been bored in the hot summer of 1970 when a group of foreign girls appeared, lasciviously dressed in swimsuits.

I moved away from him.

Almost forty years had passed since that day. I had never thought I'd be back in this place, working to defend the rights of those boys, of their children, cousins, and friends, to stay in their homes and to preserve the character of their neighborhood in the face of Israeli efforts to make it more Jewish and to thwart a two-capital, two-state resolution in Jerusalem.

The sort of molestation I'd suffered would never happen today. A NFTY group would not enter "Silwan" in order to walk in Hezekiah's Tunnel, but would pass by armed guards into the land-scaped City of David National Park, which has been established in and around the homes of the village, turning about a quarter of the neighborhood into a Jewish heritage site. The park is run not by the National Parks Authority but by the Israeli settlement organization, El-Ad, and many of the Silwan homes around the spring have been taken over by Israeli settlers after being declared "absentee properties."

Today's NFTY group would not see the spring as a place of ad-venture out of Jerusalem's variegated past, but as a part of ancient Jewish Jerusalem, a waterway connecting the city from the time of King David to its modern restoration as capital of the Jewish state. In fact, the house in the valley below was being demolished to make way for the extension of the City of David that would help transform the Palestinian Bustan neighborhood into the Kings' Valley Park. The plan required evicting hundreds of Palestinians from their homes in order to recreate the garden where King David and King Solomon were said to have composed their psalms.

Whose side am I on? I wondered yet again, glancing at the shop owner and imagining my 15-year-old self shaking with rage and shame. Because of the Judaizing of Silwan, young Jewish visitors to the Spring of Shiloah were now safe to explore their ancient heritage — but young Silwan girls and boys were growing up with private armed guards on their streets, with the Israeli police staging nighttime raids on their homes to detain them for questioning and release them in the morning, with increasing areas of their village off-limits, and with their homes in danger of demolition.

Now a bent old man in a *keffiyeh* entered the home, followed by some guards. The jackhammer inched into the yard. The man shuffled out, followed by a lumpy woman in a long, shapeless dress, her head covered with a flowered scarf, with both of them flanked by guards. As the entire village watched breathlessly from porches and roofs, the yellow Caterpillar rumbled forward and stabbed the shack, shattering its rear wall and corrugated tin roof. In moments, the home was a pile of cement and twisted metal bars — a life reduced to rubble. I heard the thin keening of the old woman as the Caterpillar rolled on to destroy an uninhabited storage shack, then swiveled and jerked back out along the road.

Then a phalanx of border patrol guards pushed us back from the wall overlooking the Bustan. A woman guard yelled, "Everyone back from the edge! Leave the area!" Shots rang out from the slope across from us. People began to push and run. A mounted policeman loomed behind us, his horse prancing nervously; I felt its sweaty flank above me. Ahmad, his black hair plastered by perspiration to his face, shoved me behind a car as the horse reared, his hoofs coming down inches from the head of an old man who had fallen in the crush.

Across the valley, a Palestinian boy on a roof heaved bricks over the side in the direction of the border police below him. They fired up in the air toward him. Plumes of tear gas rose over Silwan and settled in the Bustan valley. Like an urban shepherd, Ahmad steered us up the hill to his four-wheel drive, parked strategically on the way out of the village. His wheels spun on the steep debris-strewn road, then grabbed the pavement, and we lurched out of Silwan, out of danger.

We left behind a village littered with stones and choking on tear gas, a village being morphed from Silwan into the City of David, from Al Bustan to the Kings' Valley. How many areas of

Israel have undergone such transformations over the years? The once-Arab village of Damoun in the Western Galilee became a Jewish National Fund Forest, where I volunteered in a summer camp; the hills above Tamra became Mitzpe Aviv, where I walked with friends; the grazing lands of the Hawashleh Bedouin became the development town of Dimona. Whether in the Galilee and the Negev, where the Palestinians are citizens of Israel, or in East Jerusalem and the West Bank, where they are not, many techniques of Judaization and its raison d'être are the same.

I thought back to a conversation I'd had in Silwan while guiding African-American dancer and choreographer Bill T. Jones. Throughout our East Jerusalem tour, Jones, lithe and engaged, had posed unexpected questions, including: "Why is the Temple Mount/Al Aqsa so important?"

When I explained the current political significance, he clarified: "Why was *this* place chosen? What happened there?"

Few people had asked me that simple, metaphysical question. I described the Foundation Stone, the rock on which Abraham/ Ibrahim almost sacrificed his son Isaac (in the Jewish narrative)/ Ishmael (in the Muslim narrative), according to God's command. It is said that the Foundation Stone, symbolizing the connection between the Divine and human realms, lies at the base of the Dome of the Rock today, and underpinned the Holy of Holies, the inner sanctuary, of the great Temple.

As we had stood overlooking the Bustan, Jones, stylishly bookish in oversized black glasses, asked, "Why are Israelis and Palestinians so stuck now?"

In his troupe's provocative performance the night before, they had portrayed in dance and readings the deep divisions splitting American society in the Civil War period, and the nation's bloody, risky and fateful choice to end slavery as a sanctioned system. That choice had changed the course of history.

"We in Israel are deeply divided as well," I answered, thinking aloud, "between those who believe that we must take the risks and relinquish land in order to reach a historic separation agreement with the Palestinians, and those who believe — for religious or military reasons — that we must not. The Palestinians are similarly divided, split between worldviews represented by Hamas and Fatah." Then I came to a realization that I had never put into words before: "Until each side makes an internal determination, we will not move forward with each other. Right now, we, Jewish Israeli society, are not ready to separate into two states, and to part with enough of the territory under our control to make that viable."

"Do you think there will be civil war in Israel?" asked Jones, his piercing eyes steady on my face.

I thought of my sons. I thought of the collective inability of both Jews and Palestinians to take the most difficult steps to resolve our hundred-year-old conflict in a fair two-state solution. I thought of the stark contrast between America's civil rights struggle and the Israeli-Palestinian conflict, which was turning from a national conflict to an ethnic one — on both sides of the increasingly imaginary Green Line — as we continued to struggle with the character and values of the polity we were fencing in.

"I don't know," I said, drawing in my breath. "I hope not. But we have already seen internal political violence with the assassination of Prime Minister Yitzhak Rabin."

Jones gazed over at Silwan, then focused back on me. "I wish you strength."

Chapter 22
Memorial Day

I gaze over a sea of white shirts from the balcony of the Hebrew University High School auditorium, where my son Shai is in 12th grade. Although the hundreds of seats are filled, a hush hovers over the room, a hush heavy with collective sorrow and respect for the dead. It is a hush learned from years of standing in silence at Memorial Day ceremonies. The year is 2009, and this is Israel's 61st Memorial Day. I have been here for twenty-nine of them.

A student steps up to the microphone and announces: *"Yiz-kor."* With a wave of rustling, the audience rises as one: "The people of Israel will remember its loyal and brave sons and daughters, the soldiers of the Israel Defense Forces . . . who risked their lives in war for Israel's rebirth."

I cringe at the pathos, at the nationalistic manipulation of grief to inspire fear, loyalty and identity. Public opinion surveys done around this time each year show that a vast majority of Israelis believe that Israel is under a serious or imminent threat of destruction.

For sixteen years, on every Jewish and national holiday, I have complied with the requests of kindergarten and school teachers, and sent Shai and Liad to class in their regulation white shirts so they would fit in and belong to the Israeli collective I joined almost three decades ago. I have made them wreaths for Shavuot and hard-boiled eggs for school seders. I have slathered my sons with sunscreen so they wouldn't burn as they stood outside listening to the testimonies of Holocaust survivors on Yom HaShoah. And this morning, as they went off to school in their white shirts, it didn't cross their minds to do anything else. They are Israelis.

But I, who grew up in the land-of-the-free-and-the-home-of-the-brave, could not bring myself to dress in white. As I quickly debated with myself about whether to dress to fit in, my mother's cynical voice filtered in: "The Israelis are always boasting about their achievements, or crying about the Holocaust . . ." Now, in my dark flowered blouse, I am one of three people in the hall not wearing white. I feel out of place, embarrassed, and removed from the most powerful bond of belonging to Israeli society — collective grief and respect for the fallen, on whose graves we live today.

As we sit to hear the recital of the names of all the graduates of the school who fell in Israel's wars and terror attacks, I shrink deeper in my chair. Each name and venue of death is read slowly by a pair of students, and the face of each fallen graduate flickers by on a wide screen on stage. "Tsafona Eshbal, the Convoy to Mt. Scopus . . . Yaakov Ben-Atar, the Road to Gush Etsion . . ." Each projected face is smiling, caught in a happy moment of a young life filled with hope. "Rafi Berger, terror attack at Patt Junction . . . Achiram Bareli, Suez Canal . . ."

My late husband Shuki had almost been killed at the Suez Canal in 1973. The stuffy bunker that he left in the middle of the desert night in order to find a better place to sleep had been bombed, with all the soldiers in it killed. He'd been saved, and led his convoy across the canal — only to die of cancer at age 45.

For years, I have tried to avoid being pulled into Israel's week of manic depression — starting with the mourning of Yom Ha-Shoah (Holocaust Remembrance Day), progressing through Memorial Day, and ending in Independence Day celebrations. Since 1994, I have taken refuge from the public sorrow by commemorating my private grief over Shuki's death, which fell, ironically, on the 3rd of Iyyar, the eve of Israel's Memorial Day. I have held our family's grief apart, designing our own private ceremony that would create meaning for the three of us and for Shuki's siblings and friends. This year, however, I could not muster the strength, for the fifteenth time, to take Liad and Shai up to Kibbutz Afikim, to stand by the graveside and hear the stories of those who had grown up with Shuki, who had known him far longer than I. I could not bear the boys' sullen anger and pain over the fact that they hold no real memories of their father.

So we did not go up to the Jordan Valley — and now I'm looking out over the heads of hundreds of kids staring silently at the dead faces projected on the screen in front of us, and wondering which of these kids will be pictured on this screen in the coming years? What a waste of young lives, young talent, beautiful souls who could add so much to the future of this society, instead of dying for it!

I think of the thousands of people I have taken out to view the results of Israeli policy in East Jerusalem, and I pray that my work may nudge us closer to negotiations and perhaps save just one of these kids from dying in an unnecessary war. How many more people will die in our conflict before we get to independence for both states, Israeli and Palestinian?

Without two independences, we will never truly have one.

Shai moves out on stage with a group of young people to sing in a minor key: "A night of stars, the moon rises; you sit staring in the darkness. An hour passes, a day, a year, and still you wait for him . . ."

Tears roll down my cheeks. Shai, 18, has been called up to be in a fighting unit of the Israeli Army next year. Where will he be a year from now? Will he be lying in ambush, on a mission vital to Israel's safety — or called to humiliate Palestinian families in service of the occupation? Will some moonstruck girl sit year after year mourning for him? Will I?

After twenty nine years, I finally belong to the Israeli collective, through my sons. I cannot bring myself to put on a white shirt, but I am now offering my first-born son to the Israel Defense Forces. They will take him and do what they want with him. And Liad, my younger son, is waiting in the wings.

This is not the future I imagined for myself and my family. When Shai and Liad were born, I did not think about this day. Over the years, when the fears slid in, I banished them with the rationalizations of every Israeli mother: that by the time he is 18, there will be peace. But now Shai is 18 and there is not peace. And I am scared. I want him and Liad each to be a *mentsh,* to live a long, happy, and productive life, to become a father and enjoy his own children. I pray that they will not die in the conflict, but will live to enjoy its resolution.

Shai steps forward, in jeans and a white shirt. His clear baritone flows over the hall: "To the streams of water, with your remaining strength . . . Keep your voice from crying; there is hope in the end." I close my eyes and listen. It is not his father's voice, but it carries the same love of singing, the same resonance and conviction. I have never heard him sing in public before; perhaps he never has. Yet here he stands with calm presence and an open voice. I cry with pride and preemptive grief.

Maybe my long-time colleague, Uri, was right: that all we can do, sometimes, is lengthen the wick on the time-bomb, until the conditions are right to defuse it; to keep alive hope, and push back the creeping despair that threatens to overwhelm and paralyze us; to dream, envision, and revision. And to encourage our children to dream and follow their beliefs.

This would have been Shuki's 60th birthday. He had been born a year after Israel's Independence, and had died, forty-five years later, on his own birthday. In the hall filled with parents of fallen soldiers, and with students poised to become soldiers, my private remembering mingles with the country's sorrow and grants me a false but warm sense of belonging.

I have given the best years of my life to help make Israel a good society for all its citizens, based on its Jewish values — a vibrant place of decency and justice, where both Jewish and Arab citizens can feel reflected and empowered. I have labored for this out of a desire to be part of one of the most amazing human and Jewish dramas of the 20th century. I have done this based on the certainty that if both nations do not have a safe home they can call their own in this land, neither will.

I know how far away we are from having such a home, and how many homes have been demolished and olive trees uprooted in its stead. I have seen my sons growing up with the pain and sadness of a family home marked by death, and I feel the recurring regret of being unable to heal that fracture.

Images flash in my mind, like the slides on the screen: Imad Younis toiling in his rented room next to Mary's Well to invent his spike detector; the elegant delegation of Jordanians crossing Sheikh Hussein Bridge in the rain; Yitzhak Rabin's voice rumbling over the masses at Malkhei Yisrael Square, minutes before his death: "I have always believed that the majority of the people want peace and are ready to take risks for peace."

So many people have taken, and continue to take, seemingly unreasonable risks for this country and the ideals that built it. None of them knew what the outcome of their actions would be, and none of us know now. They made choices they thought were right, and dedicated themselves to a dream. Israel is intoxicating and captivating because of their passion.

Now I pray that we will have the courage to reconstruct our vision of this country so that we do not see our dreams destroyed.

The commemoration is over; Shai walks slowly from the stage. In my insider/outsider flowered blouse, I push my way through the jostling crowd to find him grinning shyly among proud friends. Throwing my arms around him, I hold him tight, hugging him both for myself and for Shuki, who would have been so proud. With tears in my eyes, I wonder to what dreams he will dedicate himself in the years to come, and what price he will pay for them.

Chapter 23
Thirty-Six Years Later —
A View from the Seam

After my husband died, I used to sing my toddler sons to sleep with a Joni Mitchell song, "The Circle Game":
"The years spin by and now the boy is 20.
Though his dreams have lost some grandeur coming true.
There'll be new dreams, maybe better dreams, and plenty —
before the last revolving year is through."

Shai and Liad would fall asleep, curled up together on a big mattress on the floor. "The Circle Game" came from a time when the supply of new dreams was abundant: America in the mid-1960s, my own teen years. Although things were tough for me, for them, for our country, I was sure that when they would get to age 20 there would be some sort of peace in Israel and they would be creating new dreams for themselves and their society — as would I.

That was 1995. Yitzhak Rabin was still alive. He had signed a peace agreement with Jordan and was working toward reconciliation with the Palestinians. I was 40, and the organization I had imagined and built was creating business ties throughout the Middle East, working to establish the first joint Jewish-Arab industrial zone in the Galilee, and helping Israeli Arab women design new futures for themselves with small enterprises. I believed that I would soon fall in love again, have a new life-partner, and bring a new father-figure into my sons' lives.

Now it is 2016, thirty-six years after I came to Israel to contribute to the society, sixteen years after the implosion of my political hopes in the second *intifada* and my own war with cancer. It is a time of great displacement and disillusionment in the world. Unlike in my own teen years, we no longer live with the assumption that our children's future will be better than our own.

Israel, a still-young country, is grappling with our collective identity. Right now, we seem to be running away from the hard choices that most Israelis, deep down, know we have to make. In order for our country to continue to be viable and sustainable for years to come, we know that we need to separate into two states — Palestinian and Israeli — and to recognize the Arab citizens who will remain in Israel as legitimate partners in building the Israeli state. In order not to make these choices, which involve deep compromise and risk, more and more measures are being taken to repress and delegitimize the voices that remind us of the consequences of our actions and inactions.

After living in Israel for almost forty years — including years in which I carried a gas mask for fear of chemical attack from Saddam Hussein, and years in which I feared to drink coffee in a café lest I be blown up by a suicide bomber — I believe that we are slipping away from our last chance in a long time to have a

Sarah, Liad and Shai

256

society with both a liberal Jewish character and vibrant democracy. If we don't end Israel's fifty-year occupation of 3.5 million Palestinians and allow a Palestinian state to grow next to Israel, I fear that my sons are in for a very repressive and violent period, in which Israel will be increasingly isolated in the world community, in which fewer and fewer young Jews around the world will care about Israel, in which we will lose an important part of our moral strength.

In the war-torn Middle East, peace for Israelis and Palestinians can hardly be seen as imminent. This is as much the result of both Israelis and Palestinians being deeply internally divided about their visions for the future of their own societies as it is the result of Mideast chaos. Until each nation makes a determination about its own future vision, and how it sees sharing/dividing the Land between the Jordan River and the sea, we will not have peace. For Israel, we can have any two of the three things we want: a healthy Jewish society, a democratic state, the whole Land of Israel. We cannot have all three.

What would I tell my mother now, after thirty-six years of joy and loss, satisfaction and disappointment, about my choice to live in Israel?

Mom: These years trying to make Israel a more just society have been intensely meaningful. My ability to join in the Zionist dream of building a just and safe haven for the Jewish people in this land has given me a modest place in Jewish history. There was beauty, and perhaps necessity, in having poetic faith in Israel's creation story.

In my own middle age, I believe that it is better to examine the contradictions inherent in the old Zionist dream, and to learn the tragedies of our past and our present, in order to stop recreating them. Such contradictions — between maintaining a dominant religious, ethnic or national character and upholding universal values of equality and democracy — are hardly unique to Israel. Rather, they lie at the heart of many conflicts in the world today.

Much of the DNA of Israeli society is intensely Jewish; we don't have to mandate it. It is Jewish in the way we argue, the way we sing, the way we bunch together instead of standing in queues. It is Jewish in valuing family life on a par with work life. It is Jewish in providing immediate disaster relief to Nepal or Rwanda. It is Jewish in its still-remaining socialist roots and social sensibility.

A lot of what makes Israel Jewish was developed in diaspora, where we lived as minorities. But as we, in Israel, get further away from our Diaspora roots, we forget what it was like to live as a minority. In the 2009 election, fifteen Knesset members won their seats on an openly anti-Arab platform: "no citizenship without loyalty." In 2015, Benjamin Netanyahu squeaked back into office with last-minute alarmist rhetoric about Arab Israelis flooding the polling places. Such rhetoric about the need to punish Arab disloyalty, or to trade away Umm el Fahm in any future peace deal, or about the dangers posed by the Arab minority organizing itself, could easily have been used by the world's worst despots against their Jewish minorities.

Over my years in Israel, I have participated in building Israeli society by living on the seam between its Arab and Jewish parts. From that place, in the midst of paradox and pain, I have hope for Israel's future — because our country today is actually a joint venture of Arab and Jewish citizens, albeit still not equitable.

This reality is publicly rejected today precisely because it is undeniable. In the hospitals of Haifa, Jerusalem, Beersheva, where Jewish and Arab doctors save the lives of Jewish and Arab patients, Israel is a joint venture. In the shopping malls, where Jewish and Arab families mingle to buy and sell name-brand clothes, Israel is a joint venture. Despite the often-rabid rhetoric, in the Israeli Knesset, where seventeen of 120 members are Arab, Israel is a joint venture.

Embracing Israel as a joint venture involves a paradigm shift: accepting and legitimizing the right of Arab citizens to live in equality and dignity in Israel, and not seeking to further limit the amount of space they take up or their ability to influence the county's future and identity. Our country in 2016 has a much different demography than when I came in 1980. Israeli President Reuven Rivlin speaks of the existence of four disparate tribes in Israel today — secular, national-religious, and Haredi Jews, and Arab Israelis —and urges the building of connections and social cohesion among them. Embracing this reality will help us build strong and viable vision for the future.

Coming from the field of economic development, I have seen and helped thousands of businesspeople — Israeli Jews and Arabs, Palestinians, Jordanians, Egyptians — brokering deals. Their pragmatism in finding ways of meeting their varying interests while crafting workable joint ventures is encouraging and sometimes inspiring.

Now we Israelis need to broker our vision of the future. And the people engaged in this argument will not all be Jews. Nor will they all be Ashkenazi, or secular, as were Israel's founders. It may be frightening, even terrifying, to give up some of the dreams and illusions upon which Israel was founded, and to reorient the balance of power. But we must find the courage to do so.

My years have spun by, and I am now in a loving relationship with a wonderful man. Shai and Liad are in their twenties, exploring the world and building their lives. Upon entering the army, they wrestled with questions I never had to face at their age. Sometimes, as I look at them, I think of my father. It saddens me that he was not able to meet his grandsons and to give them some of his love and great sensibility. I remember him looking at me through his big tortoise-shell spectacles, smiling and quoting Rabbi Tarfon from the Pirkei Avot: "It is not incumbent upon you to complete the task, but neither are you free to desist from it."

For me, not desisting from the task means continuing the struggle. I work now at Beit Berl College, where Israel's joint venture unfolds as students in jeans learn with students in *hijabs*, and an Arab professor teaches ultra-Orthodox Jewish students of education.

The task is no less than to come together across the divides, to generate competing visions, and to broker a renewed working vision for the joint venture that is our country. It is not incumbent upon us to agree upon one, but we must open our eyes, talk with each other, think aloud, and legitimize the argument for peace and a shared society. I believe we can define and develop a vibrant joint venture that will serve all our children well.

Notes

p. 21, "'to strengthen the Jewish hold on this region'"
1977 Ministry of Housing plan, "Accelerated Urban Development in Galilee"; also quoted in *State Practices & Zionist Images,* David A. Wesley, Berghahn Books, 2006.

p. 63, "a theory for improving intergroup relations"
Theories we used are reviewed in Rabah Halabi, editor, *Israeli and Palestinian Identities in Dialogue: The School for Peace Approach*, Rutgers University Press, English edition, 2004.

p. 90, "closures along Israel's border"
Zeev Rosenhek writes in *Incorporating Migrant Workers into the Israeli Labour Market?*, page 3: "The shortage of cheap labour was exacerbated by Rabin's government decision in 1993 to impose closures on the occupied territories as a deterrent to terrorist actions within Israel. Under the Rabin government one of the principles applied to the Peace Process was that new, stable relations with the Palestinians should be based on a separation between Israel and the Palestinian entity. See www.carim.org/Publications/CARIM-AS06_10-Rosenhek.pdf.

p. 93: ". . . we have something to say about the terms . . ."
Saeb Bamya can be seen speaking at the Peres Center for Peace at www.youtube.com/watch?v= B_YDCvIhM00.

p.138: "not as a nationalist conflict"
See the policy brief of the Association for Civil Rights in Israel, http://www.acri.org.il/en/wp-content/uploads/2011/09/Prawer-Policy-Brief-FINAL-ENG.pdf.

p. 139: "'the Law of Return must be rescinded'"

261

A. Shavit, "Citizen Azmi: an Interview with Azmi Bishara," *Haaretz*, May 29, 1998. Available at http://azmibishara.com/site/topics/article.asp?cu_no=1&item_no=249&version=1&template_id=294&parent_id=29.

p. 142: "70,000 engineers"
See http://www.globes.co.il/en/article-258771&fid=954.

p. 144: "Ka'adans to acquire land in Katzir"
Israeli High Court decision 6698/95, *Ka'adan vs. Israel Lands Authority*

p. 145: "'prevent the establishment of the State of Israel'"
The Present Absentee: Palestinian Refugees in Israel since 1948, by Hillel Cohen, Van Leer Institute, 2000. See Hillel Cohen's article, "The Internal Refugees in the State of Israel: Israeli Citizens, Palestinian Refugees," http://www.pij.org/details.php?id=159.

p. 145: "agricultural land of *kibbutzim*"
See *State Practices & Zionist Images,* David A. Wesley, Bergahn Books, 2006, chapter 4, "Land, Territory, and Jurisdiction."

p. 148: "'all invested the same amount of money'"
"Israeli High-Tech Incubator Provides Platform for Arab Startups," http://nocamels.com/2011/09/israeli-high-tech-incubator-provides-platform-for-arab-startups.

p. 151: "limiting the number of Palestinians who could get in to work"
"Economics of Palestinian Return Migration," Ward Sayre , Jennifer Olmsted, Middle East Research and Information Project, http://www.merip.org/mer/mer212/economics-palestinian-return-migration.

p. 156: "crowded into cramped houses"
CIA World Factbook, 2005

p. 156: "one-tenth the Israeli level"
"Palestinian Economy and the Oslo 'Peace Proces,'" by Leila Farsakh, Trans-Arab Research Institute, Boston, and "Under Siege: Closure, Separation and the Palestinian Economy," by Leila Farsakh, Middle East Research and Information Project, http://www.merip.org/mer/mer217/under-siege.

p. 159: "the high-tech sector leading the advance"
Siemens company report, http://www.siemens.com/investor/pool/en/investor_relations/downloadcenter/gb1999_d_1365092.pdf.

p. 157: "Palestinian real GDP per capita fell by one third"
CIA World Factbook, 2000. More on the Palestinian economy at http://

www-wds.worldbank.org/servlet/WDSContentServer/WDSP/IB/1993/09 /01/000009265_3970311123238/Rendered/PDF/multi0page.pdf.

p. 161: before "taking things into their own hands."
Jerusalem Post, September 13, 2000.

p. 162: "wounded over one hundred in the area of Al Aqsa mosque" See Or Commission report, Section One, paragraph 154, http://elyon1. court.gov.il/heb/veadot/or/inside1.htm#c. p. 179. This and other incidents described in Chapter 15 are documented in the Or Commission Report, summarized in English at http://www.jewishvirtuallibrary.org/jsource/Society_&_Culture.

http://www.jewishvirtuallibrary.org/jsource/Society_&_Culture/

p. 230: "'a united Jerusalem, to be subject to terrorism.'"
David Makovsky, "How To Build a Fence," *Foreign Affairs* 83: 2, pages 50-64.

p. 231: "severing many Palestinian families from their olive groves" B'Tselem report on Separation Barrier, http://www.btselem.org/separation_barrier.

p. 236: "litter-strewn neighborhood of 25,000 people" See https://www.ochaopt.org/documents/opt_prot_ipcc_Old_City_urban _fabric_geopo_implications_2009.pdf.

p. 243: "there will not be a political process with the Palestinians" See http://www.haaretz.com/top-pm-aide-gaza-plan-aims-to-freeze-the-peace-process-1.136686.

p. 245: "homes of thousands of Palestinian Jerusalemites" "A Layman's Guide to Home Demolitions," Ir Amim, 2009, http://eng.ir-amim.org.il/?CategoryID=254.

p. 246: "demolition of eighty-eight Palestinian homes" "Shady Dealings in Sliwan," Ir Amim, May 2009, http://eng.ir-amim.org. il/?CategoryID=254.

Sarah Kreimer founded The Center for Jewish-Arab Economic Development in 1988 and co-directed it with an Israeli Arab colleague for fourteen years. The Center continues to advance economic development in the Arab sector in Israel, and has catalyzed economic cooperation between Jews and Arabs within Israel and in the Middle East.

From 2002 to 2004 she was a Fellow in the Mandel School for Educational Leadership in Jerusalem, during which time she studied models and mechanisms of multicultural societies. From 2004 to 2012, she was part of the team that established and ran Ir Amim, which works for a more equitable, stable and sustainable Jerusalem for Israelis and Palestinians who share the city.

In recent years, she advised numerous social ventures working toward affordable housing, community development and Arab-Jewish equality, including Injaz Center for Professional Arab Local Governance. She has also served on the board of the Association of Civil Rights in Israel, and was a founding member of Tsofen High Technology Centers, for which she still serves on the board. Currently she works as Director of External Relations and Resource Development at Beit Berl College.

Sarah was awarded the 2002 Speaker of the Knesset's Award for Quality of Life in the Field of Tolerance. She and her two sons live in Jerusalem.